Storytelling in Luxury Fashion

This book examines the ways in which luxury fashion brands use their heritage in their digital storytelling and marketing.

With chapters from authors in China and Macau (PRC), India, Romania, Turkey, the United Kingdom, and the United States, covering British, Chinese, French, Japanese, Indian, Italian, and Turkish brands, this truly global collection is the first book of its kind devoted solely to the emerging study of digital heritage storytelling. This method of reaching potential consumers and perpetuating brand identity is a hugely important factor in the marketing of luxury brands and has yet to be studied comprehensively.

The book will be of interest to scholars working in fashion studies, fashion history, design history, design studies, digital humanities, and fashion marketing.

Amanda Sikarskie is Lecturer in the Department of Art and Art History at the University of Michigan–Flint and in the Comprehensive Studies Program at the University of Michigan–Ann Arbor.

Cover image: Model in a choker and blue top. Image by South African photographer Ash Cork

Routledge Research in Design Studies

Routledge Research in Design Studies is a new series focusing on the study of design and its effects using analytical and practical methods of inquiry. Proposals for monographs and edited collections on this topic are welcomed.

Thinking Design Through Literature
Susan Yelavich

Labor and Creativity in New York's Global Fashion Industry
Christina H. Moon

Wayfinding, Consumption, and Air Terminal Design
Menno Hubregtse

Narrative Environments and Experience Design
Space as a Medium of Communication
Tricia Austin

Contemporary Processes of Text Typeface Design
Michael Harkins

Design and Political Dissent
Spaces, Visuals, Materialities
Edited by Jilly Traganou

The Ontology of Design Research
Miguel Ángel Herrera Batista

Storytelling in Luxury Fashion
Brands, Visual Cultures, and Technologies
Edited by Amanda Sikarskie

For more information about this series, please visit: www.routledge.com/Routledge-Research-in-Design-Studies/book-series/RRDS

Storytelling in Luxury Fashion

Brands, Visual Cultures, and Technologies

Edited by Amanda Sikarskie

Routledge
Taylor & Francis Group
NEW YORK AND LONDON

First published 2021
by Routledge
605 Third Avenue, New York, NY 10017

and by Routledge
2 Park Square, Milton Park, Abingdon, Oxon, OX14 4RN

First issued in paperback 2022

Routledge is an imprint of the Taylor & Francis Group, an informa business

Library of Congress Cataloging-in-Publication Data
Names: Sikarskie, Amanda Grace, 1982– editor.
Title: Storytelling in luxury fashion : brands, visual cultures, and technologies / edited by Amanda Sikarskie.
Description: New York, NY : Routledge, 2021. | Series: Routledge research in design studies | Includes bibliographical references and index.
Identifiers: LCCN 2020028495 (print) | LCCN 2020028496 (ebook) | ISBN 9780367901288 (hardback) | ISBN 9781003022794 (ebook)
Subjects: LCSH: Fashion merchandising. | Luxuries—Marketing. | Branding (Marketing)
Classification: LCC HD9940.A2 S78 2021 (print) | LCC HD9940.A2 (ebook) | DDC 746.9/20688—dc23
LC record available at https://lccn.loc.gov/2020028495
LC ebook record available at https://lccn.loc.gov/2020028496

ISBN: 978-0-367-63805-4 (pbk)
ISBN: 978-0-367-90128-8 (hbk)
ISBN: 978-1-003-02279-4 (ebk)

DOI: 10.4324/9781003022794

Typeset in Sabon
by Apex CoVantage, LLC

We would like to dedicate this book to everyone in the luxury sector who rapidly pivoted to make masks, hand sanitizer, and other PPE essentials in 2020 in response to COVID-19 and to the garment workers, artisans, shopkeepers, and other employees in the fashion industry who lost their livelihoods due to the Coronavirus pandemic. May the fashion stories told of this trying and transformative year be ones of hope and compassion.

Contents

Acknowledgments

Thanks first and foremost to the authors—Federica Carlotto, Alice Dallabona, Stefano Giani, Zaliha İnci Karabacak, Lan Lan, Madeleine Luckel, Marina Moskowitz, Rimi Nandy, Crînguța-Irina Pelea, Peng Liu, Ayşe Aslı Sezgin, Andrea Tanner, and Alexandra Thelin—for making this such a rich and varied collection of chapters.

Thank you also to the four peer reviewers who provided highly supportive comments and concrete suggestions early on in the writing process, including a new title for this collection!

Many thanks to our editorial team at Routledge—to Robert Langham for spotting the potential of this project, to Acquisitions Editor Heidi Lowther for guiding this project to the Routledge Research in Design Studies series, and a huge thank you to our editor at Routledge, Isabella Vitti, and her editorial assistant Katie Armstrong for guiding us through the steps toward publication, especially in light of the coronavirus crisis that stood the world on its head in 2020. Like most everyone else, our editors at Routledge had to work at home through much of the editorial process of this book, and they did so with much patience and aplomb.

Many thanks also to colleagues around the world who helped to circulate the call for papers for this collection—Holly Kent, Regina Lee Blaszyzck, and many others. And thanks so much to Colleen Hill for your input along the way in the editorial process. Thank you to the Los Angeles County Museum of Art (LACMA) and the Metropolitan Museum of Art, New York, for use of images from your collection as illustrations in this book. Thank you also to Ash Cork, photographer of the cover image, for donating your beautiful photograph to the public domain.

Finally, thanks to Stomping Grounds in Durand, MI—where, prior to the coronavirus crisis, several of the chapters in this volume were edited—for the many iced lattes and the tranquil atmosphere.

Images

Figures

Contributors

Federica Carlotto is Cultural Strategist and Course Leader of the Art of Luxury program at Sotheby's Institute of Art. Her research and consultancy activity uncovers the sociocultural underpinnings of branding and consumption in the luxury, fashion, and other super-value industries.

Alice Dallabona is a lecturer within the School of Design at the University of Leeds. Her work examines issues related to luxury fashion, fashion communication and marketing, digital media, and new technologies but also branding and national identity, employing an interdisciplinary methodology that attributes a privileged role to semiotics.

Stefano Giani is an assistant professor in high-performance computing within the Department of Engineering at Durham University and is an expert in computational methods. His research interests lie in the mathematical and practical development of highly efficient and accurate numerical methods applied to a variety of areas.

Zaliha İnci Karabacak is an associate professor in the Faculty of Architecture and Design, the Department of Visual Communication Design, at TOBB University of Economics and Technology/Turkey, where she has been a faculty member since 2014. Her research interests lie in the area of advertising, visual communication, new media, and photography.

Lan Lan is Senior Lecturer at Beijing Institute of Fashion Technology (BIFT). She received her MA in women's wear design at London College of Fashion (LCF). Her research and writing are devoted to fashion education.

Peng Liu is Assistant Professor at Macau University of Science and Technology (M.U.S.T.). He received his Ph.D. in visual art at Curtin University, Australia. His artworks have been exhibited internationally, working with wide range of mediums. He writes academic journals papers and book chapters in the field of cultural study and visual culture.

Madeleine Luckel is an editor at *Architectural Digest*, where she covers national and international design news for online. Previously, Madeleine worked at *Vogue* and Vogue.com, where she covered a variety of design-related topics. Madeleine holds a Master of Arts in Costume Studies from NYU and a Bachelor of Arts in Classics from Brown University.

Marina Moskowitz is the Lynn and Gary Mecklenburg Chair in Textiles, Material Culture, and Design at the University of Wisconsin-Madison. She is International

Co-Investigator on the research project "Fleece to Fashion: Economies and Cultures of Knitting in Modern Scotland," funded by the UK Arts and Humanities Research Council.

Rimi Nandy is presently working as an assistant professor at Adamas University, India, in the Department of English Language and Literature (School of Liberal Arts and Culture Studies). She is also pursuing a Ph.D. from the School of Media, Communication and Culture, Jadavpur University. Her research areas include cultural studies and social media narratives.

Crînguța-Irina Pelea is a lecturer at the Department of Communication and Public Relations, Titu Maiorescu University, Bucharest, Romania, where she has been a faculty member since 2018. Pelea is proficient in the Japanese language and has published a volume and research articles, which address a wide spectrum of subjects ranging from Japanese contemporary popular culture and the globalization of cultural icons to the problematics of protecting one's cultural identity.

Ayşe Aslı Sezgin is an associate professor in the Department of Communication Sciences at the Çukurova University Faculty of Communication. Ayşe Aslı Sezgin completed her Ph.D. at Gazi University, Ankara, Turkey. Her research interests lie in the area of new media, communication technologies, social media, political communication, and media literacy.

Amanda Sikarskie is a fashion historian whose work investigates the methods and best practices for doing the history of dress and textiles in a digital age. Since receiving her Ph.D. in 2011, she has published three books—*The Duprees of Spitalfields* (Amazon CreateSpace, 2015), *Textile Collections* (Rowman & Littlefield, 2016), and *Digital Research Methods for Fashion Studies* (Bloomsbury, 2020)—and taught undergraduate and graduate-level courses in fashion, art and design history, and museum studies. She is the editor of this volume, *Digital Storytelling in Luxury Fashion Marketing*, as well as planning a book on idols as brand ambassadors in China. In her spare time, she loves music—especially the Rolling Stones—thrifting, cats, squirrels, and flowers. Follow her on Instagram @sikarska.

Andrea Tanner is Company Archivist at Fortnum & Mason, Senior Research Fellow at the Institute of Historical Research, and Honorary Archivist at Great Ormond Street Hospital for Children. A Scot by birth, she is a Londoner by adoption and has spent her working life researching this fascinating city.

Alexandra Jordan Thelin is a fashion historian using a multidisciplinary approach to combine fashion, popular culture, and art history. A Ph.D. student in history and culture at Drew University, she previously earned an M.A. in fashion and textile studies (Fashion Institute of Technology) in addition to a B.A. in art history and an M.A. in theatre (Montclair State University).

Preface

A Sea Change

> Full fathom five thy father lies;
> Of his bones are coral made;
> Those are pearls that were his eyes:
> Nothing of him that doth fade
> But doth suffer a sea-change
> Into something rich and strange.
> —William Shakespeare,
> *The Tempest*

In Ariel's song from *The Tempest*, Ferdinand's father, who was believed to have been lost at sea, is described as undergoing a profound metamorphosis after bodily death, not fading away but rather becoming the luxurious natural materials coral and pearl. For much of the year 2020, we were metaphorically lost at sea, quarantined in our homes away from family and friends and unable to carry on with much of our work. But, like Ferdinand, we are reemerging. How has this transformative experience of the coronavirus pandemic changed us? Have we, and the luxury fashion industry, become something better? Will we continue our quarantine frugality, spending less and making do with what we have, treating our purchases as something precious? Will we treat the people who make our clothes better? Will we, and the fashion industry, take better care of the Earth, which has enjoyed a brief respite from our constant, carbon-filled comings and goings? Or will rampant greenwashing continue?

Surely the fashion industry shares a portion of the blame for the twenty-first-century climate crisis; hopefully the industry had no hand in the genesis of the novel coronavirus. As Joshua Katcher, author of *Fashion Animals*, wrote in an op-ed for *Business of Fashion*, however

> there is a very large and specific problem at the intersection of luxury goods and animal welfare. For millennia, the display of animal parts has been a way to showcase power and wealth; the rarer an animal, the more valuable a material is often perceived to be. Meanwhile, the cruelties and ecological consequences of these goods remain largely hidden in the supply chain, shrouded by millions of dollars in aspirational marketing and industry lobbyists.[1]

Even though fashion was not what brought that fateful pangolin or bat to the Wuhan wild animal market, luxury certainly shares the blame for the trafficking of wild animals. And, as Katcher notes, aspirational marketing—much like the digital heritage storytelling discussed in this book—can be used to both create and perpetuate desire for these animal objects and to obfuscate their origins by changing the narrative. Ultimately, brands that are successful in the 2020s and beyond will likely be those that can tell stories from 2020 of sustainability-driven (and increasingly vegan) transformation.

Amanda Sikarskie, University of Michigan

Note

1. Joshua Katcher, "Luxury Fashion's Link to the Illegal Wildlife Trade," *Business of Fashion*, May 29, 2020, www.businessoffashion.com/articles/opinion/op-ed-luxury-fashions-link-to-the-illegal-wildlife-trade

Introduction

Amanda Sikarskie

Fashion in the Time of Coronavirus

As this book neared completion in March 2020, the coronavirus pandemic took over the world, bringing fashion, education, and most other industries to a standstill. Several authors of this book were unable to work on their research and writing during this time, which was instead spent quickly retooling our university classes to be taught online, and for some of us on childcare and homeschooling. Our university workloads basically tripled between reading and replying to discussion forums, tech troubleshooting with students, and emergency faculty meetings on Zoom every week. Luxury and fashion suddenly seemed like afterthoughts, save those brands that were changing over their production to produce essentials for doctors and nurses like masks and hand sanitizer. But I was reminded of one of Florentino's lines in *Love in the Time of Cholera*: "Love is the only thing that interests me."[1] Just like romantic love remains vital in spite of, and even because of, an epidemic, so too, I think, does fashion. Governments have placed great emphasis on deciding what is and is not an essential industry, and while many state and national governments did not see it this way, and perhaps it was not in the life-and-death definitions of basic needs, fashion is essential as a basic expression of self and as a cultural and economic force.

Many problems loom in the fashion sector as a result of the coronavirus. There is legitimate fear among brands and retailers that consumers will see retail clothing stores as a vector for disease. We are seeing massive supply chain disruptions in places like Bangladesh. As of the writing of this book, we are in danger of losing the infrastructure of start-up designers and artisanal producers. In spite of these anxieties, responses to the crisis make this an exciting time for fashion. In 2020, retailers will be shipping their spring/summer product in June and July rather than March and April. This need not be a problem, however, but an opportunity, as that is how the majority of consumers (who buy now to wear now) have always shopped anyway. If the industry can change the cadence of retail and push forward each season by two or three months, major losses can be averted.

Another opportunity are the new retail technologies that will almost certainly be brought to bear to avoid tactile interactions and promote social distancing, such as telecommuting in the workplace and, in retail stores, smart mirrors and other augmented reality. Museums, too, will have to meet these problems as opportunities in order to thrive in a touchless, post-COVID-19 world. "Touchless" has come to describe objects or processes that, through technological advances, have become automated, as with car washes, or hands free, as with mobile phone calls synced through an automobile. In these instances, we take touchless to be a good thing . . . we embrace touchlessness.

In fashion exhibitions, however, the inability to touch on object on display has long frustrated museum visitors, especially the young and the young at heart. This longing to touch is compounded when the object's surface looks particularly tactile. Textile collections, in particular, incite our desire to touch. Access to such collections online, even when accessed via touchscreen on a phone or tablet, does little to sate our desire to touch. The cool, smooth screen of a device is a poor mimic of the soft texture of fabric. Luxury and museum professionals now have an unprecedented opportunity to work together to deliver touchless tech that still communicates the sensuality of fashion objects.

This book deals largely with digital approaches to heritage storytelling for luxury fashion. On account of the coronavirus crisis, fashion has become an irrevocably more digital industry. How brands have responded to the coronavirus crisis will define them for a generation or more, if not longer. The brands that responded well will likely incorporate this pivotal time into their brand stories in the future. We have just witnessed an incredible moment in global fashion history. This book has truly come out at a very interesting moment in history, the moment when we have just emerged from a global pandemic (in which the world failed to mount a globalized response) that, in addition to the heartbreaking human toll, shut down fashion, academia, museums, and most other industries. And I think that this book, and every book coming out in the next couple of years, cannot help but be read through the lens of the coronavirus crisis. I hope that in reading this book, you find that, just like love still mattered in spite of, or perhaps because of, the cholera epidemic, fashion continues to matter, now more than ever.

About This Book: What Is Digital Heritage Storytelling?

To introduce a book about storytelling for luxury fashion brands, it first bears defining just what digital heritage storytelling is. *Digital heritage storytelling may be defined as appropriating past visual culture—fine art, advertising, dress, and the built environment—to tell a story about luxury goods in the present.* It usually (though not always) differs from cultural appropriation and its negative connotations because the appropriation is of one's own culture, in the case of a brand still tied strongly to the founding designer's vision, or, in the case of larger, older brands, the culture of the brand's own country. Digital heritage storytelling is growing in relevance for luxury brands, not only because of the digital, mobile, and social nature of the media-mediated 2020s but also because, as I wrote in "Digital Heritage Storytelling at Mulberry,"

> The late 2010s have shown themselves to be years of cultural and financial uncertainty, with Brexit representing the tip of the iceberg in a sea of shifting political and economic alliances. Add to this climate the reality that the luxury market is becoming increasingly aspirational as housing prices soar and purchasing power stagnates and the fact that the younger generations seem less interested in accruing possessions than even the Gen Xers before them. In this period of flux, luxury giants—such as Chanel, Dior, Gucci, Halston Heritage, Mulberry, Saint Laurent, and Versace—must prioritize safeguarding their brand loyalty and recognition.[2]

While I was writing a case study on digital heritage storytelling at Mulberry for *Bloomsbury Fashion Business Cases*, I realized that there was a gap in the market for an edited collection that brings together many different case studies representing not only various brands but also various academic disciplines. With contributors from disciplines ranging from fashion studies to archival science to communication to the digital humanities, the group of authors represented in this volume was well positioned to bring together a useful anthology for students, industry professionals, and academics alike. With chapters from authors in China and Macau (PRC), India, Romania, Turkey, the United Kingdom, and the United States, covering Chinese, English, French, Japanese, Indian, Italian, Scottish, and Turkish brands, this truly global collection is the first book of its kind devoted solely to the emerging study of digital heritage storytelling.

While fashion studies still has ground to gain in the digital humanities community, the study of fashion is long established as an academic discipline. The position of luxury is a bit murkier in academia, and finding resources on specifically on luxury studies remains more difficult than it ought to be. In the preface of their 2016 book, *Luxury: A Rich History*, Peter McNeil and Giorgio Riello note that, "While fashion has a long history and has now amassed a large body of studies, luxury—we observed—had received little attention. What seemed to be missing was an analysis of the meaning and importance of luxury across time."[3] While McNeil and Riello's recent book does a marvelous job at presenting luxury's rich past, it does not address luxury's digital future. With *Storytelling in Luxury Fashion Marketing: Visual Cultures and Digital Technology*, we propose to do just that.

The Purpose of Heritage Storytelling for Luxury

In 2014, I was a residential research fellow at the International Quilt Study Center and Museum at the University of Nebraska-Lincoln when I discovered that several generations of Rolling Stone Keith Richards' family on his mother's side were Huguenot silk weavers. In 2015, I self-published a trade non-fiction book based on that research, *The Duprees of Spitalfields: Silk Brocade in the Family Tree of Rolling Stone Keith Richards*. Inspired not only by writing *The Duprees of Spitalfields* but also by seeing fashion collections such as Sarah Burton's nod to historic silk for Alexander McQueen (RTW Spring 2016) and L'Wren Scott's rococo-inspired S/S 2010 collection *Madame du Barry*, I had an intuition that fashion and accessories celebrating the look of late seventeenth- and early eighteenth-century English Huguenot silk—picture brocades with oversized vegetal motifs; delicate floral designs in silver gilt thread; and sharp color contrasts between subtle ivories and jewel-toned burgundies, purples, greens, and blues—would hit the runways and luxury retail shops sooner rather than later. In the 2019 summer escape issue of *Porter* Magazine, fashion editor Helen Broadfoot counted floral dresses featuring tapestry inspired-brocades and antique prints on luxe jacquard silks among the escape essentials of the season. What Broadfoot was describing were pieces akin to what I had written about in *Duprees of Spitalfields*. The problem with the escape essentials photo-essay was in the shoot itself. Models were photographed wearing their seventeenth- and eighteenth-century-inspired floral prints in front of palm trees and swimming pools. No doubt the sorts of environs in which the dresses will be worn by their consumers this summer, but the designs lost much of their luster of historicism and elegance in such an atmosphere. A setting in a historic house, surrounded by antiques, would undoubtedly have set the dresses off to better effect and better told the story of the floral designs' rich heritage. As stated on the popular Instagram account @thefashionlaw,

> The context is so important, and, let's face it, when you're selling luxury, you're not selling a product. No one is buying a Dior handbag for Euro 3,000 because of its incredible utility. You're buying it because the culture of Dior has meaning.[4]

This, in a nutshell, is heritage storytelling, albeit an analog example. One sees it in print form in magazines, shop windows, and billboards, but lately more commonly online in Instagram posts and stories, on retail websites, and on YouTube channels.

Heritage storytelling fundamentally connotes a usage of the past that is purposeful and commerce driven, not just nostalgia for nostalgia's sake. Globally, the most popular historical costume drama of 2019[5] was undoubtedly *The Untamed* (*Chen Qing Ling*[6]), starring Chinese boy band idols Wang Yibo (also the co-host of popular Chinese TV show *Day Day Up* and the dance mentor on the reality show *Produce 101*) and Xiao Zhan. The series takes place in ancient China, and while taking place in a fantastical (*Xianxia*) China that never really existed, the location of Gusu (near modern Shanghai) and the clan-based social and political system are evocative of the Zhou Dynasty, particularly the Spring and Autumn Period, circa 771–476 BCE, while the presence of a Guanyin Buddhist temple in the final arc of the series suggests a time period several centuries later. Great attention to detail was paid in the costuming—the robes, long wigs, and elaborate headpieces and hairpins—which evoke a variety of time periods from ancient and early Imperial Chinese history.

A photoshoot that went viral on social media for the July 2019 issue of *Harper's Bazaar China* features Wang and Xiao in contemporary dress styled to suggest the costuming of *The Untamed*. The settings of the shoot, with faux lotuses and a *guqin* (a classical zither), further set the mood.

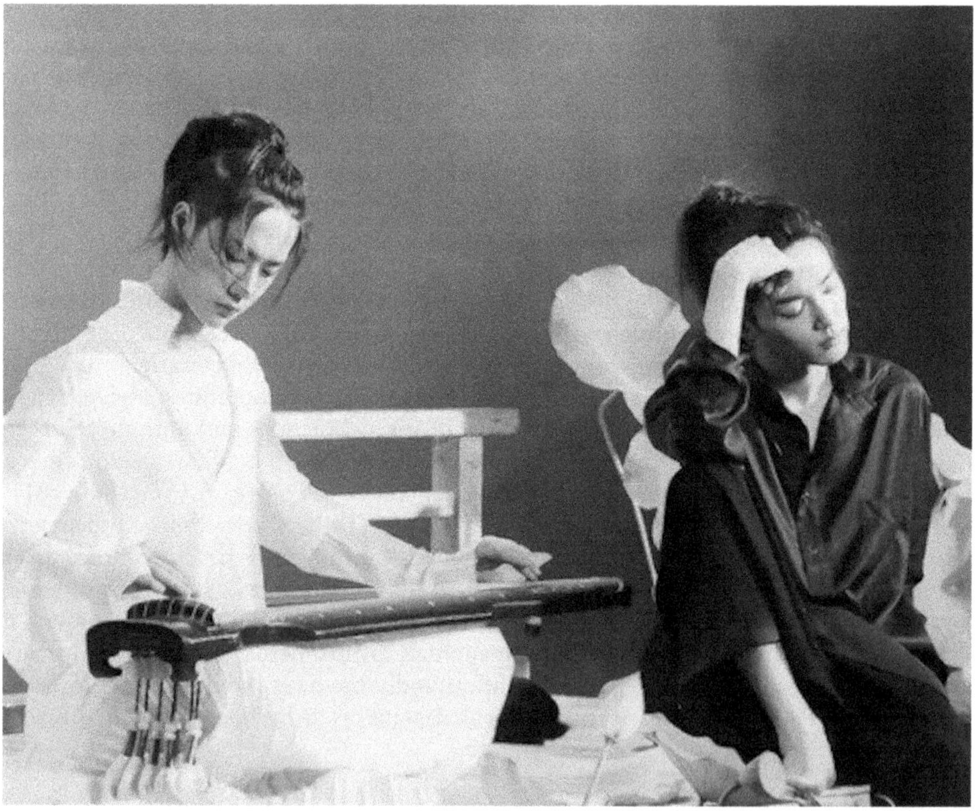

Figure 0.1 Wang Yibo and Xiao Zhan, still from the promotional video for *The Untamed x Harper's Bazaar*, China, July 2019.

While artistically styled and playfully drawing upon Chinese history, the purpose of the shoot is ultimately a commercial one—to advertise the TV series. The differencc between referencing the past in art and referencing the past in fashion photography is chiefly the latter's purpose: to hock goods. This second approach was recently employed in Calvin Klein's use of quilts in advertising and as luxury objects for sale. A separate but related practice is curatorial heritage storytelling. Curatorial heritage storytelling, such as Manolo Blahnik shoes exhibited in front of Fragonard's rococo painting *The Swing*—begins in the gallery rather than on a location fashion shoot, then gets splashed all over Instagram.[7]

Defining Luxury

"Roland Barthes defined luxury as 'le mousseux': in other words, whatever is foamy, frothy, light, airy, and useless."[8] What Barthes described was basically the essence of the rococo style of the eighteenth century. A pair of Manolo Blahnik shoes or a Fragonard painting are certainly luxurious, but what is luxury, exactly? The word 'luxury' has a complex and challenging etymology. McNeil and Riello note that,

> Since Roman times the very definition of luxury has been based on a semantic slippage between the words *luxus* (meaning splendor, pomp, but also sensuality) and its derivative *Luxuria* (riot, excess, extravagance). Neither word had a positive connotation, and luxury was therefore held to be problematic and negative on many levels.[9]

The unintentionally comic figure of Hyacinth Bucket and her obsession with her hand-painted Royal Doulton periwinkles come to mind. Academics, too, have historically been more or less dismissive of luxury. According to McNeil and Riello:

> A decade ago, this issue would have been easily dismissed by arguing that luxury was either a niche topic—the whimsical choices of the elites—or of little interest to either serious scholars or the majority of readers. Yet, in the last few years, luxury has become a 'hot topic.' In an age of rampant individualism, of rising economic inequality, and of puritanical attitudes to social mores, luxury has become commonplace in our daily newspapers, lamenting the vulgarity of the super-rich, in billboards advertising the same commodities that are supposed to be so vulgar, and in the general desire to aim for something better, something different, and something exclusive.[10]

Digital heritage storytelling rehabilitates this negative image of luxury, tying it to beauty, yes, but also to tradition, lineage, and country—all of which figure heavily in this book.

Is luxury immoral? That is, is luxury still an affront to (puritanical) middle-class values, as it was in the eighteenth-century rococo epoch referenced by Roland Barthes? Fashion houses strive to tell stories, and those told of modern and contemporary luxury generally feature a bit more utility and less frothiness, though there are always exceptions to the rule (for example, several recent Moschino collections or Viktor and Rolf's fluffy and cumbersome gowns printed with texts like 'No'). The chapters in this book, in fact, present the case that luxury is no longer synonymous with the quite personal, inward-focused characteristics of impurity, immorality, overindulgence, and other personal excesses that one might associate with the court of Louis XV but rather with larger, more outward-looking, and politicized concepts of tradition, the middle-class work ethic and national identity and pride but also globalism and aspirationalism. Global economic and racial inequality is, of course, the elephant in the room here. Readers of this book must ultimately decide for themselves where they stand on the ethics of luxury.

Europe and Silk: A Micro-History of Luxury

In terms of tradition, lineage, and national identity, Italian silk is particularly evocative of luxury. Its history can be read as a micro-history of luxury itself. In the European mind, the Orient has long been associated with luxury and sumptuousness. Perhaps nothing embodies this more than silk. The history of silk in Europe dates back at least to the 300s BCE, when the conquests of Alexander the Great brought the Hellenistic world into direct contact with India.[11] The Romans had silk, trading with China from the first century CE.[12] It was the Byzantine Emperor Justinian the Great, however, who was responsible for the first sumptuary laws regarding textiles in the 500s CE.[13] This is hardly surprising, given the fact that Constantinople was a cultural melting pot, serving as the gateway between East and West. Also, the lavish tastes of the early Byzantine period, not only for silks but also for gold jewelry and precious stones and expensive dyes, such as a royal purple made from whelks, are legendary. (British readers may at this point be thinking of a joke about Justinian not even being able to run a whelk stall.) Concerned that his subjects spent too much money on silk, Justinian forbade its import, causing his courtiers to complain about the chafing of coarser woolen undergarments and leading some exasperated monks to smuggle silkworms into the city in 552.[14]

Before the fall of Constantinople in the 1400s, Venice got its silk mostly from Central Asia, especially Azerbaijan, via the Byzantines. Venetian traders then took the silk north into Europe. After the fall of the Byzantine Empire to the Ottomans, Beirut, Damascus, Tripoli, and Aleppo in Syria briefly became the new sources of top-quality silk before European silk production got underway in earnest.[15] Recall the lines from *Othello*:

> And say, besides, that in Aleppo once,
> Where a malignant and turban'd Turk
> Beat a Venetian and traduc'd the state.[16]

Unlike the Near East and North Africa, silk production on the European continent was scant during the middle ages. The Umayyads established a few silk mills in the south of Spain, around Grenada,[17] and in Italy, a small degree of silk production was largely confined to the south of the peninsula. Sericulture began in Italy in the 800s, and many of the early workers in the industry were foreigners or otherwise Other—Arabs, Greeks, and Jews.[18]

It was during the Renaissance that the Terraferma, the mainland of northern Italy near that city of Venice, established itself as the major center of the European silk industry, an industry that grew to rival the silk production of even Persia and China.[19] The cities of Verona and Vicenza were particularly important to the new, burgeoning industry in Europe.[20] According to Luca Mola, author of *Silk Industry of Renaissance Venice*, "the advance of the mulberry tree in Italy paralleled in many respects the advance of the silk industry."[21] By the 1530s, the sericultural industry was widespread, even in the north of Italy.[22] To give a sense of the scale of the industry, in 1554, Padua alone produced 31,000 pounds of silk, and by the early seventeenth century, Padua was producing at minimum 40,000 pounds of silk per year.[23]

Silk production was a part of life for all social classes of the Terraferma. Mola notes that,

> from the second half of the fifteenth century onward, the interest of Italian princes and feudal lords in mulberry trees and silkworms grew enormously, becoming no less than a fashion in its own right for the aristocratic classes of the peninsula.[24]

Aristocratic men were not alone in this pursuit; it became fashionable for aristocratic women to involve themselves in sericulture as well. Around 1470, Barbara of Brandenburg received as a present several mulberry seeds, along with a basket of quinces, and "in Piedmont, around 1490, Duchess Bianca of Monferrato procured mulberry leaves for her own personal silkworm raising, which she entrusted to a Catalan specialist, and bought cauldrons from a Greek woman who unwound the cocoons."[25] Besides aristocrats of both sexes, merchants too sought to cash in on the sericulture craze.[26] *Pavaglioni*, urban markets in which merchants and peasants alike traded in cocoons, took place in cities and towns throughout northern Italy.[27] Peasants, of course, also played a vital role in sericulture, doing most of the actual labor, from the planting of mulberries to the unwinding of cocoons.

Because of silk's tremendous importance to the economy, political leaders sought to control the export of silkworms. Agostino Barbarigo, the Doge of Venice in the 1480s, for example, prohibited the export of silkworms from the Venetian state.[28] The import of silk textiles from other states was also strictly controlled. Chronicles from the period indicate the primary importance of silk to the local economy. "Sericulture became an even more distinctive feature of Vicenza's economy in the next century, as attested by the many references in descriptions of the region to the presence of 'innumerable' mulberries."[29] Vincenza was the first city in the Terraferma to engage in the production of silk threads, with operational mills by 1418.[30] "The territory of Verona, too, witnessed the spread of mulberry cultivation in the first part of the fifteenth century. Actually, mulberry trees represented the only new crop in the Veronese agriculture of the day."[31] Verona, too, engaged in silk spinning along with sericulture, as evidenced by twelve different individuals registered as silk spinners in tax documents from the 1450s.[32] Women were key to the silk industry in both cities. As Mola notes,

> during the sixteenth century, the example of Vicenza and Verona stimulated other cities and towns of the Terraferma to launch the silk-spinning craft in order to take advantage of the local production of raw silk and to create new jobs, especially for women, who were a driving force behind the spread of the silk industry in Renaissance Europe.[33]

Silk amounted to such big business, in fact, that spun silk was the main item of trade in both Vicenza and Verona around the turn of the seventeenth century.

Among the silk produced in the Terraferma, there were two types: "true silk" (*seta leale*) and "double silk" (*seta di doppi*). True silk (which amounted to about 80% of production in Italy) was the first-choice material, suitable for weaving, while double silk, which accounted for the other 20%, was the seconds, created when two silkworms got too close to one another and ended up in the same cocoon, resulting in raw silk that was only suited to making silk thread and other notions.[34] The best-quality true silk from the Terrraferma was said to be even finer than Chinese silk.[35]

Spun silk was initially consumed mostly within the Italian peninsula itself, but by the early seventeenth century, much of the silk from Vicenza and Verona was destined for places such as Lyon in the south of France, an up-and-coming center of silk weaving, as well as Flanders and Germany.[36] Adam Geczy notes that,

> the swathe of land from Flanders to Lyon belonging to the Dukes of Burgundy—a region not only contested militarily but attracting merchants and workers from all over Europe—was one of the most prosperous regions of secondary and tertiary fabric production by the fifteenth and sixteenth centuries.[37]

French cities, not only Lyon, but also cities like Nimes, Orleans, and Tours, came to rival the spun silk production of the Terraferma. Indeed, by the middle of the sixteenth century, Lyon had taken its place as one of the world's leading silk producers, though Geczy argues that its produce was lacking in terms of quality and consistency in comparison to the silks produced in the Venetian Terraferma.[38] Just as the silk industry was the foundation of the Terraferma's economic power, the loom became the symbol of France's economic power, and while raw silk was still largely associated with Italy, France became the leading exporter of woven silk.[39] And, as in Italy, southern French cities, including Orleans and Nimes, were prohibited from exporting raw textile materials or importing certain finished stuffs, including silk taffeta.[40] The potential of the French silk industry would have been much greater, though, had King Louis XIV not revoked the Edict of Nantes in 1685, driving many of the top French silk spinners and weavers, most of whom were Huguenots (Protestant Calvinists), from France. According to Geczy, "Burgundy was debilitated as a result."[41] France's loss was England's gain, as many of the Huguenot silk weavers set up shop in the London neighborhood of Spitalfields, helping to create an English silk industry to rival France and surpass that of Italy.

Roadmap to the Book: Part 1: Luxury Brands

This book begins with chapters by scholars each explore how a single brand approaches heritage storytelling. The brands featured in the chapters in Part 1 of this book—Hermès, Dolce & Gabbana, and Gucci—are all synonymous with European luxury, and Hermès in particular with European silk. As Madeleine Luckel explores, Hermès has utilized digital technology to create experiential events telling new stories of European silk.

1. Madeleine Luckel, *Architectural Digest*, USA,
   "Picture Perfect: Hermès, Its Silk Scarves, and Twenty-First-Century Experiential Events"
2. Alice Dallabona, University of Leeds, UK, and Stefano Giani, Durham University, "The Good, the Bad, and the Ugly: Dolce & Gabbana and Narratives of Heritage and National Identity"

3. Amanda Sikarskie, University of Michigan, USA,
   "Gucci Beauty, Nur Jahan, and Mining the History of Art for Global Beauty Icons for the Twenty-First Century"

Roadmap to the Book: Part 2: Visual Cultures

Part 2 features chapters that explore how brands use the visual culture of their own nation's past or appropriate the visual culture of other past civilizations in their digital heritage storytelling, especially as settings and props. Examples include exoticism and the visual culture of India and twentieth-century visual culture—especially advertising—in India, Scotland, Turkey, France, and Japan, as used in heritage storytelling.

4. Rimi Nandy, Adamas University, India,
   "The Exotic As Luxury: Visual Narrative Advertisements of Indian Luxury Goods on Instagram"
5. Marina Moskowitz, University of Wisconsin-Madison, USA
   " 'Terrain of Every Hue:' Locating the Luxury Knitwear Trade in Scotland's Landscapes"
6. Zaliha İnci Karabacak, TOBB University of Economics and Technology, Turkey, and Ayşe Aslı Sezgin, Çukurova University, Turkey,
   "Stories of Turkish Cultural Heritage Motifs Subject to Digital Marketing in Fashion"
7. Alexandra Jordan Thelin, Drew University, USA,
   "Louboutin's Red: Using Color to Connect France's Past and Present"
8. Crînguța-Irina Pelea, University Titu Maiorescu, Romania,
   "Japan's Fashion Subculture: Lolita, From Cuteness to Feminist Revolution and Escapism"

Rimi Nandy's chapter, which begins this section of this book, deals with Indianness, what Tereza Kuldova calls "the buzzword of contemporary Indian fashion design."[42] Kuldova writes

> These days, all Indian designers know that if they do not attempt to capture the *essence* [italics original] of being Indian in one way or another in their designs they are likely to be out of business. Therefore, even the most extravagant and artistic designs often claim to express that mysterious quality of Indianness. . . . And so, the more blatantly obvious this displayed Indianness is, most often taking the form of heavy embellishments, craftwork and hand-woven cloth, the better.[43]

The fashion for Indian embroidery and dress in the West has its roots in a bohemian movement immediately traceable to the countercultural era of the 1960s and '70s but which has existed in some form since at least the early nineteenth century. From the European Continent to the British Isles to America, Bohemian youth in the West was fascinated with Indian textiles in the late 1960s and into the '70s. German supermodel and symbol of the leftist 68er movement Uschi Obermaier traveled extensively through Afghanistan, Pakistan, and India in the early 1970s. Her traditional Indian wedding to German explorer Dieter Bockhorn further popularized Indian dress and textiles in the West. Writing in the nineteenth century, French poet, dramatist, and art critic Théophile Gautier described Indian embroidery in Romantic terms:

> Indian embroidery seeks to engage in a contest with the sun, to have a duel to the death with the blinding light and the glowing sky. . . . At all costs its duty is to shine and glitter and to send forth the prismatic rays; it must be blazing, blinding, and phosphorescent—and so the sun acknowledges defeat.[44]

Western consumers began to read Indian and Pakistani luxury goods as something out of a fairy tale, as the bedazzling quality of many Indian textiles seemed to echo traditional European ideas of luxury.

From Indianness to Scottishness (and Frenchness, Turkishness, and Japaneseness), the other chapters in this section on visual cultures all deal in some way with luxury storytelling and national identity as well. As John P. T. Walsh, of British luxury woolen goods brand Abraham Moon and Sons, said, "The luxury brands want authenticity and a story. Now we are a brand. We are selling that identity."[45] Storytelling is at the heart of Marina Moskowitz's chapter on Scottish luxury knitwear, as seen in the author's discussion of the 'Pringle Moments' brand strategy. Another important aspect of Scottish luxury seen in her chapter, the 'Made in Scotland' mark, like the 'Made in Italy' country of origin label seen in the chapters on Dolce & Gabbana and Gucci in Part 1 of this book, reflects the continuing tension between nationalism and globalism in twenty-first-century luxury storytelling.

Today of course, in the age of Instagram, street-style images coexist more or less as equals alongside traditional fashion photographs. Perhaps nowhere is street-style fashion photography more important than Tokyo, particularly in Harajuku, where fashions of the various youth subcultures there are always on display. Crînguța-Irina Pelea describes one of these subcultures—the Lolitas, or simply 'Lolis'—in her chapter, "Japan's Fashion Subculture: Lolita, from Cuteness to Feminist Revolution and Escapism."[46]

Roadmap to the Book: Part 3: Spaces and Technologies

The final third of this book looks particularly to the emerging technologies that make digital heritage storytelling possible, featuring chapters that explore how various brands utilize a particular technology in digital heritage storytelling. This could be something as simple as YouTube videos or Instagram stories or something as complex as the use of augmented reality in digital heritage and spatial storytelling.

9. Peng Liu, Macau University of Science and Technology, Macau, PRC, and Lan Lan, Beijing Institute of Fashion and Technology, China,
   "Digital Storytelling in an Affective Space: A Case Study on Bodily Engagement With a Chinese Luxury Brand Through Spatial and Heritage Storytelling"
10. Federica Carlotto, Sotheby's Institute of Art, UK, and Andrea Tanner, Fortnum & Mason, UK,
    "New Old Stories: The Temporal Salience of Fortnum & Mason's Digital Heritage Storytelling"

In Part 1 of this book, Madeleine Luckel presented the participatory spectacle of Hermèsmatic. In Part 3, which explores luxury storytelling and technologies, Peng Liu and Lan Lan and Federica Carlotto and Andrea Tanner consider the role of affective, immersive spaces in brand storytelling. In her book *Luxury Indian Fashion*, Tereza Kuldova writes that

> Affective spaces and experience design are the current mantra of fashion design and marketing. Forget direct advertising, this is the era of the advertiser (Serazio 2013), of invisible consumer governance that tries to seduce our unconscious and capture and direct our desires. It operates through affective ambient design and emotionally charged ritualized spectacles carefully staged within such theatrical spaces.[47]

These affective, experiential spaces may be considered what Joanne Roberts and John Armitage have termed the third realm of luxury.

> For our analysis we refer to the real places of luxury as the 'first realm of luxury' and the imaginary spaces of luxury as the 'second realm of luxury.' To these we add a 'third realm of luxury' where the first two realms exist and connect to generate a real-imaginary space of luxury.[48]

What is the future of luxury, especially in the post–COVID-19 era? Does luxury even really exist anymore? Verena Andermatt Conley suggests that perhaps what was once considered luxurious—the gilded, shiny object or the 'it' bag—has now become middle class and banal:

> True luxury—what would be unique, ineffable, unnecessary, without purpose—if it still exists, has withdrawn from view. Most 'luxury' has been standardized and (at the risk of falling into the Marxian idiom) its exchange value carefully calibrated. The ongoing shift in what, thanks to ubiquitous marketing, passes for luxury can be best discerned in the entangled words and images of advertisement.[49]

Perhaps in the future, the heart of luxury will lie in its attention to the self, less in the stuff, the objects, and the material culture and more in transformative and uplifting spaces and experiences.

Accidentally Wes Anderson: A Fresh Take on Luxury Storytelling

Heritage storytelling images generally conjure up a particular visual culture or historical period, and we will see in this book brands making use of a wide array of visual narratives, from Scottish Highlands style to Japan's Lolita culture. In a single image, and through the careful choice and placement of objets d'art, a stylist can take us to Italy, as in the case of this model posing with a pièta, or evoke the Belle Epoque, as with this model posing with ormolu statuary.

Often, we can easily recognize a particular stylist, designer, photographer, or filmmaker's unique vision of the near or distant past. The popular Instagram account @ accidentallywesanderson invites the public to hashtag photographs that look like they could be something out of a Wes Anderson film and then reblogs the best posts to the account. Images that have nothing to do with Anderson's films yet share the aesthetic of Royal Tennenbaums fashion, the historical accuracy and painstaking but whimsical

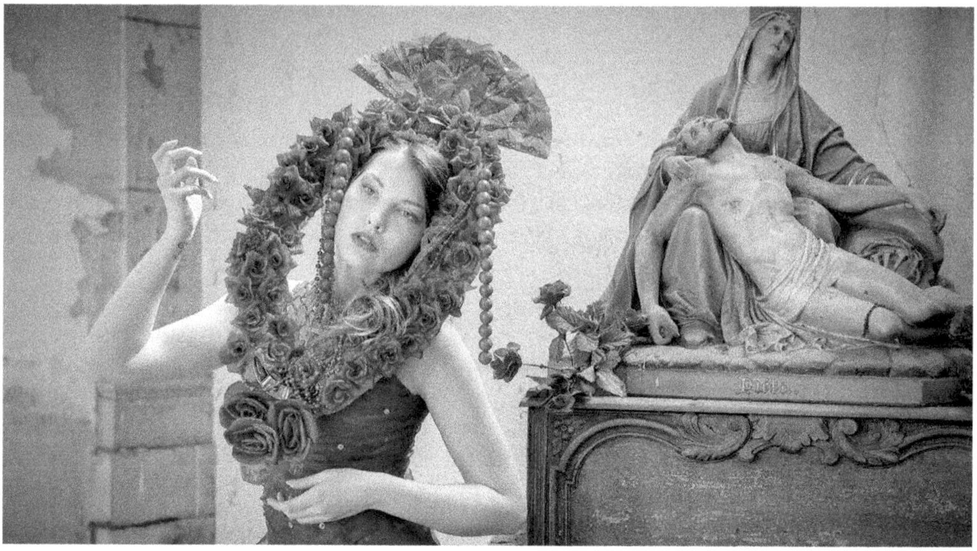

Figure 0.2 Model posing alongside a pièta, Pixabay, Pexels.com.

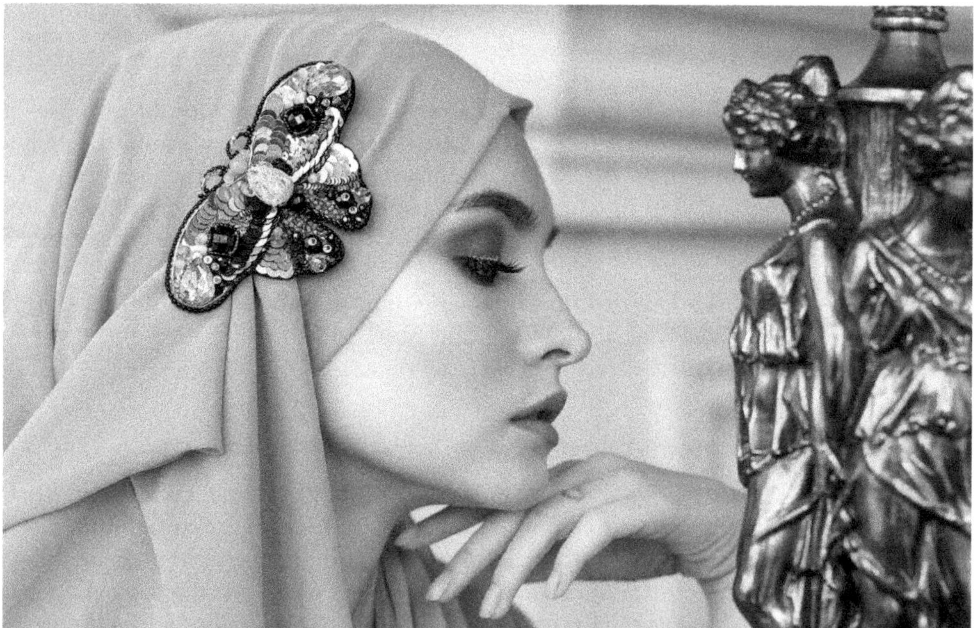

Figure 0.3 Model in a veil, posing with ormolu, Pixabay, Pexels.com.

1960s detail of Moonrise Kingdom, the faded splendor of Grand Budapest Hotel, and the like are popular, judging by the account's over 845,000 followers as of November 14, 2019. This photograph of a young woman with a pink peacoat, high socks, and umbrella, standing in front of a sort of chalet is the sort of popular contemporary fashion image that fits the bill as #accidentallywesanderson.

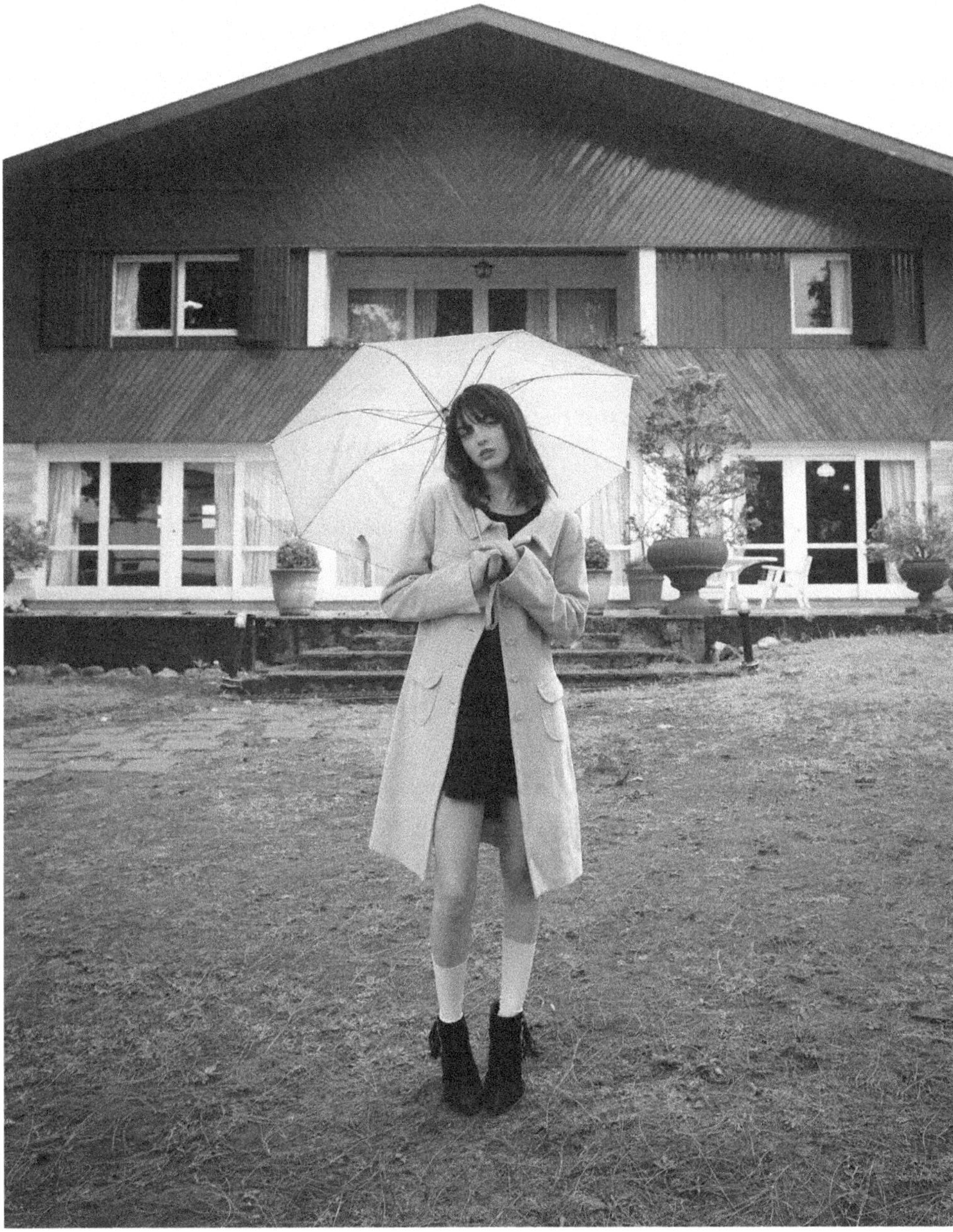

Figure 0.4 'Accidentally Wes Anderson'—Girl in a pink coat with umbrella, Pedro Sandrini, Pexels.com.

This fresh, spirited approach to luxury storytelling is reflected in this book's brilliant cover image by Irish photographer Ash Cork. It is my hope that this book, like these images, shows luxury heritage storytelling not to be stodgy and haughty but rather new, vital, and alive.

Notes

1. Gabriel García Márquez, *Love in the Time of Cholera*, Trans. Edith Grossman, New York: Vintage, 2003, 4.10.
2. Amanda Grace Sikarskie, "Digital Heritage Storytelling at Mulberry," In *Bloomsbury Fashion Business Cases*, London: Bloomsbury Academic, 2018.
3. Peter McNeil and Giorgio Riello, *Luxury: A Rich History*, Oxford: Oxford University Press, 2016, VII.
4. @thefashionlaw Instagram.
5. "Idol-Led Chinese Drama 'The Untamed' Lands on Netflix This Week," *Radii China*, October 22, 2019, https://radiichina.com/untamed-netflix-xiao-zhan-wang-yibo/
6. Based on the book *Mo Dao Zu Shi.*
7. I saw the Blahnik-Fragonard mashup first on Suzy Menkes's blog.
8. Roland Barthes, qtd. in Joanne Roberts and John Armitage, eds., *The Third Realm of Luxury: Connecting Real Places and Imaginary Spaces*, London: Bloomsbury, 2020, 67.
9. McNeil and Riello, *Luxury*, 17.
10. Ibid, VII.
11. Adam Geczy, *Fashion and Orientalism: Dress, Textiles and Culture From the 17th to the 21st Century*, London: Bloomsbury, 2013, 16.
12. Ibid, 17–18.
13. Ibid, 17.
14. Ibid.
15. Ibid, 21.
16. See William Shakespeare's *Othello*, Oxford: Clarendon Press, 1975.
17. Geczy, *Fashion and Orientalism*, 19.
18. Ibid, 21.
19. Ibid.
20. See Luca Mola's, *Silk Industry of Renaissance Venice*, Baltimore: Johns Hopkins University Press, 2000, 220.
21. Ibid, 217.
22. Ibid, 224.
23. Ibid, 225.
24. Ibid, 217.
25. Ibid.
26. Ibid, 218.
27. Ibid, 219.
28. Ibid.
29. Ibid, 221.
30. Ibid, 237.
31. Ibid, 221.
32. Ibid, 237.
33. Ibid, 238.
34. Ibid, 233.
35. Ibid, 244.
36. Ibid.
37. Geczy, *Fashion and Orientalism*, 25.
38. Ibid, 24.
39. Ibid, 25.
40. Ibid.
41. Ibid.
42. Tereza Kuldova, *Luxury Indian Fashion: A Social Critique*, London: Bloomsbury, 2016, 12.

43. Ibid.
44. Théophile Gaultier, qtd. in Robbie and Tony Fanning, *Here and Now Stitchery From Other Times and Places*, New York: Butterick Publications, 1978, 110.
45. Regina Lee Blaszczyk, *Fashionability: Abraham Moon and the Creation of British Cloth for the Global Market*, Manchester: Manchester University Press, 2017, 236.
46. Patrick Macias and Izumi Evers' book *Japanese Schoolgirl Inferno: Tokyo Teen Fashion Subculture Handbook* is a helpful resource for background on Lolis and other subcultures. One can learn, for example, that Vivienne Westwood shoes are "Long the favorite choice of footwear for Lolitas and Goth kids alike."
47. Tereza Kuldova, *Luxury Indian Fashion: A Social Critique*, London: Bloomsbury, 2016, 2.
48. Joanne Roberts and John Armitage, eds., *The Third Realm of Luxury: Connecting Real Places and Imaginary Spaces*, London: Bloomsbury, 2020, 1.
49. Verena Andermatt Conley, "Inhabiting Luxury Spaces," in Joanne Roberts and John Armitage, eds., *The Third Realm of Luxury: Connecting Real Places and Imaginary Spaces*, London: Bloomsbury, 2020, 78.

Part I

Brands

1 Picture Perfect

Hermès, Its Silk Scarves, and Twenty-First-Century Experiential Events

Madeleine Luckel

Luxury marketing scholar Jean-Noël Kapferer once wrote, "Products are communication, and communication should be undertaken with the same exceptional exigency for style, for ultra-qualitative details[,] as any of the products."[1] Undoubtedly, French luxury fashion house Hermès embodies that sentiment, from its carefully crafted goods to each and every manner in which they are displayed. Recently, the brand's visual footprint has been greatly expanded thanks to Instagram and, more specifically, to the thousands of posts shared with the hashtags #hermeesmatic or #carreclub.

Long before the digital revolution, Thierry Hermès founded his namesake brand as a purveyor of high-quality horseback riding equipment in 1837.[2] One hundred years later, the French house released its first square silk scarves, which, like so many Hermès products, grew out of craft-oriented roots.[3] But scarves, and other equestrian accessories, are not the historic domain of Hermès alone.[4] Other European luxury houses, including Gucci and Ferragamo, have been producing colorfully patterned silk scarves for decades.[5] Nonetheless, Hermès has succeeded in maintaining its reputation as the *ne plus ultra* destination for this specific accessory, thanks in large part to the house's deft ability to position itself as such.

The company's brand identity is predicated on high-end luxury and an enduring commitment to craft-based manufacturing techniques. These values have echoed through the company's two recent traveling, transitory, and highly visual scarf-focused events—Hermèsmatic, a dip-dyeing pop-up, and the Carré Club, a more general peripatetic endeavor.[6] (The word "Carré," it is important to note, is French for square. However, in the Hermès universe, it is often used as a synonym for scarf.[7]) These ephemeral events, which traveled to New York, Los Angeles, Austin, Rome, and Singapore—among other destinations—indicate that the company has pivoted to embrace experiential and inclusive strategies that are inherently linked to social media use. Luxury theory, and specifically works by Thomaï Serdari and Jean-Noël Kapferer, can help explain the ways in which these current digital marketing efforts build upon preexisting precedents, reflecting past efforts by Hermès and the luxury retail industry at large.

In 2016 and 2017, visitors were invited to bring their own, often old, Hermès scarves to be re-dyed in one of three colors at Hermèsmatic.[8] While the seemingly inclusive service was free of charge, it promoted the consumption of high-end luxury accessories with direct and indirect messaging. Hermèsmatic pop-ups created momentary communities in which ownership of an Hermès scarf was an unofficial prerequisite for entry.[9] Although the remaking of scarves was the ostensible purpose of these pop-ups, visitors were not involved in the process beyond the initial color selection.[10] Instead, the interiors of the pop-ups, which featured orange washing machines in which the scarves were dyed, facilitated the creation of social media content.[11]

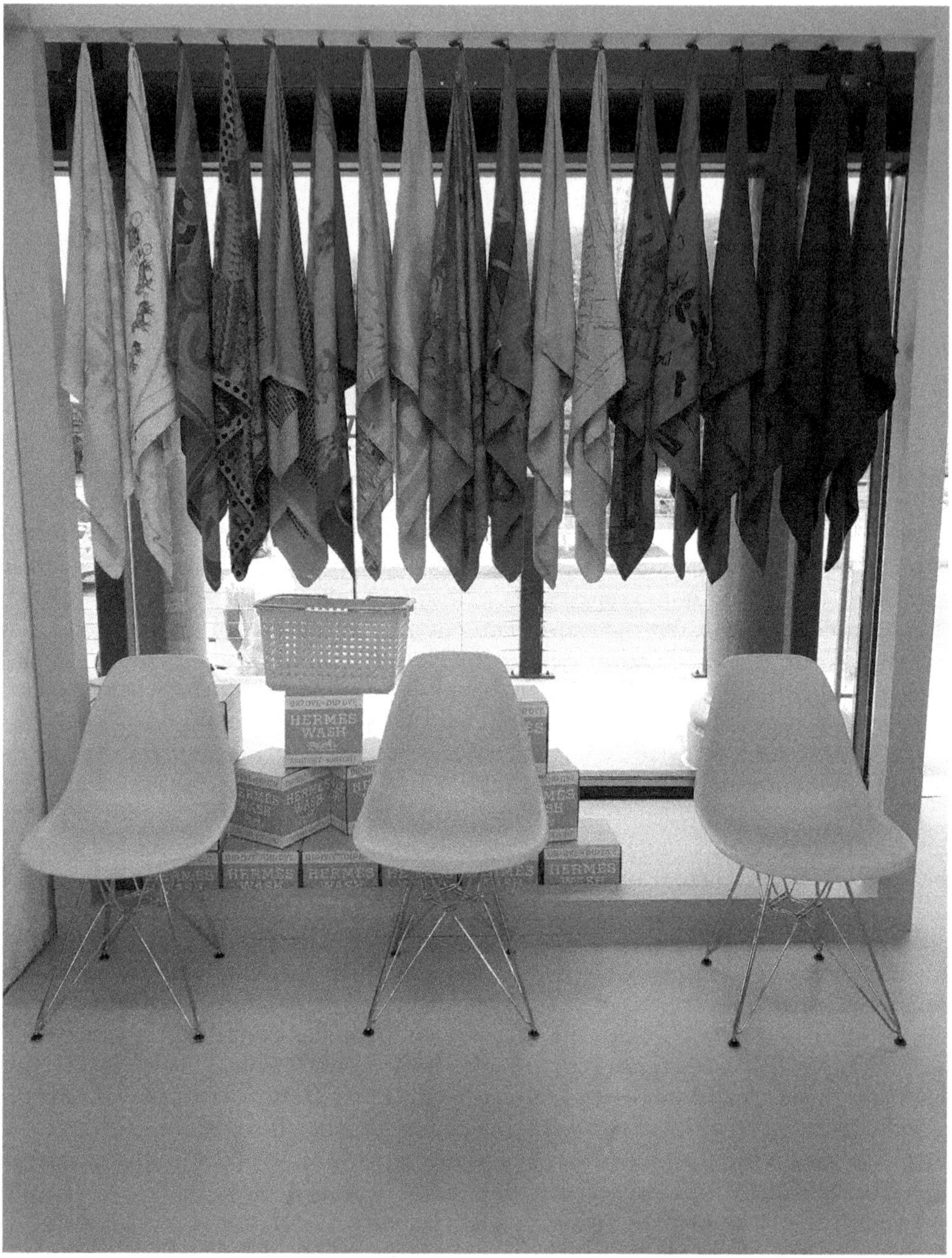

Figure 1.1 Inside the New York edition of Hermèsmatic.
Source: Photographed by Madeleine Luckel.

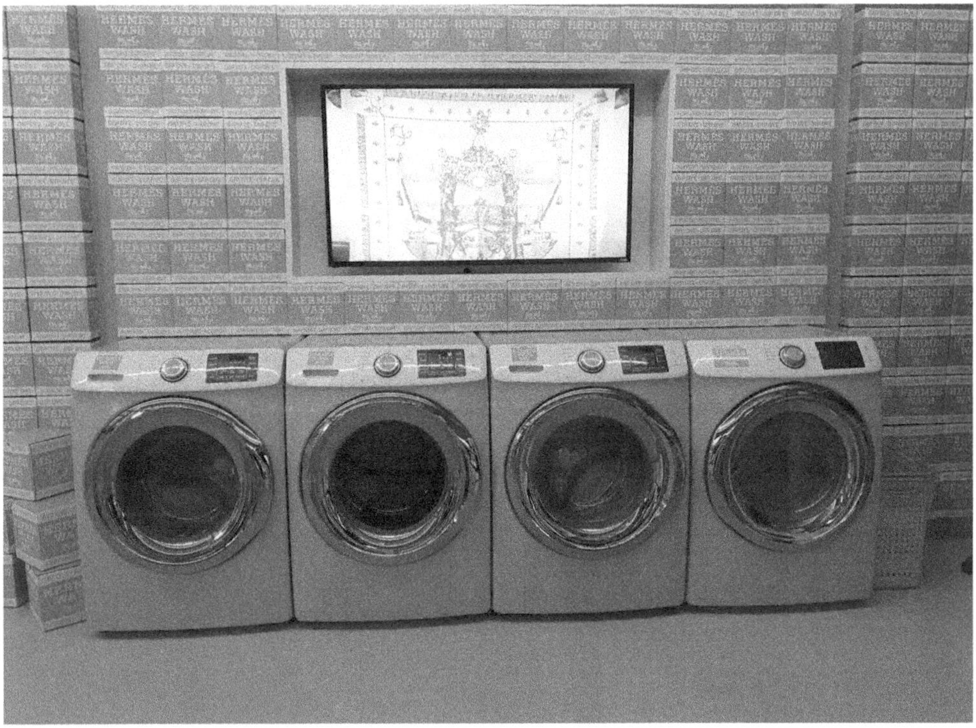

Figure 1.2 Washing machines in which the scarves were dyed.

Source: Photographed by Madeleine Luckel.

In 2018, Hermès broadened this model by organizing its globetrotting Carré Club. Once again, these events, which continued into 2019, were free and open to the public and included an area in which visitors could purchase an Hermès scarf.[12] Unlike Hermèsmatic, the apparent goal of the Carré Club was more simply for visitors to see, photograph, and share images related to the company's scarves. Visitors were encouraged to orbit around the main areas of the pop-ups, where some of Hermès' most successful freelance silk scarf designers were working and available for interaction.[13] In this way, Hermès drew attention to its longstanding and frequently touted commitment to craft while focusing visitors' attention on the house's relationship with artists and its products' apparent links to fine art.[14]

It would be naïve to hypothesize that any of these productions are arbitrary and exist within a vacuum. They are instead excellent examples of experiential marketing, a subset of rational choice theory within microeconomics that emphasizes experiences in an attempt to appeal to consumers' emotions and memory.[15] The significance of this study is fourfold. First, the history of Hermès scarves is a rich topic that has not been thoroughly explored within academic texts. Second, experiential events are a growing trend within the luxury industry and have yet to be sufficiently examined in academic publications related to fashion marketing. Third, these events merit deeper investigation, as they and their digital footprints bring up and expand upon elements

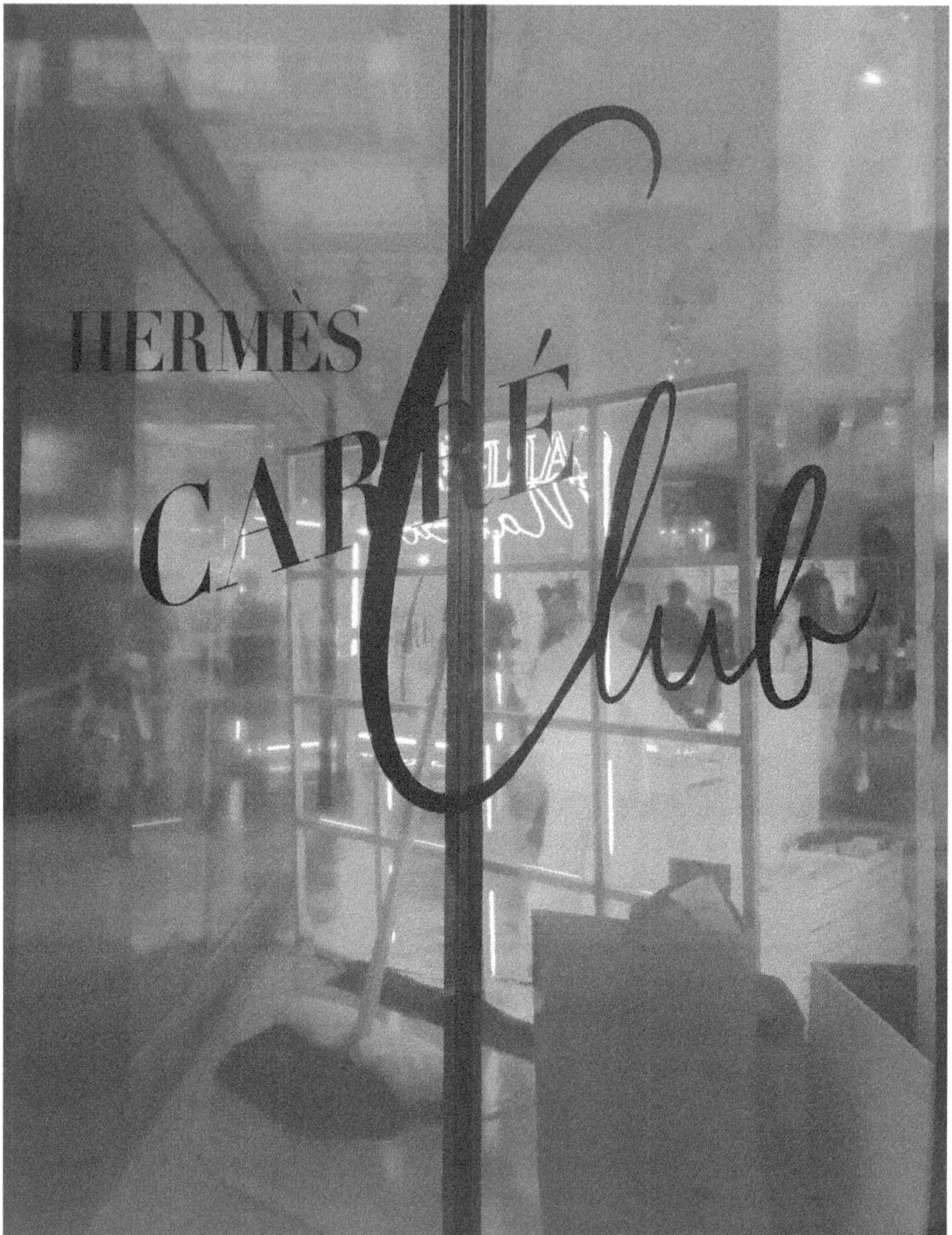

Figure 1.3 The exterior of Manhattan's Carré Club, located in the Meatpacking District.
Source: Photographed by Madeleine Luckel.

of traditional luxury and luxury marketing theories. Finally, Hermès' events appear to be pioneering efforts within this industry and may influence subsequent efforts by other companies to communicate their own narratives.

This investigation uses a case study methodology while also relying on the idea of reception theory. Reception theory, a phrase largely associated with Wolfgang Kemp's *The Methodology of the Aesthetic Reception*, plants the focus of an investigation firmly on the reaction to an object by the spectator rather than on the object itself.[16] This chapter concentrates on Hermès' recent ephemeral events and the reactions of visitors, as opposed to Hermès scarves as objects worthy of art historical interpretation. Photographs taken at the events, as well as social media posts created by others, make up the majority of primary sources cited. The events are analyzed through the lens of theories espoused by luxury and luxury marketing scholars. Guy Debord's idea of the spectacle and Jonas Hoffman and Ivan Coste-Manière's writings are considered.[17] However, Jean-Noël Kapferer's *Kapferer on Luxury: How Luxury Brands Can Grow Yet Remain Rare* and Thomaï Serdari's article "Experiments in Suchness: Hiroshi Sugimoto's Silk Shiki for Hermès" form the primary basis of this study's analysis.[18]

Thomaï Serdari and Jean-Noël Kapferer, among others, have posited interesting, and potentially foundational, ideas related to luxury and luxury marketing theory. In her text, Serdari appears to rebut Thorstein Veblen's famed *The Theory of the Leisure Class*, expounding upon luxury's ability to delight while also citing the work of Kapferer, whom she herself considers a pioneer within the field.[19] While Kapferer is a prolific author, his 2015Ref_60_FILE150314136001 book *Kapferer on Luxury: How Luxury Brands Can Grow Yet Remain Rare* compiles some of his most notable texts, inserting sections of new material in some instances.[20] Kapferer's work is an excellent foundation for understanding luxury companies and, in particular, family-run French brands.[21] What is more, it is his unique marrying of business and the humanities that positions his work as an influential example to others and as a helpful model for this chapter.[22]

While tangible products are essential to luxury industry businesses, intangible ideas best explain how the field is functioning in an increasingly digital era. This chapter discusses aspirations and dreams within the context of luxury marketing theory, as well as the ways in which these ideas are evident in the Hermèsmatic and Carré Club events. Excess, scarcity, and exclusivity are also examined—with attention paid toward their contradictions—as are ideas related to the store as an environment for spectacle. Finally, the role that fine art and artisans often play in the luxury fashion industry is addressed.

Aspiration and Dreams

While marketing is generally understood as the practice of promoting products to the outside world, Hermès has consistently insisted in the press that it does not have a marketing department.[23] Since Hermès does not conduct market research, such as organizing focus groups or soliciting and responding to consumer feedback, this is technically true.[24] Instead, for brand and product development, the house relies directly on its employees, artists, artisans, and craftspeople, who are trusted unreservedly.[25] Yet outside sources routinely discuss the company's marketing practices, glossing over this nuance. A *Business of Fashion* article, titled "Hermès' Anti-Marketing Marketing," focused on the nature of the company's marketing work within the context of the Carré Club.[26] In another *Business of Fashion* article, Hermès family member and Chief Executive Axel Dumas stated,

> One thing I deeply dislike is . . . trying to manipulate people's minds. Everything we do [at Hermès], we do it because we believe in it—it has to be meaningful and relate to what we are trying to express.[27]

Dumas' words hint at the negative implications luxury brands often associate with marketing practices.[28]

As Kapferer has astutely noted, luxury brands advertise to stimulate dreams, as opposed to selling products.[29] While luxury companies are increasingly employing Instagram to achieve this objective, Hermès has a long history of overtly linking itself to this concept.[30] Pierre-Alexis Dumas has said, "I want our customers to indulge in a moment of pure lightness, because it is in those moments of dream where you have insights into life, and into the future."[31] This ethos is regularly communicated on Hermès' official Instagram account in ways that touch upon its diverse range of product sectors.[32]

It is an important distinction that Hermès is a luxury, as opposed to a fashion, brand.[33] Desire within the context of fashion requires almost immediate gratification, as the trend cycle moves quickly from focus to focus.[34] In contrast, a luxury brand like Hermès can afford to capitalize on dreams that require a longer amount of time to be satisfied.[35] But while a lengthy period is allotted for actual purchases, as well as for acquiring new customers, ephemeral events such as Hermèsmatic and the Carré Club give relatively instantaneous gratification. And yet, despite the quick satisfaction that comes from an Hermèsmatic visitor's number of Instagram likes, these events are at their core focused on cultivating long-term dreams. By allowing for consumers to experience and learn about the brand, Hermès plants the seeds for future aspirational purchases.

The central component of the so-called dream equation within luxury theory is, according to Kapferer, that the brand is known by many, or all, and bought by few.[36] At the crux of this maxim is the concept that individuals familiar with a luxury brand dream of one day possessing its products. Instagram is rightfully used by Hermès as a tool by which this aphorism can be achieved. In accordance, the company regularly posts dream-inflected images and captions. When fans of the brand and average individuals see Instagram content related to Hermès, as is the case with its experiential, scarf-focused events as well, the pool of consumers who "know" Hermès is expanded in ways that the brand itself would not otherwise be able to achieve.

Desire, Kapferer has noted, spreads like a contagion.[37] Brand-generated content no longer wields total influence over consumers' decisions to purchase.[38] Instagrams posted by Hermès' own account testify to how the house uses the platform with these facts in mind. In one post, a scarf jumpsuit–clad employee is seen at the New York pop-up, in a photograph captioned "Loving silk from head to toe."[39] On an independent account, Chou Chou, an influencer with over one million followers, posted a slideshow of photographs of herself at the Singapore Carré Club.[40] In this case, the post functions like an advertisement, setting off a chain reaction in which followers aspire to attend the event, post images to social media about the experience, and procure an Hermès scarf to wear. The immediacy of social media is in this way curiously at odds with the many years Hermès is willing to wait for a new customer to make an aspirational purchase.

In the short term, the main purpose of Hermèsmatic and the Carré Club is not to sell scarves. At the New York iteration of the Carré Club, a woman was seen in the store component of the event asking an employee to take her photograph against the colorful, and branded, backdrop.[41] She displayed no interest in making a purchase or in perusing the goods on display.[42] The actions, and posts, of visitors illustrate short-term decision-making yet speak to another intrinsic truth within luxury and luxury marketing theory: As Thomas observed of the luxury climate in 2007, the brand, as opposed to the specific good, is what the customer seeks to own.[43] In the case of Hermèsmatic and the Carré Club, visitors are clearly more interested in linking themselves to Hermès than they are in associating themselves with any specific scarf. To take a picture of an orange, highly branded interior—and to share it on one's own Instagram profile—is in a sense to possess a small piece of Hermès.

Excess, Scarcity, and Exclusivity

Luxury is traditionally associated with excellence. In many ways, Hermès, and its scarves in particular, embody this distinction of merit. Pierre-Alexis Dumas has recognized as much, citing his family's "desire for excellence—and maybe something a little bit obsessive and mad about detail."[44] However, within the luxury industry, excellence is often the direct result of excess—an arguably better metric by which to judge individual products.[45] As Serdari argues, it is "[e]xcess that propels creative thinking, craftsmanship, art[,] and production of timeless objects with cultural significance."[46]

Within the context of Hermès' scarves, excess can be most easily detected in the time that the company invests in its production processes. Notably, Hermès does not impose any time limits or production quotas on its artisans or designers and is often willing to wait years for a finalized design from a freelance artist.[47] What is more, once a scarf's design has been completed, it takes eighteen months for it to be produced in Lyon, with an average of 750 hours alone going toward the engraving of an individual silk screen.[48]

The idea of excess is evident not only in Hermès' own choices but also in those of its targeted visitors. The structure of Hermèsmatic presumed that visitors had an extra Hermès scarf available for artistic, if potentially risky, experimentation. This, of course, assumes a high level of personal wealth, which was corroborated by visitors' Instagram posts.[49] In one such post, a visitor who evidently brought multiple Hermès scarves to the event captioned her photograph by writing, "My scarves look amazing!!! New, chic[,] and totally updated!!!"[50]

Serdari believes that the concept of excess, as a propeller of luxury, is also inherently linked to isolation.[51] In her text, "Experiments in Suchness: Hiroshi Sugimoto's Silk Shiki for Hermès," Serdari writes,

> Objects with excessive physical traits that bring out unexpected and pleasing physical experiences absorb the person fully in what that experience is. They may isolate the individual from the social, and therefore from questions of equality and inequality, fairness and injustice.[52]

At first, the concept of isolation may appear to be antithetical to the use of social media and to Instagram in particular. However, Instagram is a tool that allows its users to cordon themselves off within homogenous communities of their own making.

What is more, posting on social media is first and foremost an individual, as opposed to group, action. To partake in it requires, as does the enjoyment of any sort of luxury, a certain amount of leisure time. Finally, the act of using Instagram, whether by posting content or scrolling through one's feed, stories, or explore pages, is an immersive, solo activity.

As Kapferer and Veblen both emphasize, luxury is a product of its era.[53] Besides serving as a symbolism of status, luxury goods can speak volumes about the specific period, place, and society in which they were created.[54] It is therefore fitting that Hermès' ephemeral events appear to be so heavily tailored around the use and pervasive nature of Instagram. The Carré Club's photo booth was an especially overt nod to this focus.[55] As countless Instagram posts prove, the photo booth was not an anachronistic feature of the peripatetic pop-up but instead one that invited digital sharing, down to its text-based, caption-worthy props.[56] Similarly, at the Hermèsmatic events, Hermès closely linked itself to the current craft-based zeitgeist in the ways in which it associated itself with DIY culture.[57] As the house wrote on its website, "Come visit with your Hermès scarves and give them an entirely new feel and look. . . . Whether it's denim blue, fuchsia pink or intense violet, the choice is yours!"[58]

While scarcity is known to increase value as a general economic principle, luxury is unique in its association with rarity.[59] Scholars agree that a key component of the appeal of a luxury item is the recognition the consumer receives from those who do not own the product.[60] The social media posts produced by visitors to the Hermèsmatic and Carré Club events indicate that this was a crucial motivating factor in consumers' interest in attending the events.[61] Of course, part of the seductive appeal lies in the fact that taking a photograph was far more accessible, and sharable, than taking a costly purchase home. Nevertheless, in one post, a visitor shared a photograph of herself at the Carré Club, captioning the image, "Join the club."[62] In the image, the user wears an Hermès scarf. This action identifies her in the eyes of her non–scarf owning followers as a possessor of this good while hinting at the event's implicit barriers to entry.

The luxury industry's innate link to scarcity and exclusivity is at direct odds with its current emphasis on inclusivity.[63] In recent years, Gucci's Alessandro Michele has been praised for his inclusive brand approach and is often held up as a harbinger of the current era.[64] While Hermès has increased exclusivity in some areas of its retail business, most notably by limiting the number of people who can enter its Paris store at one time, the experiential events appear to be a direct attempt to infuse its brand image with a more democratic and welcoming ethos.[65] Both the Carré Club and Hermèsmatic were free and open to the public.[66] What is more, once a visitor made his or her way into the Carré Club, none of the club's various vignettes were ostensibly designed to intimidate the guest. In one particularly whimsical case, a fictitious illustrated character named Mino clearly linked the event to the brand's playful and carefully cultivated identity.[67]

The Spectacle and the Store

In Brian Nelson's introduction to his 1993 translation of Emile Zola's influential novel, *The Ladies' Paradise*, Nelson compares the newfangled and fast-paced way in which passing nineteenth-century customers viewed department store goods to the manner in which then-novel trains affected passengers' vision.[68] In both cases, rapid movement blurs the foreground while allowing the goods or horizon in the distance to come into focus.[69] Today, Instagram functions somewhat analogously, in that the constant scroll enabled by its home screen feed allows users to see images shared by the likes of Hermès in one collective blur. Only when many posts of the same topic are shared—as is the ostensible goal of hosting photogenic experiential events such as the Carré Club—do a brand's wares reach a critical mass and come into focus.

Despite the growing influence of the Internet, the store as a physical space has retained its power within luxury marketing. As Kapferer notes, "The luxury retail experience is supposed to be a delight—justifying in itself the visit to the stores."[70] In addition to providing a visual and documentable concrete form of spectacle, the store produces further discernible benefits of its own.[71] As Kapferer has stated, the goal of the store is to "develop direct, one-to-one relationships with clients. Luxury means treating all clients as VIPs. This necessitates direct, personalized, one-to-one interaction, ideally in exclusive stores that represent the dream in 3D."[72] This sentiment appears to be directly in line with the role of the Carré Club's concierge. In Hermès' first official Instagram post announcing the Carré Club, the brand featured a picture of the concierge—an apparent employee-actor.[73] The caption read "Join the Club, s'il vous plaît."[74] Making an overt connection himself, Florian Craen, executive vice president of sales and distribution at Hermès, addressed the presence of the concierge, or "membership desk," by stating in a *Business of Fashion* article: "It creates a one-to-one, personal relationship. We want to re-engage people."[75]

Hermès seeks to both subtly whip up and suppress frenzied in-store and virtual scenes in a manner that stays true to both the luxury business model and the appeal of spectacles.[76] At Hermès' Paris Faubourg flagship, the company recently started limiting the number of customers that can enter the space at once in order to avoid a sense of crowding.[77] Conversely, visitors streamed into both Hermèsmatic and the Carré Club, thanks in large part to the events' disparate, somewhat populist, collective ethos. As Guy Debord argued in his seminal 1967Ref_53_FILE150314136001 work, *The Society of the Spectacle*, the spectacle has the power to transform an object from its purely economic identity to one that also wields greater emblematic and communicative power thanks to its appearance, or visual impression.[78] Retail, and luxury retail in particular, perfectly illustrate Debord's point. The power of an Hermès silk scarf is indeed far more than its literal $415 price tag.[79] Instead, the spectacle that is the pop-up store and experiential event imbues the square piece of silk with heightened appeal and authority. The high volume of consumers that populated and digitally documented Hermèsmatic and the Carré Club is a testament to Hermès' success in creating both a product worthy of idolization and corresponding events capable of catalyzing autonomous interest.

Art

In this century, fashion brands have increasingly sought to associate themselves with fine art.[80] This is no arbitrary coincidence and instead dovetails with dominant luxury marketing theories.[81] In this way, luxury retail products can transcend the at times somewhat pejorative associations of capitalism, emerging as objects worthy of cultural respect. While some luxury houses, such as Prada and Louis Vuitton, have placed physical works in museum-like foundations, far more have incorporated fine art into their designs.[82] Nevertheless, within this milieu, Hermès is unique in its overt embrace of craft and art.

The Hermès scarf is a particularly apt item to absorb the revered associations of art and design. As the company itself has noted, a square silk scarf is its own blank canvas and is therefore an especially harmonious assignment for any artist.[83] In its press materials, Pierre-Alexis Dumas notes, "From the beginning, the Hermès *carré* was imagined as an object, and not as an accessory."[84] This initial intention has proved prescient, as today consumers are known to sometimes frame their scarves instead of wearing them as fashionable accessories.[85] In this way, the *carré* often transcends the craftsmanship behind its design and construction to function as an *objet d'art*.

Hermès' ephemeral events, which, in the case of Hermèsmatic, took pains to brand itself in different historic architectural styles around the globe, further positioned the scarves as such. At the time of Hermèsmatic, one savvy Instagram user compared the brand's stacked boxes of Hermès Wash to Andy Warhol's famous Brillo Box works.[86] Although the caption, "When Warhol meets Hermès marketing officers," expressed a slightly cynical tone, it implied that Hermès' events exist on the contemporary art continuum and partially equated the company's work with that of the avant-garde tradition of readymades.[87]

Hermèsmatic and the Carré Club highlighted the rarity of Hermès' artistically produced scarves—as Instagram users made clear. The scarves for sale at the store components of both events were, like all of the company's designs, only available for a limited number of seasons.[88] What is more, after visiting the Carré Club, numerous consumers noted on Instagram the amount of time that went into the production of such works. In doing so, visitors made clear that they had absorbed the implicit message that new Hermès scarf designs are infrequently produced, despite the capabilities of modern textile production.[89] In one noteworthy example, a visitor posted a picture of herself with Hermès freelance artist Alice Shirley, noting her love of Shirley's work, and the fact that she eagerly anticipated seeing her next scarf.[90] The visitor therefore made clear that she views Hermès scarves to be rare collectables well worth a lengthy wait.

In theory, Hermès did not have to limit Hermèsmatic and the Carré Club to a finite time period or a limited number of places. Therefore, these events can be understood as extensions of the brand's effort to make itself seem more rare. At the time of Hermèsmatic, one visitor posted that she had celebrated her mother's birthday early by making a special trip to the event.[91] Additionally, an individual who had attended the Carré Club's opening cocktail party captioned her post, "Thank you . . . for this opportunity to learn so much more about craft and business."[92] Both Instagram posts indicate that Hermès consumers understood the events as rare opportunities, which merited their rapt attention.

Hermès succeeded in making visitors to Hermèsmatic and the Carré Club conceptualize their experiences as existing beyond a finite moment in time. When Hermèsmatic traveled to Dubai, one visitor captioned her Instagram image of herself at the pop up by writing, "Memories like this are priceless."[93] After visiting the New York Carré Club, another Instagram user shared a detail of a scarf design seen at the event, captioning the image, "Midsummer Night's Dream as silky inspiration."[94] While the dreamlike quality of the post suspends the traditional idea of time to a certain extent, the very nature of inspiration implies a lasting and nonlinear effect.[95] Similarly, a treasured, or priceless, memory lives on beyond its initial, catalyzing moment to become timeless in its own right.

Art is capable of imbuing brands with seemingly universal appeal.[96] It is therefore perfectly logical that Hermès would position art-making stations around the Carré

Club. In one especially large "drawing machine" station, the brand invited guests to watch a series of wheels spit out fully fledged creations.[97] The fact that Hermès chose to post Instagram content specifically about this component of the club reiterates how integral the making of art was to its overall goals.[98] While the Carré Club garnered enthusiastic response on social media in general, posts indicate that its interactive and artmaking components were particularly well received.[99] A station where visitors could have their portraits sketched in the house's familiar shades of orange and chocolate brown was one of the most popular components documented on social media.[100] Moreover, an area where visitors could name their own color received similar levels of attention.[101] In both cases, the stations required equally low initial barriers to entry and required skill sets.

Serdari argues that continued creativity is essential to maintaining the luxury identity of any brand.[102] Therefore, as Serdari asserts, heritage-based houses cannot afford to rest on the laurels of their lofty pasts.[103] This context can help further explain Hermès' choice to work with freelance artists in order to create continuously varied, and visually diverse, scarves.[104] It also helps explain Hermès' experiential events. The act of organizing these costly creative endeavors is essentially an act of preserving luxury through reaffirming the importance of novelty to Hermès. Therefore, it cultivates long-term strategic thinking in the business as well. As Serdari similarly asserts, in luxury, constant creativity is necessary, as opposed to stagnation.[105] Pierre-Alexis Dumas clearly understands this principle and, by extension, its relevance to his company. In a *Business of Fashion* article, he states, "Craft can only survive if it finds a natural application and if it finds a market. What a craft produces has to be relevant to the world we live in today. . . . If craft does not reinvent itself, it dies."[106]

The Artisan

Kapferer recognizes that the role of the artisan is often central to the story of the luxury house.[107] Therefore, whether these creative individuals are viewed as artists or artisans, it is perfectly rational that they would be intimately involved with the brand's experiential events. As Serdari notes of Hermès' recent Hermèsmatic and Carré Club pop-ups, they are far from still lifes and impress upon people the integral importance of process.[108] One Instagram video, shared by the brand, captured the principal way in which the Carré Club put its artists on display.[109] In the video, an artist paints his illustration while applying what appears to be gold leaf or foil.[110] It is clear that visitors to the New York Carré Club positively responded to the presence of artists and artisans at the event. One visitor captioned her image, "I love that @Hermès is giving so much exposure to young and brilliant illustrators!"[111]

Visitors to Hermèsmatic were more centrally involved in the ideas of process and artisanal production than those at the Carré Club. Yet, crucially, while the brand invited consumers to come dye their own old scarves, visitors themselves were not involved in the dyeing process.[112] Upon arrival, customers simply selected which of three colors they would like their scarf to be completely submerged in.[113] Then, anonymous employees, clad in white jumpsuits that evoked painters' uniforms, performed the actual work.[114] Individuals' scarves were dyed in bright orange washing machines, which functioned as the event's main attraction.[115] However, visitors had to drop their scarves off and were not actually present when their own scarf was dyed.[116] In a series of Instagram videos, Hermès shared individual vignettes of the process that employees undertook.[117] However, none of these videos contained any detailed or informational footage that might explain the process or allow others to replicate the dyeing at home.[118]

Instagrams posted by visitors to both events evidenced a diverse range of responses to their various process-oriented components. One New York Carré Club attendee registered surprise on social media when informed about how long it took to produce the house's scarves.[119] Another, like many other fellow visitors, chose to pose for an Instagram picture within an artist's work space.[120] Analogously, at Hermèsmatic, a visitor posed as if he himself was taking dyed scarves out of a washing machine—despite the fact that he and other visitors had no such role in the process.[121] Both choices imply a desire to pretend to be, or at least momentarily play, a talented artist or artisan working for Hermès. Perhaps most interesting of all is the nature of the work the Carré Club artists set out to accomplish. Images taken of freelance artist Virginie Jamin at the New York version of the pop-up indicate that she spent the majority of her time working on a new border to a preexisting scarf design.[122] Although this may at first imply that the entirety of her work was an unproductive ruse, one visitor shared on social media that Hermès will indeed ultimately produce this updated scarf design—although it has yet to appear.[123]

While craft, and its current link to DIY culture, was palpable at both recent Hermès experiential events, it was particularly prevalent at Hermèsmatic. The very idea of dyeing a scarf taps into current DIY practices, which have seen an increase in the popularity of tie dye, shibori, and other dyeing techniques. One visitor took the remaking process even further, ultimately fashioning a dyed scarf into a shirt and sharing it on social media—ridding the object of any final preciousness.[124] Additionally, while scarf dyeing was undoubtedly the primary focus of the event, the pop-ups also featured stations where visitors could make, and post about, splatter paintings with Hermès-branded supplies.[125] Unsurprisingly, such paintings have experienced a wave of popularity in recent years—especially on social media.[126]

Conclusions

The Internet has undoubtedly helped luxury brands expand to reach greater, and more widespread, audiences.[127] While academic discourse may not have reached a consensus on this point, the Internet allows brands to—at least in theory—reach any individual in the world.[128] However, the Internet establishes an innate, and frequently discussed, paradox for luxury brands, in that it makes products universally accessible to see and to purchase. In response, many luxury companies have purposefully chosen to partially or entirely limit the number and type of products available on the web—Hermès included. Hermèsmatic and the Carré Club demonstrated this principle as well by greatly limiting the type and variety of products available to a circumscribed set of scarves.[129] Therefore, somewhat ironically, these experiential events behaved more like ecommerce spaces than traditional brick-and-mortar stores, echoing their intrinsic connection to the Internet.

As Kapferer emphasizes, "Too many people equate the concepts of 'community' and 'social'[;] this is a mistake."[130] Today, luxury brands aim to build engaged followings, as opposed to a sheer large number of followers.[131] This can be understood as analogous to Hermès' approach to experiential events. The company is building a specific community with its pop-ups instead of targeting the entire population surrounding its various urban, ephemeral outposts. This was illuminated by the Carré Club concierge and membership desk. On the surface, this component appears to be service oriented and democratic in its welcoming nature. However, email addresses given to the New York concierge as part of the event's basic sign-in process were intended to be used for customer outreach when the brand opened its then-upcoming and nearby Meatpacking District store.[132] In this way, it is clear that the Carré Club aimed to help form and later access a tribe of potentially loyal Hermès consumers living in affluent Manhattan neighborhoods.

Undoubtedly, Hermès will continue to produce experiential events aimed at a specific set of consumers. It is also likely that the company's scarves will continue to be a focus of future endeavors. Nevertheless, it is highly plausible that Hermès will employ the model it created at Hermèsmatic and further developed at the Carré Club to non-scarf–related pop-ups. It is conceivable as well that other luxury fashion brands may look to mimic and build upon the template that Hermès has helped pioneer. Despite the fact that Hermès has a relatively small social media following compared to its peers, Hermèsmatic and the Carré Club netted a noticeably large total media impact.[133] In future instances, the theories espoused by Thomaï Serdari, Jean-Noël Kapferer, and others will be helpful tools through which such events can be analyzed.[134] While the arguments laid out in their respective texts may gain or decrease in resonance as the years go on, they will always shed illuminating and clarifying light on Hermèsmatic and the Carré Club. This academic approach is particularly apt when it comes to Hermès. As Nadège Vanhee-Cybulski, creative director of womenswear at the French house, said, "We never talk about luxury inside Hermès. We talk about intelligence."[135]

Notes

1. Kapferer, *Kapferer on Luxury*, 60.
2. Dumas-Hermès, *A Little of Hermès Philosophy*, 12.
3. Dumas-Hermès, 17; Bennedsen, Crawford, and Hoefer, "Hermes Paris," 2–3.
4. Albrechtsen and Solanke, *Scarves*, 12.
5. Baseman and Carlton, *The Scarf*, 14, 17.
6. Hermès, "Hermès Carré Club;" Hermès, "Hermèsmatic in Austin."
7. Hermès, *Carrés: Behind the Scenes*.
8. Hermès, "Hermèsmatic in Austin."
9. Ibid; Luckel, *Untitled photographs from Hermèsmatic event in New York*.
10. Ibid.
11. Hermès, "Set your machine to colour wash #Hermes #Hermesmatic."
12. Tan, "The Hermès Carré Club Is Coming to Singapore!"
13. Luckel, *Untitled photograph from Carré Club*.
14. Hoffman and Coste-Manière, ed., *Luxury Strategy in Action*, 78.
15. Walsh, "Experiential Marketing."
16. Serdari, "Experiments in Suchness," 3.
17. Debord, *The Society of the Spectacle*; Hoffman and Coste-Manière, ed., *Luxury Strategy in Action*.
18. Kapferer, *Kapferer on Luxury*; Serdari, "Experiments in Suchness," 1–14.
19. Serdari, "Experiments in Suchness," 4; Veblen, *The Theory of the Leisure Class*; Serdari, "Kapferer on Luxury," 128–129.
20. Kapferer, *Kapferer on Luxury*; Serdari, "Kapferer on Luxury," 129.
21. Serdari, 128–129.
22. Ibid.
23. Sherman, "Hermès' Anti-Marketing Marketing."

24. Serdari, “Conversation with author,” January 9, 2019.
25. Ibid.
26. Sherman, “Hermès’ Anti-Marketing Marketing.”
27. Anaya, “The Humanity of Hermès.”
28. Sicard, *Luxury, Lies and Marketing*, XI.
29. Kapferer, *Kapferer on Luxury*, 47.
30. Hoffman and Coste-Manière, ed., *Luxury Strategy in Action*, 136.
31. Anaya, “The Humanity of Hermès.”
32. Hermès, “Look up!”
33. Kapferer, *Kapferer on Luxury*, 59.
34. Ibid, 21, 58–59.
35. Ibid, 21.
36. Ibid, 30, 52.
37. Ibid, 3.
38. Ibid.
39. Hermès, “Loving silk from head to toe.”
40. Chou, “Carré Club—checked in!”
41. Luckel, *Untitled photographs from Carré Club*.
42. Ibid.
43. Thomas, *Deluxe*, 280.
44. Anaya, “The Humanity of Hermès.”
45. Serdari, “Experiments in Suchness,” 5.
46. Ibid, 4.
47. Craik, “Meet the Maker;” Brinkley, “Every Scarf Has a Story.”
48. Brinkley, “Every Scarf Has a Story.”
49. Threadgill, “Such Fun at the Hermesmatic!!!”
50. Ibid.
51. Serdari, “Experiments in Suchness,” 6.
52. Ibid.
53. Kapferer, *Kapferer on Luxury*, 12.
54. Ibid.
55. Franzecca&Co, “Born to be square.”
56. Ibid.
57. Hermès, “Hermèsmatic in Austin.”
58. Ibid.
59. Kapferer, *Kapferer on Luxury*, 1, 41.
60. Ibid, 1, 47.
61. Pigazzini, “Join the Club.”
62. Ibid.
63. Mintel, “The Affluent and High Net Worth Premium Brand and Luxury Consumer;” Driscoll, “Panel: Luxury Now x Future;” Lacy, “Panel: Luxury Now x Future;” Solca, “Is Inclusivity the New Exclusivity?”
64. Solca, “Is Inclusivity the New Exclusivity?”
65. Serdari, “Conversation with author,” January 9, 2019.
66. Tan, “The Hermès Carré Club Is Coming to Singapore!” Sherman, “Hermès’ Anti-Marketing Marketing;” Hermès, “Hermès Carré Club.”
67. Hermès, “Mino, our special guest.”
68. Nelson, “Introduction,” XII-XIII.
69. Ibid.
70. Kapferer, *Kapferer on Luxury*, 21.
71. Debord, *Society of the Spectacle*.
72. Kapferer, *Kapferer on Luxury*, 47.
73. Hermès, “Join the Club.”
74. Ibid.
75. Sherman, “Hermès’ Anti-Marketing Marketing.”
76. Debord, *Society of the Spectacle*; Kapferer, *Kapferer on Luxury*, 44, 47; Sicard, *Luxury, Lies and Marketing*, 47.

77. Hermès, "Welcome to Hermès."
78. Debord, *Society of the Spectacle.*
79. Hermès, *Centered Rhyme de Elaine Lustig Cohen Scarf 90.*
80. Serdari, "Experiments in Suchness," 131–132.
81. Kapferer, *Kapferer on Luxury*, 59.
82. Foundation Louis Vuitton, "The Foundation Louis Vuitton;" Fondazione Prada, "Milan."
83. Hermès, *History in Carrés.*
84. Ibid.
85. 1stdibs, "Framed Hermès Scarves."
86. Nana_Venturine, "When Warhol meets Hermès marketing officers."
87. Ibid.
88. Hermès, "Scarves and Silk Accessories."
89. Corrigan, "After @jamin.virginie completes her painting;" Iamhumbertofong, "Got to meet the artist from Paris."
90. Icedteacat, "Over the moon meeting my favorite Hermes scarves designer."
91. Psihramis, "Celebrating my mom's birthday."
92. Clarke, "Thank you @hermes."
93. Groenendijk, "Memories Like This Are Priceless."
94. Taylor, "Midsummer Night's Dream as Silky Inspiration."
95. Ibid.
96. Kapferer, *Kapferer on Luxury*, 63, 73; Serdari, "Experiments in Suchness," 4, 5, 11, 13.
97. Hermès, "Welcome to the Hermès Carré Club."
98. Ibid.
99. Rainbow_riki_surprise, "The aesthetic;" Malachi, "Amazing illustration in process."
100. Rainbow_riki_surprise, "The aesthetic."
101. Mit_chin. "Name your own H colour!"
102. Serdari, "Experiments in Suchness," 8.
103. Ibid.
104. Hermès, "Scarves and Silk Accessories."
105. Serdari, "Experiments in Suchness," 12.
106. Anaya, "The Humanity of Hermès."
107. Kapferer, *Kapferer on Luxury*, 63–83.
108. Serdari, "Conversation with Author," January 9, 2019.
109. Hermès, "Blue Brushstrokes."
110. Ibid.
111. Ladylemonade25, "I Have Always Loved Silk Scarf."
112. Luckel, *Untitled photographs from Carré Club.*
113. Ibid.
114. Ibid.
115. Ibid.
116. Ibid.
117. Hermès, "Set your machine to colour wash;" Hermès, "Ding! It's ready;" Hermès, "New life for a scarf;" Hermès, "Find the dyed one;" Hermès, "Hermèsmatic team;" Hermès, "Shake Shake!"
118. Ibid.
119. Pukusawa, "Friday Night at @hermes Pop Up Store."
120. Traiwatanapong, "H E R M È S Carré Moment."
121. Victoire.lvg, "Surteinte."
122. Moukarzel Giordano, "Hermès Carre Pop Up Store."
123. Fedoruk, "More from Hermès pop up!"
124. Choc_and_lace. "J'entends déjà vos voix."
125. Pialoux, "J'aurais voulu être un artiste."
126. Instagram, "#spinpainting."
127. Hoffman and Coste-Manière, ed., *Luxury Strategy in Action*, 75.
128. Ibid.
129. Luckel, *Untitled photographs from Carré Club.*
130. Kapferer, *Kapferer on Luxury*, 31.

131. Lacy, "Panel: Luxury Now x Future."
132. Sherman, "Hermès' Anti-Marketing Marketing."
133. Smith, "Hermès, Artisan of the Birkin Bag."
134. Serdari, "Experiments in Suchness;" Kapferer, *Kapferer on Luxury*.
135. Hass, "Hermès's Refusal to Change Is Its Most Radical Gesture Yet."

Bibliography

Primary Sources

Choc_and_lace. "J'entends déjà vos voix s'écrier au scandale d'avoir osé prendre de la teinture et une paire de ciseaux face à un carré Hermès . . ." *Instagram*, November 13, 2018. www.instagram.com/p/BqIOF1xFL9y/.

Chou, Chou. "Carré Club—checked in! #hermes #carreclub #hermes #tamson #tamsonfashion #tamsonwatchandjewelry." *Instagram*, October 19, 2018. www.instagram.com/p/BpHLnp3Fx0Y/.

Clarke, Alex. "Thank you @hermes & @buildanest for this opportunity to learn so much more about craft and business. Also, thank you for this cocktail party #carreclub." *Instagram*, September 13, 2018. www.instagram.com/p/BnsFQ-XlGBE/.

Corrigan, Kiera. "After @jamin.virginie completes her painting it's a two year process to make the @hermes scarves!" *Instagram*, September 16, 2018. www.instagram.com/p/BnypC5IBUuB/.

Dumas-Hermès, Jean-Louis . . . *A Little of Hermès Philosophy*. Paris: Hermès, 2014.

Fedoruk, Kristina. "More from Hermès pop up!" *Instagram*, September 16, 2018. www.instagram.com/p/BnzbFO6BVFv/.

Franzecca&Co. "Born to be square." *Instagram*, November 27, 2018. www.instagram.com/p/Bqs0rlFl1-Z/.

Groenendijk, Per. "Blue brushstrokes #CarreClub." *Instagram*, September 14, 2018. www.instagram.com/p/BntmZTeHlKv/.

———. *Carrés: Behind the Scenes*. Paris: Hermès Éditions, 2008.

———. Designed by Elaine Lustig Cohen. *Centered Rhyme de Elaine Lustig Cohen Scarf 90*. Scarf in silk twill with hand rolled edges. 36 × 36 in. www.hermes.com/us/en/product/centered-rhyme-de-elaine-lustig-cohen-scarf-90-H003139Sv07/.

———. "Ding! It's ready #Hermes #Hermesmatic." *Instagram*, June 7, 2017. www.instagram.com/p/BVC5_WzlFYR/.

———. "Find the dyed one #Hermes #Hermesmatic." *Instagram*, June 8, 2018. www.instagram.com/p/BVFMhXUl3Un/.

———. *Hermès Carré Club*. Paris: Hermès, 2018.

———. "Hermèsmatic in Austin." www.hermes.com/us/en/story/107636-hermesmatic/.

———. *History in Carrés*. Paris: Hermès Éditions, 2008.

———. "Join the Club, s'il vous plaît. #CarreClub." *Instagram*, September 12, 2018, www.instagram.com/p/Bnpd2UUHdX-/.

———. "Look up! #Hermes #petith." *Instagram*, December 29, 2016, www.instagram.com/p/BOnORrFD3w1/.

———. "Loving silk from head to toe. #CarreClub." *Instagram*, September 14, 2018, www.instagram.com/p/BntuNZqHuPT/.

———. "Memories like this are priceless." *Instagram*, July 27, 2018. www.instagram.com/p/BluZEB0lqnE/.

———. "Mino, our special guest. #CarreClub." *Instagram*, September 12, 2018, www.instagram.com/p/BnpkoNoHoJt/.

———. "New life for a scarf #Hermes #Hermesmatic." *Instagram*, June 7, 2017. www.instagram.com/p/BVDRlEWFtDe/.

———. "Scarves and Silk Accessories." *Women Scarves Creations and Silk Accessories for Women—Hermès*. www.hermes.com/us/en/women/scarves-and-silk-accessories/?gclsrc=aw.ds&&gclid=CjwKCAjwpKveBRAwEiwAo4Pqmx-g_NCXZJbth9ly9sf0yEh5NM8d-K90jIIshtxUbxGvfiq-D3CXuRoCYBEQAvD_BwE&gclsrc=aw.ds#fh_view_size=108&country=us&fh_location=--%2Fcategories%3C%7Bcatalog01_women%7D%2Fcategories%3C%7Bcatalog01_women_womensilkscarvesetc%7D%2Ftheme%3E%7Bs_collectionneur%7D%2Fobject_type_filter%3E%7Bcarres_90_x_90%7D||Category,Theme.

———. "Set your machine to colour wash #Hermes #Hermesmatic." *Instagram*, June 6, 2017. www.instagram.com/p/BVAZKlclNFy/?taken-by=hermes.

———. "Shake Shake! #Hermes #Hermesmatic." *Instagram*, June 9, 2017. www.instagram.com/p/BVIGbFjleq_/.

———. "The Hermèsmatic team #Hermes #Hermesmatic." *Instagram*, June 8, 2017. www.instagram.com/p/BVFbOSDFi1R/.

———. "Welcome to Hermès–Le Faubourg Saint-Honoré." www.hermesfaubourg.com/client/register.

———. "Welcome to the Hermès Carré Club. Feast your eyes on the fantastical Drawing Machine. #CarreClub." *Instagram*, September 12, 2018. www.instagram.com/p/BnpZFrGndDL/.

Iamhumbertofong. "Got to meet the artist from Paris. I will buy this when it come out . . [.] estimate production 18 months." *Instagram*, September 15, 2018. www.instagram.com/p/Bnw8lT8Fyqh/?utm_source=ig_embed&ig_mid=XGNGhgABAAGVRKjliZ_TyiAHyiF6.

Icedteacat. "Over the moon meeting my favorite Hermes scarves designer. Thank you, Alice! I can't wait for your next design!" *Instagram*, September 16, 2018. www.instagram.com/p/BnzcjCtDUMa/.

Ladylemonade25. "I have always loved silk scarf and have a large collection that dates back to my college years. I love that @Hermès is giving so much exposure to young and brilliant illustrators! #carreclub." *Instagram*, September 16, 2018. www.instagram.com/p/BnydAUKnQOP/.

Luckel, Madeleine. *Untitled photographs from Carré Club event in New York*. 2018. Digital photographs taken on iPhone.

———. *Untitled photographs from Hermèsmatic event in New York*. 2017. Digital photographs taken on iPhone.

Malachi, Peter. "Amazing illustration in process @hermes #carreclub." *Instagram*, September 15, 2018. www.instagram.com/p/BnwjMUwFQ9Z/.

Mit_chin. "Name your own H colour!" *Instagram*, September 15, 2018. www.instagram.com/p/BnvA9_XnKnn/.

Moukarzel Giordano, Yasmina. "Hermès Carre pop up store . . . amazing artists . . . attention to detail." *Instagram*, September 16, 2018. www.instagram.com/p/BnyqtfKhs4F/.

Nana_Venturine. "When Warhol meets Hermès marketing officers." *Instagram*, June 15, 2017. www.instagram.com/p/BVXuyKqFlA5/?utm_source=ig_share_sheet&igshid=.

Pialoux, Florian. "J'aurais voulu être un artiste." *Instagram*, June 15, 2017. www.instagram.com/p/BVXtYGHh-OP/.

Pigazzini, Elisa. "Join the club #Hermes#CarreClub #bethereorbesquare#notsosquare #joinwatchfeel #celebration." *Instagram*, December 2, 2018. www.instagram.com/p/Bq5mrIVnJ3x/.

Psihramis, Lisa. "Celebrating my mom's birthday a little early at the #hermes pop-up shop #hermesmatic These scarves are going to be over dyed pink!" *Instagram*, March 14, 2018. www.instagram.com/p/BgUslT5jwoQ/.

Pukusawa, "Friday night at @hermes Pop up store." *Instagram*, September 16, 2018. www.instagram.com/p/BnymztCHnBR/.

Rainbow_riki_surprise. "The aesthetic. The appreciation. The art. The ARTISTS!!" *Instagram*, September 15, 2018. www.instagram.com/p/BnvAllRnGdU/.

Taylor, Lillis. "Midsummer Night's Dream as silky inspiration . . . #carréclub #carreclub." *Instagram*, September 16, 2018. www.instagram.com/p/BnzXuXmnpbY/.

Threadgill, Cheri-Kay. "Such fun at the Hermesmatic!!!" *Instagram*, November 18, 2017. www.instagram.com/p/Bbo4i0GFzvw/.

Traiwatanapong, Toon. "H E R M È S Carré moment." *Instagram*, September 15, 2018. www.instagram.com/jidatoon/?hl=en.

Victoire.lvg. "Surteinte." *Instagram*, June 6, 2017. www.instagram.com/victoire.lvg/.

Secondary Sources

1stdibs. "Framed Hermès Scarves." www.1stdibs.com/buy/framed-hermes-scarves/.

Albrechtsen, Nicky and Fola Solanke. *Scarves*. New York: Thames & Hudson, 2011.

Anaya, Suleman. "The Humanity of Hermès." *The Business of Fashion*, April 29, 2014, Intelligence. www.businessoffashion.com/articles/intelligence/humanity-hermes.

Baseman, Andrew and Harold Carlton. *The Scarf*. New York: Stewart, Tabori & Chang, 1989.

Bennedsen, Morten, Robert Crawford, and Rolf Hoefer. "Hermes Paris." *Harvard Business Review*, April 28, 2014, Case Study. https://hbr.org/product/recommended/an/INS508-PDF-ENG?referral=02527&cm_vc=rr_item_page.articles.

Brinkley, Christina. "Every Scarf Has a Story." *The Wall Street Journal*, May 22, 2013, On Style. www.wsj.com/articles/SB10001424127887323975004578499110750076242.

Craik, Laura. "Meet the Maker: Hermès Scarf Designer Alice Shirley." *The Telegraph*, October 27, 2017, Luxury, Women's Style. www.telegraph.co.uk/luxury/womens-style/hermes-scarf-designer-alice-shirley/.

Debord, Guy. *The Society of the Spectacle*. London: Bread and Circuses Publishing, 1967.

Driscoll, Marie. "Panel: Luxury Now x Future." Panel Participant at Parsons School of Design "Redefining Luxury" Conference, New York, October 5, 2018.

Fondazione Prada. "Milan." www.fondazioneprada.org/visit/visit-milan/?lang=en.

Foundation Louis Vuitton. "The Foundation Louis Vuitton." www.fondationlouisvuitton.fr/en.html.

Hass, Nancy. "Hermès's Refusal to Change Is Its Most Radical Gesture Yet." *The New York Times Style Magazine*, February 15, 2019. www.nytimes.com/2019/02/15/t-magazine/hermes.html.

Hoffman, Jonas and Ivan Coste-Manière, ed. *Luxury Strategy in Action*. London: Palgrave Macmillan, 2012.

Instagram. "#spinpainting." www.instagram.com/explore/tags/spinpainting/.

Kapferer, Jean-Noël. *Kapferer on Luxury: How Luxury Brands Can Grow Yet Remain Rare*. London: Kogan Page, 2015.

Lacy, Christopher. "Panel: Luxury Now x Future." Panel Participant at Parsons School of Design "Redefining Luxury" Conference, New York, October 5, 2018.

Mintel. "The Affluent and High Net Worth Premium Brand and Luxury Consumer–US—December 2016." http://academic.mintel.com.proxy.library.nyu.edu/display/806467/.

Nelson, Brian. "Introduction." In *The Ladies' Paradise*. By Émile Zola. Translated by Brian Nelson. Oxford: Oxford University Press, 1993.

Serdari, Thomaï. "Kapferer on Luxury, Brands Can Grow Yet Remain Rare." *Luxury* 2, no. 2 (2015), 127–132.

———. "Conversation with Author." January 9, 2019. NYU Stern School of Business.

———. "Experiments in Suchness: Hiroshi Sugimoto's Silk Shiki for Hermès." In *Critical Luxury Studies: Art, Design, Media*. By John Armitage and Joanne Roberts. Edinburgh: Edinburgh Scholarship Online, 2017, 1–18.

Sherman, Lauren. "Hermès' Anti-Marketing Marketing." *Business of Fashion*, September 27, 2018, Intelligence. www.businessoffashion.com/articles/professional/hermes-anti-marketing-marketing.

Sicard, Marie-Claude. *Luxury, Lies and Marketing: Shattering the Illusions of the Luxury Brand*. Translated by Trevor Cribben Merill. London: Palgrave Macmillan, 2013.

Smith, Ray A. "Hermès, Artisan of the Birkin Bag, Rolls Out a Fanny Pack." *The Wall Street Journal*, April 3, 2019, Life & Style. www.wsj.com/articles/hermes-artisan-of-the-birkin-bag-rolls-out-a-fanny-pack-11554313767.

Solca, Luca. "Is Inclusivity the New Exclusivity? Gucci Certainly Thinks So." *Business of Fashion*, July 25, 2018, Luca's Letter. www.businessoffashion.com/articles/professional/is-inclusivity-the-new-exclusivity-gucci-certainly-thinks-so.

Tan, Pakkee. "The Hermès Carré Club Is Coming to Singapore!" *Harper's Bazaar Singapore*, October 5, 2018. www.harpersbazaar.com.sg/fashion/hermes-carre-club-singapore-details-dates/.

Thomas, Dana. *Deluxe: How Luxury Lost Its Luster*. New York: Penguin Press, 2007.

Veblen, Thorstein. *The Theory of the Leisure Class*. Edited by Martha Banta. Oxford: Oxford University Press, 2007.

Walsh, John, PhD. "Experiential Marketing." *Salem Press Encyclopedia*, 2017. http://proxy.library.nyu.edu/login?url=http://search.ebscohost.com/login.aspx?direct=true&db=ers&AN=90558320&site=eds-live.

Zola, Émile. *The Ladies' Paradise*. Translated by Brian Nelson. Oxford: Oxford University Press, 1993.

2 The Good, the Bad, and the Ugly

Dolce & Gabbana and Narratives of Heritage and National Identity

Alice Dallabona and Stefano Giani

Dolce & Gabbana and Italianicity

Dolce & Gabbana is an Italian luxury fashion label founded in 1985 by Domenico Dolce and Stefano Gabbana. The label is renowned with regard to womenswear for its sensual and bold looks. Dolce & Gabbana, in terms of brand identity, heavily relies on references to its country of origin, Italy, and in particular on the culture of Sicily and its Mediterranean heritage. References to those elements are consistently featured by the label in every aspect of its marketing and communication strategy and constitute, in semiotic terms, an isotopy. An isotopy is something that could be described as a recurring 'theme' or 'motif,' a fil rouge providing *continuity and coherence to storytelling and that can involve all levels of meaning, from the textual surface to the deeper structures of the generative trajectory* (Greimas and Courtés 1986, Nöth 1995, Bronwen and Ringham 2006).

The narratives employed by Dolce & Gabbana, which feature characterizing traits of Italian national identity, are considered here not in terms of Italianness but in terms of Italinicity (Barthes 1977), as we want to draw attention to the fact that the elements that are linked to Italy and considered salient traits of national identity are not fixed once and for all but change in time and space to include new and different elements where sometimes reality and imagination merge and are closely intertwined.

The focus on Italianicity of Dolce & Gabbana is easy to see in the label's communication strategies, its products, and its advertising campaigns but also its store environments. For example, Dolce & Gabbana features, in its flagship stores and selling points in upmarket retailers, an abundance of frescos, brocade textiles, and marble but also bright Sicilian carts and majolica pottery. Lately, the link between Dolce & Gabbana and Italian identity has been emphasized further with culinary collaborations that have seen the label first offering a 'Limited Edition Dolce & Gabbana pasta' collection with Valvona Crolla in 2017 and then, in 2019, expanding on this with a collection of *panettoni* (a type of Italian Christmas cake) with Fiasconi, all featuring packaging in the bright colors and patterns so closely associated with Sicily and, more broadly, the south of Italy and the Mediterranean area. Moreover, Dolce & Gabbana's advertising campaigns feature countless signs of Italianicity, from 'pizza, pasta and mandolino' to bread, big multigenerational families, and parties in the streets. However, despite the differences in the elements featured, a common theme emerges, and that is an image of Italy as a place outside of modernity (Parkins 2004), frozen in an idealized past centered around conviviality and tradition. This is particularly evident in the brand's digital storytelling strategies, which will be examined in the next section through the analysis of a series of videos focusing on the craftsmanship of Dolce & Gabbana that once again capitalize on certain traits linked to Italy to provide prestige and a competitive advantage to its products.

However, if relying on traits of national identity that are familiar to consumers has significant advantages, there are also risks involved. National identity can be an incredibly valuable reserve for brand culture, as seen in the next section with regard to the use of narratives of craftsmanship, but sometimes situations of cultural opportunism (Dallabona 2015) that see brands appropriating, and taking advantage of, cultural elements can go wrong if those are perceived as offensive by certain communities. That was the case for the furious backlash received by Dolce & Gabbana with regard to a campaign focusing on China in 2018, which is discussed later on in the chapter.

Digital Storytelling and Italian Craftsmanship

Dolce & Gabbana, unlike older labels like Gucci, does not originate in workshops, nor is it rooted in the craftsmanship traditionally associated with Italian fashion and which contributed to creating the reputation of the country as a homeland of fashion in the first place. Nonetheless, Dolce & Gabbana refers to this pivotal aspect of Italian heritage while at the same time also portraying other elements of Italian national identity in its marketing strategies. Here, we focus in particular on the over 40 videos published by the brand on its official YouTube channel, which focus on how the goods associated with the label are produced, with the aim to examine references to traditional Italian craftsmanship. It will be argued that the label has emphasized, in its online communication, the handmade craftsmanship involved in the creation of its products. However, it will be observed how that element is presented only in association with certain types of goods and not to the totality of products that are associated with the name of the fashion brand. It is important to notice how the vast majority of the videos published by Dolce & Gabbana primarily show its most expensive products, from haute couture pieces to shoes and handbags but also jewelry and watches. There are only a couple of videos focusing on cheaper items, like eyewear. Even cheaper products, like cosmetics or fragrances, are actually not represented at all. Nonetheless, the videos share many common elements. They are represented by a focus on handmade production, references to practices that are hundreds of years old, and very limited references to modern methods of production.

In all of the videos focusing on the production of Dolce & Gabbana's haute couture, for example, we only see workers performing tasks completely by hand. First, we are shown people drawing the design on paper; then we see the different materials getting cut and sewed before decorations and embroidery are applied. Even though we actually see some faces at times, it's interesting to notice how the focus of the videos is actually represented by the hands of many expert artisans slowly and carefully performing a series of actions. For example, in a video focusing on the brand's jewelry line (Dolce & Gabbana 2011), we only see the hands of the artisans making the product and working on the different pieces, melting metal, mounting stones, creating delicate filigree, and finishing the products. The same can be observed when it's shoes or handbags being made, as we see different people, and many hands, in a workshop setting performing a series of actions, from cutting to sewing, from embroidering to applying decorative elements and painting, alongside gluing materials, hammering leather with nails, and assembling the final products. Interestingly, many of the hands featured in the videos proudly showcase signs of ageing (wrinkles and age spots), alluding to the link between years of experience and the ability to master all the delicate phases of the production of Dolce & Gabbana products. Moreover, the focus on the hands of craftspeople also functions to present them as an anonymous and 'eternal' force that is intrinsically linked to 'Made in Italy' and that can provide history and additional value to Dolce & Gabbana products.

This dimension is further emphasized in a small series of videos that focus not on the in-house production practices of Dolce & Gabbana but on the different artisans and companies that supply the brand when it comes to some specific products or materials. That is, for example, the case for certain types of silk (Dolce & Gabbana 2019a), brocade (Dolce & Gabbana 2019b), or velvet (Dolce & Gabbana 2019c). With regard to the latter, the video is described as an insider's look into the handmade production of *soprarizzo* velvet, "an ancient handcraft renowned for its use of two different irons: an intricate and delicate process that enhances the homespun manufacturing of this unique textile" and that has been produced in Venice's Canal Grande by Bevilacqua Weaving since the fifteenth century. It has to be noted that, while the production videos posted by Dolce & Gabbana feature classical music as soundtrack, the videos focusing on the traditional craftsmanship of its suppliers are actually narrated in Italian by the people involved in the production of goods. The videos present English subtitles to make them accessible to a wider public, and it is argued here that the choice not to use a voice-over in English but to privilege the first-person account of the Italian people actually involved in the production of traditional textiles, or employing jewelry techniques that are centuries old, functions to convey ideas of authentic Italianicity. Those notions of authenticity are in this sense the result of narrative strategies that support such modality of discourse (Greimas 1984) and not the product of some intrinsic characteristics (Spooner 1986, Bruner 1991, Silver 1993, Wang 1999).

It has to be observed that such dimensions of handmade craftsmanship and workshops are often used for promotional purposes by Italian companies (Ross 2004), and that is especially the case for the small- and medium-sized enterprises (SMEs) that constitute the backbone of the Italian fashion industry (Dunford 2006). The prestige and good reputation attributed to Italian craftsmanship have been long established thanks to centuries of experience in the field of textile production (White 2000), embroidery (Giordani-Aragno 1983, Steele 2003, Rocca 2006), tailoring, and accessory production, in particular leather goods (Jackson 2004), and it precedes the rise of Italian fashion in the post-war period. It is precisely on this tradition that Dolce & Gabbana is capitalizing by presenting, in its digital storytelling, narratives of traditional Italian craftsmanship.

As examined by Dallabona (2014), craftsmanship is an element often employed by Italian luxury fashion brands in their communication and marketing practices, as it is considered a powerful tool in terms of associating the products, and the label, with positive values and connotations, supporting their appeal and presenting them as part of an invaluable long-established heritage. More generally, craftsmanship is also considered a distinctive trait that characterizes luxury fashion brands (Dubois and Paternault 1995, Tungate 2005, Berthon et al. 2009, Fionda and Moore 2009), and the assumption is that the luxury products are unique (Dubois et al. 2001) as a result of the fact that specialized artisans make those products by hand (Chevalier and Mazzalovo 2008). However, that is only one facet of how the goods associated with luxury fashion labels are actually made, even though people prefer not to believe that (Chevalier and Mazzalovo 2008). In fact, not all the products associated with luxury fashion brands are made by hand, and a number of goods bearing the names of luxury fashion labels are mass manufactured. That is especially the case for diffusion lines and the less expensive facets of the brands, such as accessories and cosmetics (Dallabona 2014). This is in line with conceptualizations that state how there are nowadays different levels of luxury in the industry. In this sense, Kapferer (2004) identifies, for example, the level of the *griffe*, where the products are the result of the unique work of the designer; the level of the workshops, which is the one that the videos by Dolce & Gabbana discussed previously refers to; and last the level of mass manufacture, which is very different from the other two and is the type of production used, for example, in eyewear.

On its official YouTube channel, Dolce & Gabbana feature a number of videos depicting the production of its glasses, and those are the only videos where technology and mass manufacture are actually seen. For example, in two videos focusing on the making of the Domenico and Lace frames (Dolce & Gabbana 2019d, 2019e), we see the design for the eyewear pieces being drawn by hand, but then the frame and temples of glasses are machine made. This might seem problematic in terms of the narratives of traditional Italian craftsmanship that the label is employing in the other videos, but at the same time, this is counterbalanced by two elements. In fact, alongside notions of traditional handmade craftsmanship, the reputation of Italian luxury fashion labels, and more broadly Italian fashion, is also strictly associated with ideas of technological advancements (Steele 2003). And, moreover, Dolce & Gabbana still focus on conveying ideas of tradition and craftsmanship even when it comes to products that are usually mass manufactured through videos depicting special editions where handmade production has a more prominent role. With regard to eyewear, that is, for example, the case of DG Crystal Sunglasses (Dolce & Gabbana 2019f), which feature stones individually applied to the frame by hand, or in the case of the Mosaico (Dolce & Gabbana 2014) and Sicilian cart glasses (Dolce & Gabbana 2016).

The video for the limited-edition Mosaico eyewear shows how the tassels of the mosaic are first produced, and then applied, by hand to create a colorful and detailed floral pattern. It is this process, it is claimed in the caption, that makes "this sunglass a real masterpiece, unique and highly exclusive" and an "expression of the most high Italian craftsmanship ability" (Dolce & Gabbana 2014). Another limited-edition eyewear collection was launched in 2016, called Sicilian Carretto, that is, Sicilian cart (Dolce & Gabbana 2016). The video shows a dark-haired Mediterranean-looking woman painting a wooden glass frame using rich and vibrant colors to replicate the same intricate patterns that feature on the traditional Sicilian carts but on a smaller scale. The craftswoman works slowly and meticulously, using a magnifying glass to transfer the traditional pattern and paint relief miniatures. The caption states that, "like the antique carts, every pair of glasses is a special piece: the decorator's hand renders each model completely unique," in this sense supporting the idea that the label Dolce & Gabbana is using traditional methods of production and handmade craftsmanship that originate in Italian culture, benefiting from the positive values and connotations deriving from this association. But those two videos focus on special-edition eyewear, more expensive pieces produced in limited numbers, that are not mass produced as their 'regular' counterparts are.

However, the choice by Dolce & Gabbana to focus on notions of craftsmanship and handmade production, even in this case, is functional in terms of capitalizing on the long-established reputation of Italian fashion for its heritage and quality (Steele 2003). This contributes to reinforce narratives that see Italy as the custodian of traditions and skills that pass down from generation to generation, kept alive and constantly revitalized by production practices employed in the fashion industry and, in particular, by luxury fashion brands, which are in turn presented as an essential part in conceptualizations of Italianicity. It is interesting to note that Dolce & Gabbana has actually emphasized this dimension of Italian traditional handmade craftsmanship even more after the notorious 2018 scandal concerning promotional videos presenting a controversial image of China. The label is in this sense recognizing the powerful value of such narratives in reinforcing positive elements of national identity that can, in turn, positively affect the prestige, aura, and reputation of the brand, which was, as discussed in the next section, tarnished by the controversy.

The Big Controversy: Dolce & Gabbana Loves China

As we have seen, to rely on traits of national identity that are familiar to consumers can be very beneficial, capitalizing on long-established positive associations that increase the prestige and desirability of brands and their products. But using traits of national identity can be a double-edged sword and cause offence, potentially alienating consumers and public opinion. Dolce & Gabbana has long been criticized by the Italian community for reinforcing questionable stereotypes, like the one surrounding the alleged innate boisterous and loud nature of Italians. Storytelling can use stereotypical elements to convey meaning in a concise manner and to play with elements that are familiar to the public, but there is a danger of oversimplification and, if those are not employed with cultural sensitivity, the risk of causing offense rises even more. This was the case with regard to a series of videos created by Dolce & Gabbana in November 2018 to promote its fashion show in the city of Shanghai (China), which caused a furious backlash amid accusations of racism.

The Chinese market is very important for luxury fashion labels, and Dolce & Gabbana planned to lure such consumers further by organizing a fashion show, in late 2018, that was supposed to promote the label and celebrate China at the same time (Wiener-Bronner 2018). Chinese celebrities, buyers, and movie stars were to attend, and the event was heavily promoted online through the hashtags #DGTheGreatShow and #DGLovesChina. However, as Dolce & Gabbana posted three promotional videos to Weibo (the most popular social network in China), controversy ensued.

The videos featured a young Chinese model, wearing Dolce & Gabbana clothes and accessories, facing typical Italian food, that is, pizza, spaghetti, and cannoli. The set of the videos was what has been described by many as a dark and old-fashioned Chinese interior that does not represent the true reality of the country nowadays, and the ads feature a soundtrack of stereotypical Chinese folk music that has been similarly defined as outdated (CGTN 2018). Things were not made better by the voice-over, a male speaking in Mandarin giving instructions and who appeared to be 'mansplaining' to the young girl how to use chopsticks to eat pizza, spaghetti, and cannoli as she struggled, nor by the double entendres of sexual nature (Xu 2018). The videos even featured the speaker mispronouncing the name of the label Dolce & Gabbana, in what was perceived to be a mockery of Chinese people. What was perhaps meant to be a tongue-in-cheek campaign certainly seemed to have missed the mark, as the ads were perceived as racist and disrespectful, so much so that within an hour, hashtags about boycotting Dolce and Gabbana emerged and went viral in China (France24 English 2018). In response to that, Dolce & Gabbana posted a message on its official Instagram page, but that fell just short of an apology, as it stated that the company intended to bring to Shanghai a tribute event dedicated to China that it had created with love and passion and defined the whole thing as unfortunate for all those who worked to create the event, before closing with a heartfelt thank you to the friends and guests who were planning to attend (E! Asia 2018). The brand also immediately removed the three videos from Weibo, but not from its official Instagram account, and soon the controversy gathered pace even more.

The Chinese brand ambassador resigned from the role (DW News 2018), and very quickly, celebrities and VIPs, but also model agencies, started to distance themselves from the event, declaring that they would not attend the fashion show due to Dolce & Gabbana's disrespectful attitude toward China, that they thought was being depicted as a backward and old-fashioned country ignorant of the Western way of life, so much so that its citizens were portrayed as allegedly unable to perform even simple tasks like eating pizza. The ads were branded "offensive" and accused of "spreading false stereotypes" and lacking consideration for the Chinese cultural sensibilities (Barr 2018). On the day of the fashion show, everything was ready for the grand-scale event, which saw thousands of people involved in the production and should have seen over 360 people walking the catwalk, but at the last minute, everything was cancelled, as Chinese guests and models started leaving due to another controversy (Dazed 2018). In fact, screenshots of a conversation between a journalist of Diet Prada (a popular Instagram account acting as a sort of watchdog with regard to the fashion industry) and Stefano Gabbana were circulating over the Internet, with the latter allegedly making some rather offensive remarks toward China in response to the scandal. Some refused to believe the screenshots were true, as to send such messages would have not been a wise PR move at all, but the story, again, went viral.

The alleged messages by Stefano Gabbana were quite strong, using a 'poop emoji' to define China and adding that the country was "Ignorant, Dirty Smelling Mafia" (Diet Prada 2018). Later on, Dolce & Gabbana claimed that the brand's account, and the one belonging to Stefano Gabbana, had been hacked. Afterward, Domenico Dolce and Stefano Gabbana also released a video, still available on the official YouTube channel (Dolce & Gabbana 2018), where they made a groveling apology and asked to be forgiven for the lack of respect shown toward China, claiming that this was never their intention at all and that they would learn from this mistake, making sure always to respect Chinese culture from now on. However, the damage was indeed already done, and products by Dolce & Gabbana were removed from Chinese retailers online in a move that was estimated to have cost the brand over €36 millions in just one day (Dazed 2018). It is clear to see that the brand image of Dolce & Gabbana in China was seriously tarnished by the controversy, as retailers refused to feature the label's products in their shops, and Chinese consumers returned Dolce & Gabbana items (Van Elven 2018). In China, the Weibo hashtag #DGTheGreatShowCancelled was mentioned in 74,000 discussions and seen over 540 million times (Hall and Suen 2018). But what were the repercussions in Western countries, and how did the digital narratives surrounding Dolce & Gabbana change as a result of the scandal?

We monitored the social media Twitter for one year, from November 2018 to the end of October 2019, to assess the short-term and long-term implications of the scandal. We collected live data from Twitter using the Twitter streaming APIs, and we used specific keywords related to Dolce & Gabbana to filter out unwanted or unrelated tweets. Overall, we collected more than 280k tweets between general tweets and retweets. We then performed sentiment analysis over the corpus, calculating the sentiment polarity of the tweets using VADER (Hutto and Gilbert 2015). VADER is a widely used rule-based model for general sentiment analysis. For each tweet, VADER produces four polarity scores: negative, neutral, positive, and compound. The first three indicate the grade of the polarity of the tweet in each class, whereas the fourth metric score indicates the overall polarity of the tweet. In our analysis, we used the compound score as the sentiment polarity of the tweets. The polarity values range from –1 to +1, with –1 indicating a strong negative sentiment and +1 a strong positive sentiment.

To produce Figure 2.1, we computed the aggregated polarity of all the tweets generated on each day between November 2018 and October 2019. The sentiment polarity p_d for the day d is computed using the weighted average of the sentiment polarity for all general tweets $t_{i,d}$ for the day d, with $i = 1, \ldots, N_d$, where N_d is the number of general tweets for the day d. The weighted average is computed taking into account the number of retweets $r_{i,d}$ for each general tweet:

$$p_d := \frac{\sum_{i=1}^{N_d} \left(r_{i,d} + 1\right) t_{i,d}}{\sum_{i=1}^{N_d} \left(r_{i,d} + 1\right)}.$$

The use of the number of retweets in the averaging is in line with our aim to measure the overall sentiment toward D&G for each day. We assumed that a retweet is an indication of a person expressing a sentiment aligned with the sentiment of the general tweet that is retweeted.

Looking at Figure 2.1, we can see that within the year we monitored, a major dip in the sentiment polarity for Dolce & Gabbana was seen in November 2018 as the result of the China scandal discussed previously. The dip was the biggest one for the whole

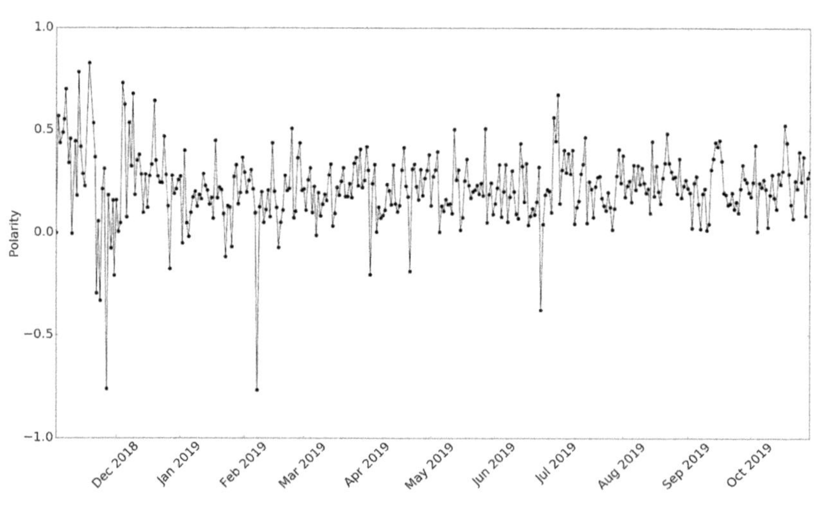

Figure 2.1 Day polarity of Dolce & Gabbana on Twitter.

year, and it is in this sense indicative of how much the controversy, and the related backlash, affected the narratives surrounding the brand Dolce & Gabbana. However, despite a clear immediate negative reaction by Twitter users, our results also show that the effects of the scandal were not felt for very long, because in just a matter of days, the narratives surrounding Dolce & Gabbana went back to being positive and in line with their standard performance. This in a certain sense contradicts earlier reports in the press, which predicted that Dolce & Gabbana would suffer, in terms of brand image, for quite some time. However, we argue, the consequences of the scandals were far from over and still active under the surface, just suspended and ready to re-emerge under the right circumstances.

Even though there were other dips, the polarity concerning Dolce & Gabbana has remained mostly positive in the aftermath of the scandal and the year after that, with only one significant exception, a major dip seen in February 2019. This was again related to the China scandal discussed previously, as it seems that Dolce & Gabbana was left vulnerable to negative narratives and prone to see the scandal re-emerge. Interestingly, in this case, the dip was the result of events that were originally completely unrelated to the brand's activities. In fact, the major dip in polarity that occurred at the beginning of February 2019, the second biggest in the year we monitored (see Figure 2.1), occurred because the Dolce & Gabbana scandal in China of November 2018 became topical once again in the aftermath of another scandal in the luxury fashion industry, this time concerning Gucci.

Gucci was accused of racism due to the peculiar design of a 'balaclava jumper,' a black sweater with a turtleneck that went over the lower face of the wearer, leaving an opening for the mouth that was surrounded by a red motif resembling lips, which was likened to blackface, causing huge controversy. The Gucci scandal attracted significant attention in the press worldwide, and the garment in question was swiftly withdrawn (Willan 2019). However, as the scandal went viral and attracted more and more attention in the press, many articles again dragged out the Dolce & Gabbana China controversy of November 2018 as a clear example of bad practice in the luxury fashion industry, which was accused of widespread cultural insensitivity (BBC 2019). The repercussions were also seen online, as we have observed that at the time, Dolce & Gabbana online discourses again became characterized by a striking negative polarity. However, just as happened at the time of the original scandal, the polarity soon went back to positive, and no similar major dips were observed again in the whole year we monitored. Nonetheless, despite the quick recovery in both cases, this means that negative impressions and narratives concerning the brand Dolce & Gabbana have not gone away for good and that they are likely to re-emerge again if other similar scandals appear in the future, not necessarily as a result of direct actions by the brand itself but also as a result of the behavior of its competitors.

National Identity: A Valuable Resource to Be Used Carefully

The core of the Dolce & Gabbana scandal of November 2018 was the disputable use of national identity traits, in a series of videos aimed at promoting a fashion show in China that presented a controversial image of the country and that was ultimately considered offensive by the public it was designed to entice. In this sense, this highlights the power such narratives hold and the issues faced when communication is not quite right in terms of cultural sensibility. It is quite interesting, then, to observe how, in the aftermath of the scandal, Dolce & Gabbana turned again to narratives of national identity to solve the issues caused by the use of national traits. In fact, if the dimension of Italianicity and a certain presence of narratives of traditional handmade craftsmanship were already present in Dolce & Gabbana's communication, they were emphasized even more after the notorious 2018 scandal. As the reputation of Dolce & Gabbana was tarnished by the Chinese controversy, the label went back to 'safer' and less contentious narratives focusing on its country of origin, in this sense recognizing and capitalizing on the effectiveness of such narratives of national identity in terms of positively affecting the prestige, aura, and reputation of the brand.

As we have seen in the beginning of this chapter, which focused on notions of traditional Italian craftsmanship employed by Dolce & Gabbana, traits of national identity can be a very valuable resource for brands, anchoring the brand image to positive narratives that are strictly associated with a certain area and rooted in people's minds, capitalizing on such associations to augment the prestige and desirability of products. In contrast to what one might think, globalization does not actually necessarily see a complete homogenization of offerings, as consumers crave diversity and see difference as an element worth pursuing (Naisbitt 1994, Pieterse 1995, Bell and Valentine 1997), especially when that is linked to entities that possess positive connotations. That is the case for images of Italy, which has historically acquired a good reputation in a variety of areas and in particular with regard to fashion, design, food, and lifestyle, being associated with narratives of quality and excellence in that respect (Snaiderbaur 2009). Positive narratives concerning countries like Italy and their heritage are widespread in the media and create a virtuous circle that enhances the reputation of luxury brands (Jackson 2004) and that contribute to creating and reinforcing such images by adopting them in their communication strategies (Moilanen and Rainisto 2009). Traits of Italianicity are in this sense powerful marketing tools that support brands in their international expansion (Moor 2007) by providing differentiation (Callon et al. 2002) and creating trust and respect (Clifton and Simmons 2003), which explains why many luxury fashion brands consistently focus, and capitalize, on their country of origin (Godey et al. 2012).

In this sense, the videos published by Dolce & Gabbana examined earlier with regard to craftsmanship present a myth of authentic Italianicity that is presented as obvious but that actually is created by purposely selecting a specific element that functions to serve the needs of the label in question. The selection of such a trait, in association with a coherent communicative strategy, ends up naturalizing such an element of Italianicity and portraying it as distinctive and 'obvious' (Barthes 1977). But one needs to remember that such myths of authentic Italianicity are far from obvious and inevitable (Martin and Ringham 2006), as they are culturally created entities that hide their nature as social and ideological constructs through an aura of reality (Barthes 1974). National identity can be sometimes be perceived as an immutable entity, but it's actually culturally created and reproduced through many mundane different elements beyond the discourses of nationalism (Edensor 2002), such as marketing practices (Borneman 1992, Billig 1995). National identity is not fixed but constantly changing, a liquid entity (Bauman 2000) that is always in process (Hall 1990) and open to reconstruction (Cubitt 1998). In this sense, brands like Dolce & Gabbana are active players in this constant redefinition of Italian national identity, creating narratives that circulate worldwide and reshape what this concept entails.

However, relying on traits of national identity in marketing is also associated with risks, as seen in the China controversy of late 2018. The narratives employed by Dolce &

Gabbana with regard to Chinese identity support the notion that discourses of nationhood in marketing are selective, as they focus on traits that are functional to convey the message the brand wants to achieve, and that this selection needs to be considered carefully to avoid pitfalls. If certain traits, like traditional Italian craftsmanship, are incontrovertibly positive and functional in reinforcing the positive image of the brands that anchor themselves to those narratives, when it comes to other traits that are potentially controversial, then the process of selection needs to be undertaken more carefully, and the cultural sensitivity of recipients needs to be considered more attentively. If this doesn't happen, brands risk being involved in controversies that can hurt their reputations and alienate consumers, therefore losing sales and suffering financially. National identity can offer valuable elements to nourish and support brand culture, as seen in the case of traditional Italian craftsmanship, but relying on other national identity traits can quickly go wrong if they are perceived as offensive by certain communities, especially if they represent the specific public brands were trying to target, as seen with regard to the controversy surrounding Dolce & Gabbana's attitudes toward China and its heritage. Brands should focus only on positive traits and reject those that could be problematic if they want to achieve their goals and avoid controversy and backlash, as everything can go viral very quickly in a world that is more and more connected. Labels' goal in this sense should be to create idealized images that contribute to reinforcing the positive image of the brands but also contribute to reshaping conceptualizations of national identity in a positive manner, as that can in turn positively affect them.

Bibliography

Barr, Sabrina. 2018. Dolce & Gabbana: Celebrities pledge to boycott designer amid racism backlash. Available at: www.independent.co.uk/life-style/fashion/dolce-gabbana-racist-boycott-chopsticks-controversy-china-instagram-video-a8646216.html.

Barthes, Roland. 1974. *Miti D'Oggi [Myth today]*. Torino: Einaudi.

Barthes, Roland. 1977. *Image-Music-Text*. London: Fontana.

Bauman, Zygmunt. 2000. *Liquid Modernity*. Cambridge: Polity Press.

BBC. 2019. Gucci withdraws jumper after 'blackface' backlash. Available at: www.bbc.co.uk/news/business-47153413.

Bell, David and Valentine, Gill. 1997. *Consuming Geographies: We Are Where We Eat*. London: Routledge.

Berthon, Pierre, Pitt, Leyland, Parent, Michael and Berthon, Jean-Paul. 2009. 'Aesthetics and Ephemerality: Observing and Preserving the Luxury Brand', *California Management Review*, 52(1): 45–66.

Billig, Michael. 1995. *Banal Nationalism*. London: Sage.

Borneman, John. 1992. *Belonging in the Two Berlins: Kin, State, Nation*. Cambridge: Cambridge University Press.

Bruner, Edward. 1991. 'Transformation of Self in Tourism', *Annals of Tourism Research*, 18(2): 238–250.

Bronwen, Martin and Ringham, Felizitas. 2006. *Key Terms in Semiotics*. London; New York: Continuum International Publishing Group Ltd.

Callon, Michael, Meadel, Cecile and Rabeharisoa, Vololona. 2002. 'The Economy of Qualities', *Economy and Society*, 31(2): 194–217.

CGTN. 2018. What's Trending on Weibo 11.21.18. Available at: www.youtube.com/watch?v=LH94vMgKgKc.

Chevalier, Michel and Mazzalovo, Gerald. 2008. *Luxury Brand Management: A World of Privilege*. Hoboken; Chicester: John Wiley and Sons.

Clifton, Rita and Simmons, John. 2003. *Brands and Branding*. London: The Economist & Profile Books.

Cubitt, Geoffrey. 1998. *Imagining Nations*. Manchester: Manchester University Press.

Dallabona, Alice. 2014. Narratives of Italian Craftsmanship and the Luxury Fashion Industry: Representations of Italianicity in Discourses of Production. In Joseph H. Hancock II, Gjoko Muratovski, Veronica Manlow and Anne Pearson-Smith, Eds., *Global Fashion Brands: Style, Luxury & History*. Chicago: Intellect.

Dallabona, Alice. 2015. 'Luxury Fashion Flagship Hotels and Cultural Opportunism: The Cases of Hotel Missoni Edinburgh and Maison Moschino', *Hospitality and Society*, 5(2–3): 117–143.

Dazed. 2018. I watched D&G's China show fall apart from the inside. Available at: www.dazeddigital.com/fashion/article/42334/1/dolce-gabbana-dg-china-cancelled-shanghai-show-model-experience.

Diet Prada. 2018. Available at: www.instagram.com/p/BqbTkY_FB7X/.

Dolce & Gabbana. 2011. Dolce&Gabbana jewellery: A love story. Available at: www.youtube.com/watch?v=0axZXFrrn3U.

Dolce & Gabbana. 2014. Dolce&Gabbana Mosaico eyewear limited edition. Available at: www.youtube.com/watch?v=6e3lbdi9JXc.

Dolce & Gabbana. 2016. Dolce&Gabbana Sicilian Carretto eyewear limited edition. Available at: www.youtube.com/watch?v=TDuqA_KCerA.

Dolce & Gabbana. 2018. Dolce&Gabbana apologizes. Available at: www.youtube.com/watch?v=7Ih62lTKicg.

Dolce & Gabbana. 2019a. Dolce&Gabbana Alta Moda brocade dress—The making of. Available at: www.youtube.com/watch?v=c8X_Ulshqzc.

Dolce & Gabbana. 2019b. Dolce&Gabbana Alta Moda corset dress—The making of. Available at: www.youtube.com/watch?v=ygHDehT2oiA.

Dolce & Gabbana. 2019c. Dolce&Gabbana's Alta Moda Soprarizzo velvet dress—The making of. Available at: www.youtube.com/watch?v=GaIbqOb6Zck.

Dolce & Gabbana. 2019d. Fatto A Mano—The making of the Domenico Frames. Available at: www.youtube.com/watch?v=Mh72mgt5z_E.

Dolce & Gabbana. 2019e. Fatto A Mano—The making of the Lace Frames. Available at: www.youtube.com/watch?v=xLj-5K7XXyw.

Dolce & Gabbana. 2019f. DG crystal sunglasses. Available at: www.youtube.com/watch?v=rGKDtsRnElA.

Dubois, Bernard and Paternault, Claire. 1995. 'Understanding the World of International Luxury Brand: The Dream Formula', *Journal of Advertising Research*, 35(4): 69–76.

Dubois, Bernard, Laurent, Gilles and Czellar, Sandor. 2001. Consumer Rapport to Luxury: Analysing Complex and Ambivalent Attitudes. *Consumer Research Working Article No.736, HEC*, Jouy-en-Josas, France, pp. 1–56.

Dunford, Michel. 2006. 'Industrial Districts, Magic Circles, and the Restructuring of the Italian Textiles and Clothing Chain', *Economic Geography*, 82(1): 27–59.

DW News. 2018. Dolce & Gabbana under fire over racism accusations. Available at: www.youtube.com/watch?v=594Q9CJQbD4&t=39s.

Edensor, Tim. 2002. *National Identity, Popular Culture and Everyday Life*. Oxford; New York: Berg Publishers.

E! Asia. 2018. Chinese Celebrities Are Boycotting Dolce & Gabbana's Shanghai Show over Racist Comments. Available at: www.eonline.com/ap/news/989456/chinese-celebrities-are-boycotting-dolce-gabbana-s-shanghai-show-over-racist-comments.

Fionda, Antoinette and Christopher, Moore. 2009. 'The Anatomy of the Luxury Fashion Brand', *Journal of Brand Management*, 16(5–6): 347–363.

France24 English. 2018. Dolce&Gabbana faces Chinese backlash after ad campaign "full of stereotypes." Available at: www.youtube.com/watch?v=ofhCu3wThCY.

Giordani-Aragno, Bonizza. 1983. *40 Years of Italian Fashion, 1940–1980: Original Drawings and Sketches of the Most Famous Italian Fashion Designers*. Rome: Made in Ltd.

Godey, Bruno, Pederzoli, Daniele, Aiello, Gaetano, Donvito, Raffaele, Chan, Priscilla, Oh, Hyunjoo, Singh, Rahul, Skorobogatykh, Irina, Tsuchiya, Junji and Witz, Bart. 2012. 'Brand and Country-of-Origin Effect on Consumers' Decision to Purchase Luxury Products', *Journal of Business Research*, 65(10): 1461–1470.

Greimas, Algirdas Julien. 1984. *Del senso 2. Narrativa, modalita; passioni. [On Sense II: Narrative, Modality, Passion]*. Milano: Bompiani.

Greimas, Algirdas Julien and Courtés, Joseph. 1986. *Semiotics and Language: An Analytical Dictionary*. Bloomington: Indiana University Press.

Hall, Casey and Suen, Zoe. 2018. Dolce & Gabbana China show cancelled amid racism outcry. Available at: www.businessoffashion.com/articles/news-analysis/racism-accusations-force-dolce-gabbana-to-cancel-chinese-fashion-show.

Hall, Stuart. 1990. Cultural Identity and Diaspora. In Jonathan Rutherford, Ed. *Identity: Community, Culture, Difference*. London: Lawrence & Wishart.

Hutto, Clayton and Gilbert, Eric. 2015. VADER: A Parsimonious Rule-Based Model for Sentiment Analysis of Social Media Text, Conference: Proceedings of the Eighth International AAAI Conference on Weblogs and Social Media.

Jackson, Tim. 2004. A Contemporary Analysis of Global Luxury Brand. In Margaret Bruce et al., Eds., *International Retail Marketing: A Case Study Approach*. Oxford: Butterworth-Heinemann, pp. 155–169.

Kapferer, Jean-Noel. 2004. *The New Strategic Brand Management: Creating and Sustaining Brand Equity Long Term*. London: Kogan Page.

Moilanen, Teemu and Rainisto, Seppu. 2009. *How to Brand Nations, Cities and Destinations: A Planning Book for Place Branding*. Basingstoke: Palgrave Macmillan.

Moor, Liz. 2007. *The Rise of Brands*. Oxford: Berg.

Naisbitt, John. 1994. *Global Paradox*. New York: Avon.

Nöth, Winfried. 1995. *Handbook of Semiotics*. Bloomington: Indiana University Press.

Parkins, Wendy. 2004. 'At Home in Tuscany: Slow Living and the Cosmopolitan Subject', *Home Cultures*, 1(3): 257–274.

Pieterse, Jan Nederveen. 1995. Globalization as Hybridization. In M. Featherstone, S. Lash and R. Robertson, Eds., *Global Modernities*. London: Sage, pp. 45–68.

Rocca, Federico. 2006. *Embroidery: Italian Fashion*. Bologna: Damiani.

Ross, Andrew. 2004. 'Made in Italy: The Trouble with Craft Capitalism', *Antipode*, 36(2): 209–21.

Silver, Ira. 1993. 'Marketing Authenticity in Third World Countries', *Annals of Tourism Research*, 20(2): 302–318.

Snaiderbaur, S. 2009. ' "Made in Italy" in China: From Country of Origin to Country Concept Branding", *The ICFAI Journal of Brand Management*, VI(3&4): 63–74.

Spooner, Brian. 1986. Weavers and Dealers; The Authenticity of an Oriental Carpet. In Arjun Appadurai, Ed., *The Social Life of Things: Commodities in Cultural Perspective*. Cambridge: Cambridge University Press, pp. 195–235.

Steele, Valerie. 2003. *Fashion, Italian Style*. New Haven: Yale University Press.

Tungate, Mark. 2005. *Fashion Brands: Branding Style from Armani to Zara*. London: Kogan Page.

Van Elven, Marjorie. 2018. Chinese stores remove Dolce & Gabbana's products, founders release apology video. Available at: https://fashionunited.uk/news/fashion/chinese-stores-remove-dolce-gabbana-s-products-founders-release-apology-video/2018112340131.

Wang, Ning. 1999. 'Rethinking Authenticity in Tourism Experience', *Annals of Tourism Research*, 26(2): 349–370.

White, Nicola. 2000. *Reconstructing Italian Fashion: America and the Development of the Italian Fashion Industry*. Oxford: Berg.

Wiener-Bronner, Danielle. Why Dolce & Gabbana's China blunder could be such a disaster. Available at: https://edition.cnn.com/2018/11/24/business/dolce-gabbana-china/index.html.

Willan, Philip. 2019. Gucci pulls $890 'blackface' jumper in racism row. Available at: www.thetimes.co.uk/article/gucci-pulls-890-blackface-jumper-w93pg0qq3.

Xu, Yuhan. 2018. Dolce & Gabbana Ad (With Chopsticks) Provokes Public Outrage in China. Available at: www.npr.org/sections/goatsandsoda/2018/12/01/671891818/dolce-gabbana-ad-with-chopsticks-provokes-public-outrage-in-china?t=1543676931772&t=1575044861042.

3 Gucci Beauty, Nur Jahan, and the Mining of the History of Art for Global Beauty Icons for the Twenty-First Century

Amanda Sikarskie

While many of today's most ubiquitous and successful luxury brands—Calvin Klein, Ralph Lauren, Stella McCartney, Vivienne Westwood, Versace—were born in the second half of the twentieth century and have a relatively short brand history upon which to draw for their digital heritage storytelling, Gucci is one of those brands—and families—that has been around for a long time. The modern House of Gucci was founded by Guccio Gucci, 1881–1953, who left Florence for England as a young man to distance himself from his parents' bankruptcy due to their failed straw hat–making firm. He found work at the Savoy Hotel and was dazzled by late Victorian England's high society, especially their glorious jewels, silks, furs, and leather goods.[1] After a few years of carrying luggage for the British elite, he learned a great deal about quality leather and what made suitcases and trunks functional—or less so—and he returned to Florence to try his hand at designing and making his own. Gucci married Aida Cavelli, seamstress and tailor's daughter, thus adding her expertise to his future business. He had not raised enough capital in England to yet go into business for himself, however, and he worked in an antique shop—again honing his eye for quality goods—and then at Franzi, a leather company in Florence, where he "learned how to select raw hides, and studied curing and tanning as well as the art of working with different hides and grades of leather."[2] After the Great War, he went into business for himself, opening Valigeria Guccio Gucci in Florence in 1921, and the House of Gucci was born.

Sarah Gay Forden writes that,

> Italians were proud of their creativity and artisan traditions and Gucci was one of those names, along with Ferragamo and Bulgari, that symbolized quality and craftsmanship. Italy had also produced some of the world's greatest designers, such as Giorgio Armani and Gianni Versace, but Gucci was a name that went back generations, before the designers had even been born.[3]

With the Guccis, there was a distinction between craftspeople and designers that—for good or ill—continues in design discourse to this day.

> To the Florentine merchant, wealth was honorable and carried with it certain obligations, such as financing public buildings, living in a grand palazzo with gorgeous gardens, and sponsoring painters, sculptors, poets, and musicians. This love of beauty and pride in creating beauty has never died despite war, plague, floods, and politics. From Giotto to Michelangelo to the craftsmen in their workshops

> today, the fruits and flowers of the arts, propagated by merchants, have flourished there.[4]

Aldo Gucci was known for his pithy wisdom on this distinction (and many other subjects): "Gucci is as Florentine as Johnnie Walker is Scotch, and there's not much that anybody can teach a Florentine about merchandising or craftsmanship."[5] The contemporary renaissancecore trend might well have appealed to Gucci's sense of humor.

Renaissancecore

Quattrocento Florence was the political, religious, and intellectual center that saw and gave rise to the birth of the Italian Renaissance. As Aldo Gucci put it, "We Guccis have been merchants since around 1410. When you say Guccis, you are not thinking of Macy's."[6] In September 2019, the style blog Man Repeller described the new trend toward dressing with a nod to Renaissance fashion as 'Renaissancecore.' The curious term's etymology derives from a back-formation of 'hardcore.' Applied to a person, the term 'hardcore' means to be a diehard or at least particularly dedicated to a given activity, while when applied to an object or event, the word suggests that which is intense, thrilling, or possibly even dangerous. Hardcore can also refer to that which is overly sexual, such as the cover of the 1998 Pulp album, *This Is Hardcore*. In common usage, hardcore has been co-opted to refer to a variety of subcultural or indie styles and scenes. The suffix '-core' is thus applied to specialized styles in music such as mumblecore and polkacore but now also to specialized styles in fashion.

In the blog post, Harling Ross describes the trend toward Renaissance styling as somehow different than the various retro trends that have marked the whims of fashion since at least the 1970s, writing,

> This simultaneous deluge is cause to consider our present culture's collective obsession with using clothes to carry us back to the past. Renaissancecore is undoubtedly the most extreme that we've witnessed thus far—transporting us centuries as opposed to decades. But unlike 90s-era chokers and slip dresses or 70s-esque flares, renaissancecore trends are not the stuff of nostalgia, memorialized in throwback photos of ourselves and our grandparents. Instead, they are fragments pulled from history itself, from textbooks and fairytales and artistic masterpieces, from an era so removed from our own it feels strangely . . . fresh, at least from a modern standpoint.[7]

In curating the GucciBeauty Instagram feed with beauty icons selected from across the history of world art, including several Renaissance portraits, such as works by Botticelli and Bronzino and a portrait of Queen Elizabeth I, Gucci does seem to be tapping into the zeitgeist.

But while the term 'renaissancecore' is new, its practice isn't, especially perhaps in Britain. For example, in the *Mighty Boosh* episode "The Power of the Crimp" (2007), Vince Noir and Howard Moon (Noel Fielding and Julian Barratt) search for the latest upcoming retro trend by going as far back as possible, appearing at a gig in vaguely Tudor-period dress and singing of "taking retro to its logical conclusion." Picking up on Man Repeller's renaissancecore concept, Hannah Marriott wrote an article for *Guardian Fashion* entitled "Renaissancecore: Why Everyone Is Dressing Like Anne Boleyn."

Marriott writes, "But the fact that the English Renaissance has been described as 'the peacock age' by some historians explains its appeal for Christmas-party season in the attention economy."[8] Marriott cites fancy, leg-of-mutton sleeves and large, jeweled or velvet headbands (the "it" accessory of autumn 2019) as evidence that, indeed, people are dressing with a nod to the Renaissance at present. Over-sized, puffy, or ballooning sleeves seem to be analogous to the shoulder pads of the 1980s, conferring on the wearer the sort of power that only size can bring. Marriott writes,

> Anne of Cleves was no style slouch either, with some saying she popularized the leg-o'-mutton sleeve. . . . Then and now, big sleeves are a way of taking up space with clothing, a power move that reverberates through the ages.[9]

The renaissance is not the only historical epoque to be given this temporary trending status in our own time, however.

We could retroactively describe the retro style of the 1970s as "rococococore" (a term of the author's own invention), what with the decade's love of Gainsborough's *Blue Boy*, Watteau prints on jewelry boxes, china shepherdess figurines, and the like. The act of naming and defining this historical retro style as "renaissancecore" represents not necessarily the novelty of historical retro but rather its novelty in the age of Instagram and fast fashion. As Harling Ross observes, "With its innately exaggerated air, its sky-high headbands and impossible-to-ignore sleeves, Renaissance-era fashion was seemingly made for social media."[10] It is fitting, then, for Gucci to put actual Renaissance fashion online rather than just AW19/20 whisperings of the renaissance.

The Italians Look to India

As we have noted, however, Gucci has long positioned itself as a global, rather than an Italian, brand. And therefore, one of its GucciBeauty muses from outside Italy, but who lived during this evocative period, seems perhaps most fitting as symbol of the GucciBeauty concept. As the Elizabethan period ticked over into the Jacobean and the Renaissance turned into the Baroque in Italy, in the Mughal Empire, Nur Jahan was Queen.

> On reaching Xanadu, Kublai Khan's summer capital of his Chinese empire, Marco Polo discovered the emperor's palace to be marble and gilt, wholly 'marvelously embellished and richly adorned.' . . . What he described had a profound influence on the European elite's understanding of Asia and their attempts to obtain some of these oriental luxuries for themselves . . . By the seventeenth century, when European kings such as Louis XIV aspired to be as wealthy, cultured, and powerful as their despotic oriental emperor 'cousins,' the relevance of Asian luxury re-emerged more strongly than ever.[11]

In our present age of rising economic superpowers in China and India and the West's relative economic decline, it makes sense that Gucci should look to Emperor Akbar and Nur Jahan as icons of luxury, beauty, and taste.

> One object in particular that captured the imagination of European readers and rulers alike: the throne of the Mughal Emperor Aurangzeb. This was no ordinary throne. It was said to be worth £4.5 million, the equivalent of more than 10 per cent of the GDP of England at the time.[12]

Nur Jahan

My mid-thirties rapidly descending into my late thirties, I was attracted to Nur Jahan as a poster woman for early middle-aged beauty.[13] If she could look more vivacious than ever in her thirties in the seventeenth century, then why can't we all? But Nur Jahan was not only known as a great beauty; she was also known for her political leadership, wisdom, and foresight—qualities that one certainly gains with age. For Nur Jahan, life really began anew at the not-so-young age of thirty-four. And, as we shall see, she is living a new kind of afterlife as a muse for Gucci on its Gucci Beauty Instagram account. The reasons for this say much about the nature of digital heritage storytelling, the continuing fascination with India in the West, the Florentine mercantile history of patronage of the arts, and the nature of beauty and the ever-shifting mark that is the ideal woman. As Ruby Lal noted in *Empress: The Astonishing Reign of Nur Jahan*,

> Historians writing in the 1960s and '70s (and even in the early 1990s, after an extensive gap) strove to cast Nur in a fuller biographical mode, as a distinguished queen on par with great rulers such as Elizabeth I or Indira Gandhi.[14]

and "Hers is a household name in South Asia. Nur Jahan has been the subject of at least eight movies, several plays, an opera, and numerous historical romances."[15] Not all scholars agree regarding Nur Jahan's military and political prowess, however, according to Lal:

> Even into the late twentieth century, academics disparaged the legend about Nur [for example, her skill as a markswoman and huntress of tigers], and leaned on love as the explanation for her extraordinary rise rather than attributing it to her talents. They dismissed Jahangir as an inebriated, ineffectual king, interested only in aesthetics, philosophy, and mind-altering substances, so besotted—with alcohol, opium, and Nur Jahan—that he handed over the running of his realm to her. Yes, the emperor was a drinker and he smoked opium. Yes, he was deeply in love with his wife. But that's not why she became a ruler to be reckoned with.[16]

A combination of feminine beauty and fierceness, like the tigers she was said to have slaughtered. A non-western personage with global appeal. This is why Nur Jahan, who lived in the 1600s, is the perfect face for Gucci Beauty in the twenty-first century.

> A generation earlier, Jahangir's father, Akbar the Great, had ordered all royal women—wives, daughters, and concubines—to be sequestered behind harem walls. He called them 'the veiled ones.' But three decades after Akbar's dictate, Nur Jahan was on view in the most male and public of places [as part of the royal hunting party.] A new kind of power was on display.[17]

This narrative of disempowered woman—hidden behind metaphorical and literal walls—not only to be emancipated, but to take the stage with males in a realm of danger and physical prowess, fits in perfectly with beauty narratives of the early twenty-first century emphasizing fierceness and power.

> Beautiful and accomplished, Nur Jahan was the daughter of nobles who'd fled persecution in Persia. She was also the widow of a court official [Sher Khan]

implicated in a plot against [Emperor] Jahangir, but that didn't stop the emperor from falling hard for her. She was thirty-four when they married, nearly middle-aged in the Mughal World. Since their wedding in 1611, the same year that Shakespeare premiered *The Tempest*, Nur Jahan (Light of the World in Persian, the name bestowed by her husband), had proved to be a devoted wife, a wise and just queen, a shrewd politician—and an expert markswoman.[18]

The GucciBeauty Instagram post from September 19, 2018, describes the queen thusly:

> This Indian portrait from c. 1725, at @LACMA, one of the #GucciPlaces, depicts an historical figure—the Muslim Mughal empress Nur Jahan, who married Emperor Jahangir in 1611, when Nur was 34 years old and a widow. The well-educated empress was at the peak of royal power when the Mughal empire was at its strongest, and Nur Jahan is said to have been the real authority over her husband for more than 15 years. "Though Nur Jahan be in form a woman,/In the ranks of men she's a tiger-slayer," a poem of the time described her stature, also reflected in this confident image.
> #GucciBeauty—@kchayka

For a brand with Italian roots to adopt a Mughal Empress as muse and beauty icon, that brand must have a global, rather than national, heritage narrative.

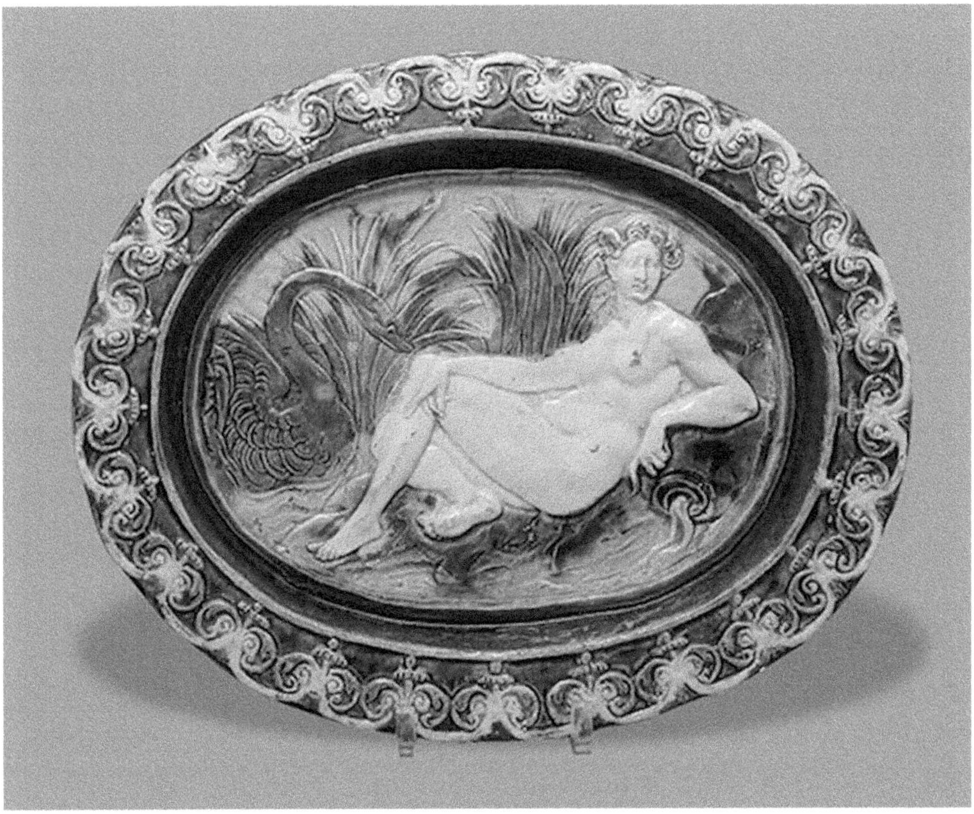

Figure 3.1 Idealized portrait of the Mughal empress Nur Jahan (1577–1645), Los Angeles County Museum of Art.

Florentine Heritage, Global Heritage

In her essay on Guccio Gucci for *The Making of Gucci*, Roberta Filippini writes,

> Some brands have been so instrumental in shaping global tastes that they have created symbols so integrated with the contemporary culture that they seem to have no origin, no human history. Who can say if the girl carrying a Bamboo bag today is aware that she is holding a piece of fashion history, or if she knows the meaning behind the two Gs facing each other in the logo of her much-loved purse?[19]

Of course, GG are the initials of Guccio Gucci, founder of the fashion house. From humble beginnings to somewhat reluctant inheritors of the Florentine artistic tradition, Gucci is truly now a global brand, claiming as its origin and history all of global art and culture that it deems good and beautiful. To create a new canon of global beauty and post it online is a powerful act of ownership. The message to Gucci customers, and those who aspire to be, is that all that is beautiful, past and present, across all cultures, is Gucci.

Just how Florentine is Gucci? Some Italian brands, like Dolce & Gabbana, focus much more on their Italian heritage in their brand storytelling than does Gucci. From almost its inception, Gucci has positioned itself as an international, now global, brand. As Emmanuele Lugli put it:

> The history of Gucci is inextricable from its connection to Florence, an enduring relationship between brand and birthplace. . . . Nonetheless, contrary to many

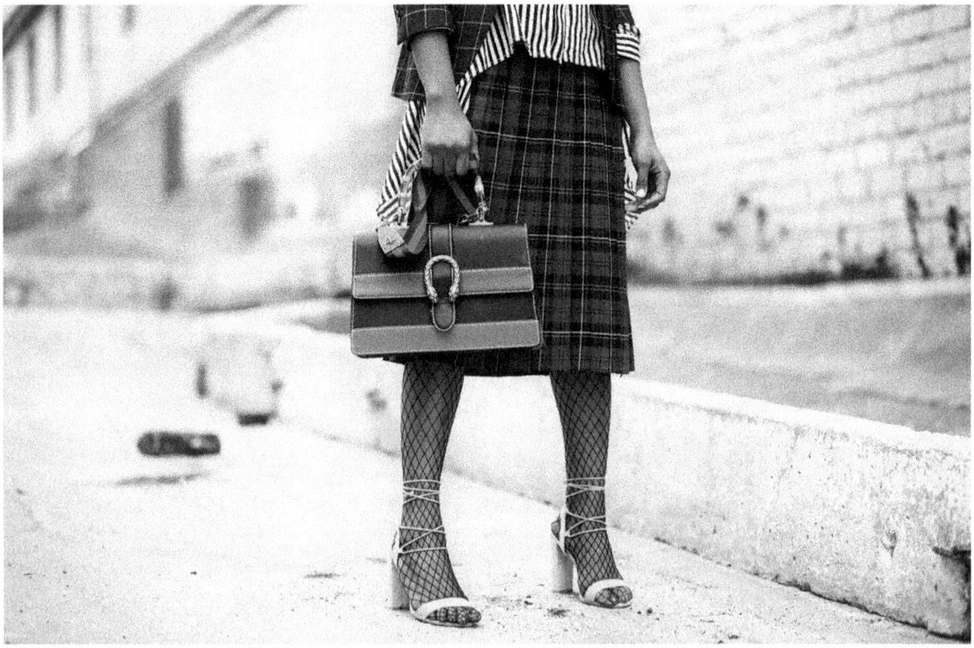

Figure 3.2 Gucci bamboo bag, as seen in a street style photograph by Godisable Jacob, Ukraine, Pexels.com.

> other companies, Gucci has always kept itself at arm's length from the city's mythology, and never has flaunted its connection through overt design references. Guccio Gucci refused to be labelled as a 'traditionalist,' and sought to distinguish himself among the plethora of leather shops in Florence by specializing in 'English-style' leather goods.[20]

Gradually, Guccio and Aida's three sons, Rodolfo, Vasco, and Aldo, took over the running of the family business. Aldo, like his father, saw not only a market for Gucci, but importantly also a story for Gucci, outside of Italy.

> Aldo was the visionary, who wanted to take Gucci outside of Italy and into the world. He opened a store in Rome, a much more cosmopolitan city than Florence, which introduced Gucci to the international jet set. That store flourished, and soon there were Gucci stores in New York, London, Paris, Palm Beach, and Los Angeles.[21]

As Simone Marchetti writes:

> The synthesis of yesterday and today, past and present, is one of the most important characteristics of contemporary fashion. Since 2000, fashion brands have been caught in a creative short circuit: on the one hand, they must continue introducing new and innovative products; on the other hand, they're called upon to rediscover tradition and the legacy of their own past to conceive new products. This apparent schizophrenic dichotomy represents the significance of heritage for Gucci and, beyond nostalgia, the recognition Gucci pays to the values and icons that have defined the house.[22]

Marchetti argues that two recent (2008) reintroductions illustrate this belief at Gucci that "the future of fashion can be found in its own archives"[23]—the *Rinascimento* Renaissance floral print developed in the 1950s and the leopard print created in the '60s for a new store on Fifth Avenue in New York.

> Today Gucci is still living the dream of a young man, who as a porter at London's Savoy Hotel, imagined returning to his native Florence to open his workshop and create products that could be respectful of tradition and craftsmanship and yet be totally new and innovative.[24]

This belief that the Gucci dream still lives, put forward by Gucci Chief Executive Patrizio di Marco in 2010, helps to explain the brand's very lofty claim that the global history of beauty is its own story.

Beauty, Imagination, Order

Paradoxically, one could argue that Gucci's history as an Italian brand is precisely that which allows it to define and claim a global ideal of beauty as its own. Writing in 2011, Elda Danese notes the role technology played (and increasingly continues to play) in the Italian luxury narrative:

> The global extension that the 'Made in Italy' movement is attempting today has emphasized the importance of new media relations and the ability to articulate a

> new and appropriate place within the spaces of virtual consumerism with an eye toward controlling the proliferation of information and potential deformation of the brand's image.[25]

Danese goes on to note that, "These imperatives are inexorably linked to the growing trend of counterfeiting and a number of polemics that question the authenticity of 'Made in Italy' goods."[26] But for eminent curator Valerie Steele, Made in Italy does not signify the global counterfeiting debacle or social media disasters but rather something much more lighthearted: "

> The charm of what fashion historian Valerie Steele calls a "playful, sexy, and effervescent" life is the driving force behind the "Made in Italy" ideal. "Made in Italy" has entered common language as a term that expresses the synthesis of quality and excellence of production in a context of hedonistic beauty.[27]

For any leather goods manufacturer, recognizable, iconic patterns that stand the test of time, yet may be adapted to the taste of the day, are an integral part of the brand story. In her essay on the history of pattern at Gucci, Alessandra Vaccari calls upon paragon of the Arts and Crafts Movement William Morris in defining what makes a good pattern: "According to the artist and theoretician William Morris, a decorative motif 'must possess three qualities: beauty, imagination, and order'."[28] Three of Gucci's best-known patterns—Diamante Canvas, Liftboy, and Rhombi—were all created in the 1930s and may all be said to feature those three attributes. Writing on "Liftboy," Angelo Flaccavento argues:

> The Liftboy, a classic symbol of the brand, is an aesthetic choice showcasing Gucci's pride in its origins. A very young Guccio Gucci held this very job at London's Savoy Hotel. The liftboy, with his livery and jaunty cap, was frequently immortalized in film during the 1930s, and has become part of our collective memory of that elegant past.[29]

Another motif, Flora, which debuted in 1966, recalls Morris' own floral pattern work of the nineteenth century, as well as hints at the Florentine artistic tradition—the mythological Flora figures in Sandro Botticelli's classic quattrocento allegory of the Renaissance, *Primavera*.

In 2019, over-sized patterns featuring renaissance portraits are in vogue. Taken together, this new canon of global beauty compiled on the Gucci Beauty Instagram account represents the beginnings of another iconic Gucci pattern. In evaluating Gucci's choices for inclusion, reader, consider whether, individually and collectively, these digital images of world portraiture embody William Morris' golden trifecta of beauty, imagination, and order.

Gucci Beauty

The first image posted to the Gucci Beauty Instagram account was of a painting in the collection of the Metropolitan Museum of Art in New York depicting an Elizabethan woman once thought by historians to be Queen Elizabeth I herself. Text accompanying the post concluded with the thought that "regardless [of the sitter's identity], the anonymous

British painter who captured her likeness did so with a striking attention to detail and level of interest in her fashion. #GucciBeauty #TheMet." Some of the other paintings and prints of women posted to the account in the fall of 2018 reflected women representing various geographic regions and time periods: a portrait of a woman by French Post-Impressionist Louis Anquetin; a mid-nineteenth-century Shanghai School portrait of a court lady; Thomas Gainsborough's portrait of Georgiana, Duchess of Devonshire; Bronzino's portrait of Maria de' Medici; Botticelli's 1485 portrait of a young woman—La Bella Simonetta; Rosetti's *Aurelia* (Fazio's Mistress) and *Monna Vanna*; Tsukioka Yoshitoshi's ukiyo-e of a lady of the Imperial court in the Kyouwa period; a Pompeiian fresco of the Roman poet Sappho; a curiously androgynous portrait of Caroline Lamb, c. 1800, by Thomas Phillips; a portrait of the actual Queen Elizabeth I from a private collection; and, of course, the idealized portrait of Empress Nur Jahan, among many others.

Reproduced subsequently are representative posts from the GucciBeauty Instagram account by art historians Tatiana Berg @tatianaberg, Britt Julious @britticisms, and Kyle Chayka @kchayka:

September 14, 2018—Anonymous sitter, a courtly lady

The Shanghai School of painting introduced a fresh alternative to the then-dominating Literati style. Western-influenced brightly colored portraiture was among the newly adopted styles, a direct reaction to the demands of Shanghai's mercantile elite who craved something distinct from the traditional aesthetics of the Chinese scholarly and gentry classes. This 19th-century portrait captures the era's distinct stylistic elements, which included a brightly-colored palette (as depicted in the blues, greens, and reds of the subject's clothing and large, dangly earrings) and exaggerated physical form.

#GucciBeauty—@britticisms

September 19, 2018—Anonymous sitter, Kyouwa period

The Japanese artist Tsukioka Yoshitoshi is known as the last great innovator of the ukiyo-e woodblock print genre before he died in 1898, having suffered depressive episodes his entire life.

Trained to draw from life, Yoshitoshi's subjects ranged from depictions of graphic violence to series of beautiful women. In hard times during his early career, the artist was often supported by his mistress, Okoto. This image, from @ LACMA, one of the #GucciPlaces, shows an ideal beauty from the Kyowa period, at the turn of the 19th century. The woman is swaddled in thick robes, her skin painted white.

#GucciBeauty—@kchayka

September 21, 2018: Sappho

Housed in the historic Naples Archaeology Museum, a woman's bright and inquisitive gaze emerges out of two-thousand-year-old paint. Pompeii's frescos are among the few examples we have left of Roman painting, and this portrait's fresh immediacy is an incredible glimpse into the past. The anonymous figure here has been identified as Sappho, a female poet who was already famous in her own

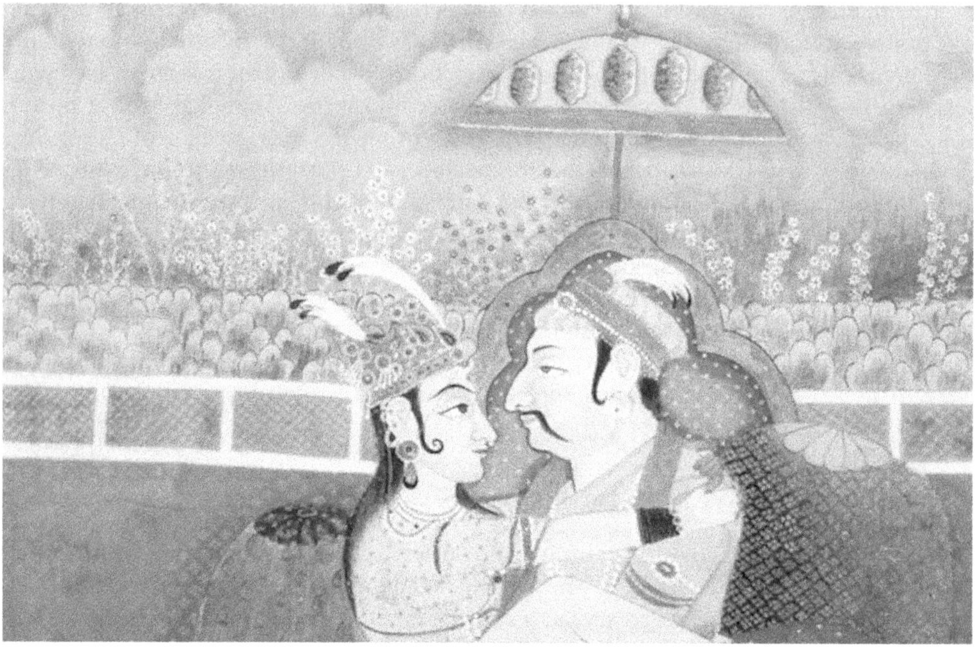

Figure 3.3 Emperor Jahangir (reigned 1605–1627) and Empress Nur Jahan in union [cropped], Nepal, circa 1830, Los Angeles County Museum of Art.

> time around 600 BC and whose work has only survived in fragments. This piece was excavated in 1760 and remains one of the most important archeological discoveries of the site. Sappho appears with a brush held to her lips, contemplating the viewer as if deciding what she'll write about us.
>
> #GucciBeauty—@tatianaberg

Sappho, a Gucci Beauty icon herself, wrote of Helen of Troy, the woman who hatched from Leda's egg to become the most beautiful woman of the Mycenaean world:

> Some say a host of horsemen, others of infantry and others
>
> of ships, is the most beautiful thing on the dark earth
> but I say, it is what you love
>
> Full easy it is to make this understood of one and all: for
>
> she that far surpassed all mortals in beauty, Helen her
> most noble husband
>
> Deserted, and went sailing to Troy, with never a thought for
>
> her daughter and dear parents.[30]

Sappho seems both critical and sympathetic toward Helen's flight from her husband and family in Sparta to find love in Troy. The idea that "the most beautiful thing on the dark earth is what you love" feels very much at home in the twenty-first century, and perhaps especially in contemporary luxury storytelling. Sex sells, of course, but so, too, does love.

Oviparity

While this chapter focuses primarily upon Gucci's digital heritage storytelling on Instagram, physical books are another component of a luxury brand's overall storytelling strategy. For its 2020 Cruise collection, Gucci released a limited-edition art book curated by Yorgos Lanthimos. Its title, *Oviparity*, means the ability of an animal (like the duck-billed platypus or echidna, as well as birds, most reptiles, and some fish) to lay eggs[31] and refers to the classical myth of *Leda and the Swan*. In the story, the beautiful Leda is seduced by Jupiter, King of the Gods, as he masquerades as her pet swan, and she later lays two eggs as a result of the union. Photographs for the book were shot in the Leda Gallery at Rome's Villa Albani Torlonia, an eighteenth-century villa, by Carlo Marchionni.

The story of Leda and the swan is an absurd tale of bestiality—the ancients did love a good laugh—comedically and unabashedly obscene. Jupiter (Zeus), in the guise of a swan, sidles up to Leda, puts a feathered wing around her hip, cranes his neck up, and warbles sweet nothings in her ear. In some versions of the story, the events that follow culminate in a rape. In other versions, however, Leda willingly gives in to the temptations . . . of her swan. The myth was often depicted in classical and renaissance art (da Vinci's painting being arguably the most famous), and its perverse, yet humorous sensuality seems to fit the tone of recent Gucci advertising campaigns under Alessandro Michele.

The word 'oviparity' suggests fertility, certainly, and in the case of mammals a reproductive flexibility bordering on universality. That out of one of Leda's eggs hatched a baby who would grow up to be Helen of Troy, legendarily the most beautiful woman in the Mycenaean world, suggests that this oviparity can be a path to the ideal. The story of the icon or ideal, the most beautiful women and men from around the globe and across history, is at the heart of Gucci's digital heritage storytelling campaign on the GucciBeauty Instagram account.

Male Beauty

When the Gucci Beauty account began in 2018, its owners posted one male muse in the form of a c. 1902 self-portrait by Maxwell Ashby Armfield.

> *September 15, 2018: Maxwell Ashby Armfield*
>
> The British artist Maxwell Ashby Armfield didn't enjoy figure drawing during his education at the Birmingham School of Art. Instead, he leapt into the Arts & Crafts Movement, which saw artists in the United Kingdom embracing decorative aesthetics, exaggerated forms, and inspiration from other cultures, including China, Japan, and the ancient Celts. In this tempera painting from 1902, from a private collection, Armfield depicts himself as a bohemian gentleman, his wavy

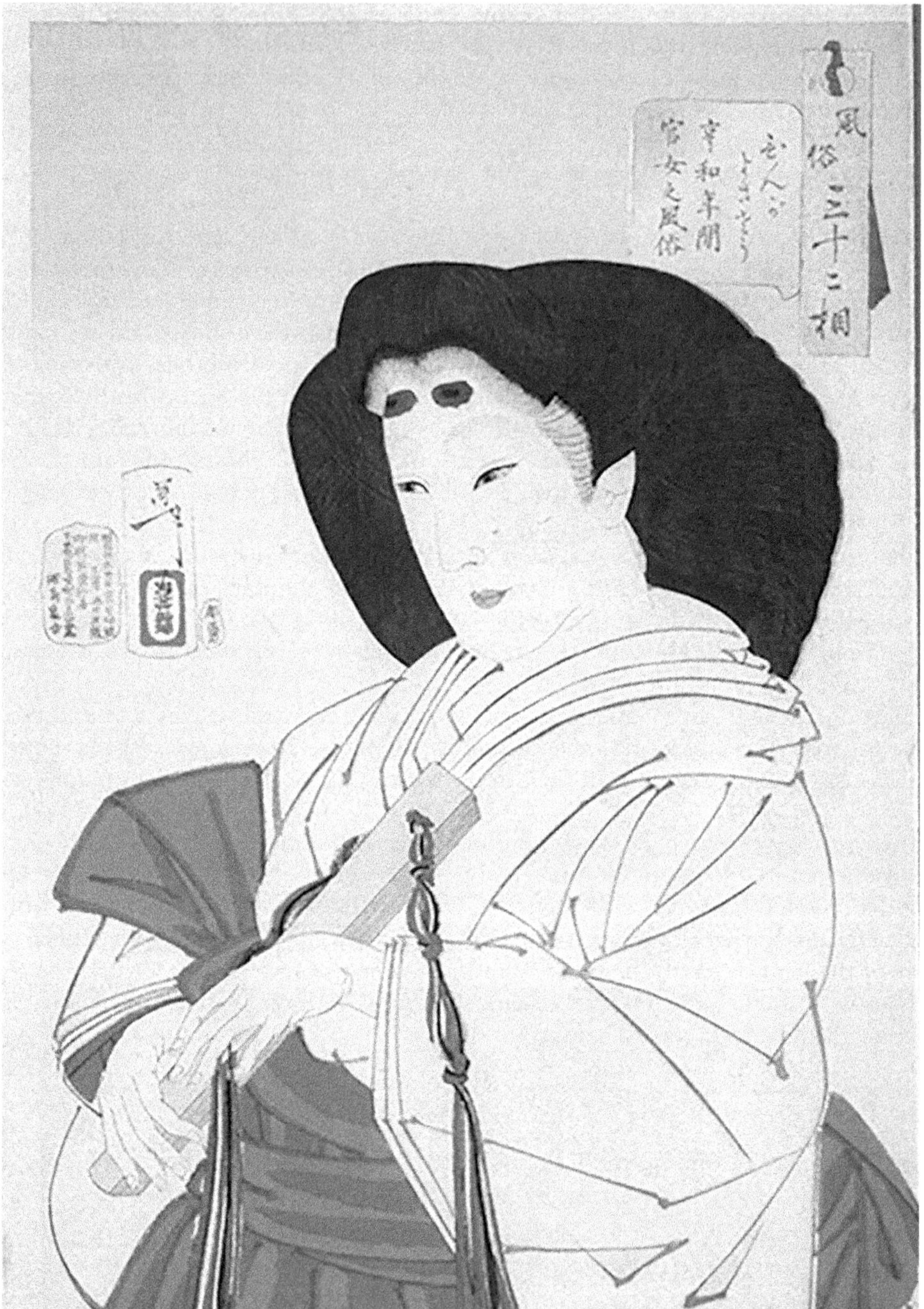

Figure 3.4 Oval dish with Leda and the swan, Palissy (after), Bernard (France, 1509–1590), Los Angeles County Museum of Art.

hair echoing the fabric of his cravat. He collaborated closely with his wife, Constance Smedley.

#GucciBeauty—@kchayka

Under the direction of Alessandro Michele, Gucci has become increasingly known for celebrating male as well as female beauty. Jared Leto and Harry Styles, juxtaposed with flowers and adorable miniature pigs, come immediately to mind. It is therefore unsurprising that in June 2019, the Gucci Beauty Instagram account took a full-fledged foray into an exploration of male beauty:

June 16, 2019: Portrait of a young man

The Florentine artist Bronzino [Agnolo di Cosimo di Mariano] painted this portrait, in the collection of the Metropolitan Museum in New York, in 1530. The portrait's subject is unknown, but what's clear is he is cultured, from the elaborate ribbons of his shirt to the book of poetry in his hand, with a finger marking his place, as if interrupted. The portrait is intimate but also a little distant. Bronzino ran in literary social circles, so this imperious young man was likely one of his friends.

—@kchayka #GucciBeauty #TheMet @alessandro_michele #AlessandroMichele

June 19, 2019: Mario Segantini

Mario Segantini is an unusual figure in the history of art. Segantini spent much of his career obsessed with mystical imagery, painting a more magical world than the one we inhabit as part of the Symbolist movement. In this colorful self-portrait from 1903, he depicts himself as a beautiful blond-haired youth, hands clasped over a bouquet of blooming flowers. This work, held in a private collection, shows how modern Segantini's work could be, especially the echoes of his signature on the left-hand side.

—@tatianaberg #GucciBeauty @alessandro_michele #AlessandroMichele
Photo © Christie's Images/Bridgeman Images

June 18, 2019: Franz Schubert

This portrait of Franz Schubert held in the Kunsthistorisches Museum in Vienna captures the composer as a brilliant but frustrated prodigy: at 17, Schubert was still bored and unchallenged as a lowly music teacher. Rendered realistically in oil paint with full lips and a tragic air, he appears lost in thought, dreamily gazing at some middle distance—perhaps dreaming up compositions, or his future creative life.

—@tatianaberg #GucciBeauty @alessandro_michele #AlessandroMichele

Predictably, youth was much less of a factor in the choice of male Gucci Beauty icons than the female ones. While Nur Jahan, in her mid-late thirties, was downright middle-aged for her time, one could hardly call her old. By contrast, multiple male sitters in portraits selected for Gucci Beauty were in an advanced age, such as Vincent Van Gogh's 1889 portrait of the *Postman Joseph Roulin*.

Vincent van Gogh, who was mostly painting landscapes at the time, set out to master portraiture through his series of twenty portraits of his neighbor, postman

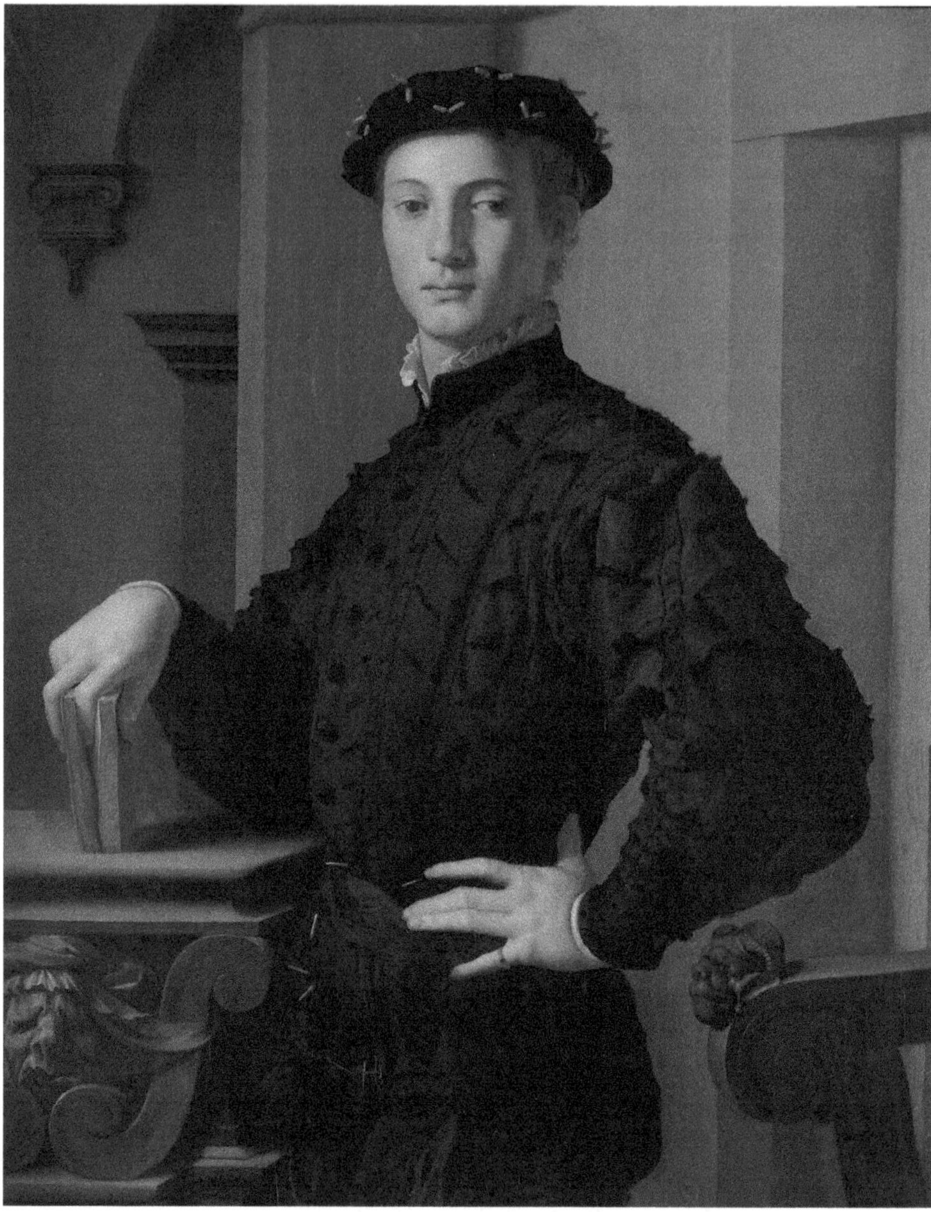

Figure 3.5 *Portrait of a Young Man*, 1530s, Bronzino (Agnolo di Cosimo di Mariano), Metropolitan Museum of Art, New York.

Joseph Roulin, and his family, including this one from 1889, in the collection of @themuseumofmodernart. In a letter to his brother, van Gogh described his joy over the portrait's emphasis on color rather than an exact copy of reality. Here, textural brush strokes give life to the portrait's intense colors, like the royal blue of Roulin's postal uniform and the bright green wallpaper scattered with pink and white flowers behind him. Roulin's robust, respectable gaze is just as piercing for the viewer as the canvas's bold hues.

—@britticisms #GucciBeauty @alessandro_michele #AlessandroMichele

By contrast, Van Gogh's portrait of Armand Roulin from 1888 shows the viewer a much younger man, one who is more emblematic of the Adonis archetype.

June 21, 2019: Armand Roulin

Van Gogh painted Armand Roulin, the son of his close friend Joseph Roulin, several times. This portrait, from the Museum Folkwang, in Essen, Germany, was painted in 1888, when Armand was only seventeen, but he has already left his family's home at this point to work as a blacksmith. Van Gogh paints him in his good clothes—a white shirt, a tie, a colorful jacket, and a fedora. But his outfit is a bit rumpled, turning downward, reflecting Armand's sideway look. There's a combination of sadness and youthful directness to the boy that van Gogh was clearly drawn to.

—@oritgat #GucciBeauty @alessandro_michele #AlessandroMichele

June 19, 2019: Actor Matsumoto Kōshirō VII as Sukeroku

In Japanese kabuki theatre, heavy makeup is used to emphasize the personality of a character rather than an individual. In this print from 1920 at the Minneapolis Institute of Arts, Matsumoto Kōshirō VII, a famous kabuki actor of the early 20th century, is shown in costume as Sukeroku, a fight-provoking samurai looking for the killer of his father. The role's makeup accentuates his angry brows; his mouth, painted red, symbolizes passion. The artist Toyonari was known for his prints of male actors. With delicate lines, Toyonari captures Sukeroku's quest: the actor's eyes gaze out of frame, searching.

—@lrsphm #GucciBeauty @alessandro_michele #AlessandroMichele

Other works of art posted included: *Boy in a Ladyfinger Shirt*, 2018, by Amoako Boafo; a self-portrait by William Rothenstein; Raphael's *Bindo Altoviti*, c.1515; *Portrait of a Young Man*, 1470, by Antonello da Messina; *Portrait of a Turk in a Turban*, c.1826, by Ferdinand Victor Eugene Delacroix; *Portrait of a Youth with a Surgical Cut in One Eye*, A.D. 190–210; Shah Ismail I, ruler of Iran 1501–1524 and founder of the Safavid Dynasty, by an anonymous Italian painter; Gottfried Lindauer's 1890 portrait of the chief of the Maori Ngāpuhi tribe Tamati Waka Nene; an English school portrait of Sir Walter Raleigh from 1588; a portrait of Maurice of Nassau, Prince of Orange, 1643 by Gerrit van Honthorst; and an Indian school portrait of Emperor Muhammad Akbar, father-in-law of Nur Jahan (the ruler who, a generation before Nur Jahan and her husband Emperor Jahangir, had ordered all court ladies veiled).

June 21, 2019: Emperor Muhammad Akbar

This portrait of the 16th-century Emperor Muhammad Akbar displays the characteristics of Indian miniature painting. Originating in Bengal, the style involved intricate patterns and geometries. The only bare expanse in the work is Akbar the

> Great's soft skin and the plain background. Captured softly and methodically, Akbar's look belies his achievements; the emperor expanded the Mughal Empire to cover much of modern-day India.
>
> —@kchayka #GucciBeauty @alessandro_michele #AlessandroMichele

In spite of the firmness of his rule, GucciBeauty chooses to celebrate the softness of his skin, rehabilitating the Emperor's historical narrative into that of a beauty icon.

What do Gucci Beauty's choices tell us between differences in ideals of male and female beauty, both of the past and today? And how do these choices impact the economic enterprise of digital heritage storytelling? The answers relate back to the definitions of 'heritage storytelling' and 'luxury' put forward in the introduction to this volume. The viewing public is seeing these works on Instagram, not for the purpose of aesthetic education, but ultimately to sell Gucci clothing, accessories, and fragrance. Leda and Helen; Mughal emperors and empresses; men and woman of the Italian Renaissance, Edo-period Japan, Tudor and Georgian England, and American high schools all serve this Italian brand's global marketing narrative.

Afterword

After this chapter was completed, Gucci went in a different direction with its beauty icons, from oviparity to equus. Bizarrely, Gucci's Spring 2020 campaign eschews human beauty for equine beauty—featuring horses in surreal print ads and profiling horse models on Instagram. Hasan (born in Austin, TX, 15 hands high, loves licorice), Batman (born in California, 13.2 hands high, favorite food cantaloupe), and other model horses subvert the traditional ideas of human beauty, desire, the gaze, and, as animals, exist outside the usual bounds of visual culture and heritage that ground and inform our reading of clothed (human) models. Perhaps this horse campaign suggests that Gucci is attempting to position itself as a universal brand, not only across culture and time, but also, audaciously, across species. Or perhaps, this is just another example of the famous Aldo Gucci sense of humor. Hasan, Batman, and the other horses can be found on Instagram using the hashtags #OfCourseAHorse and #GucciSS20.

Notes

1. Sarah Gay Forden, *The House of Gucci*, New York: William Morrow, 2000, 9.
2. Ibid, 10.
3. Ibid, 3.
4. Ibid, 9.
5. Aldo Gucci, qtd. in Ibid, 9.
6. Ibid.
7. Harling Ross, "Renaissancecore is Coming for Your Wardrobe," September 20, 2019.
8. Hannah Marriott, "Renaissancecore: Why Everyone Is Dressing Like Anne Boleyn," *Guardian Fashion*, October 16, 2019.
9. Ibid.
10. Ross, "Renaissancecore."
11. Peter McNeil and Giorgio Riello, *Luxury: A Rich History*, Oxford: Oxford University Press, 2016, 82.
12. Ibid, 82–83.
13. "At the age of thirty-seven, she realized she'd never ride through Paris in a sports car with the warm wind in her hair."—"The Ballad of Lucy Jordan."

14. Ruby Lal, *Empress: The Astonishing Reign of Nur Jahan*, New York: W. W. Norton & Co., 2018, 9–10.
15. Ibid, 6.
16. Ibid, 10.
17. Ibid, 4.
18. Ibid, 2.
19. Roberta Filippini, “Guccio Gucci,” in *The Making of Gucci*, New York: Rizzoli, 2012, 14.
20. Emmanuele Lugli, “Florence,” in *The Making of Gucci*, New York: Rizzoli, 2012, 24.
21. Rula Jebreal, “Preface,” in *The Making of Gucci*, New York: Rizzoli, 2012, 4.
22. Simone Marchetti, “Heritage,” in *The Making of Gucci*, New York: Rizzoli, 2012, 32.
23. Ibid.
24. Patrizio di Marco, qtd. in Simone Marchetti, “Heritage,” in *The Making of Gucci*, New York: Rizzoli, 2012, 32.
25. Elda Danese, “Made in Italy,” in *The Making of Gucci*, New York: Rizzoli, 2012, 36.
26. Ibid.
27. Ibid.
28. Alessandra Vaccari, “Pattern,” in *The Making of Gucci*, New York: Rizzoli, 2012, 72.
29. Angelo Flaccavento, “Liftboy,” in *The Making of Gucci*, New York: Rizzoli, 2012, 62.
30. Sappho, fragment 16. See Eva-Maria Voigt’s *Sappho et Alcaeus*.
31. This is opposed to ‘ovuliparity,’ in which fertilization is external, a distinction made by French biologist Thierry Lodé, cited in English translation in Goran Arnqvist and Locke Rowe, eds., *Sexual Conflict*, Princeton, NJ: Princeton University Press, 2005.

Bibliography

Berg, Tatiana @tatianaberg, Britt Julious @britticisms, and Kyle Chayka @kchayka. “@GucciBeauty.” *Instagram*. August 3, 2020.

Danese, Elda. “Made in Italy.” In *The Making of Gucci*. New York: Rizzoli, 2012.

Filippini, Roberta. “Guccio Gucci.” In *The Making of Gucci*. New York: Rizzoli, 2012.

Flaccavento, Angelo. “Liftboy.” In *The Making of Gucci*. New York: Rizzoli, 2012.

Forden, Sarah Gay. *The House of Gucci*. New York: William Morrow, 2000.

Jebreal, Rula. “Preface.” In *The Making of Gucci*. New York: Rizzoli, 2012.

Lal, Ruby. *Empress: The Astonishing Reign of Nur Jahan*. New York: W. W. Norton & Co., 2018.

Lugli, Emmanuele. “Florence.” In *The Making of Gucci*. New York: Rizzoli, 2012.

Marchetti, Simone. “Heritage.” In *The Making of Gucci*. New York: Rizzoli, 2012.

Marriott, Hannah. “Renaissancecore: Why Everyone Is Dressing Like Anne Boleyn.” *Guardian Fashion*. October 16, 2019.

McNeil, Peter and Giorgio Riello. *Luxury: A Rich History*. Oxford: Oxford University Press, 2016.

Ross, Harling. “Renaissancecore Is Coming for Your Wardrobe.” September 20, 2019.

Vaccari, Alessandra. “Pattern.” In *The Making of Gucci*. New York: Rizzoli, 2012.

Part II

Visual Cultures

4 The Exotic as Luxury

Visual Narrative Advertisements of Indian Luxury Goods on Instagram

Rimi Nandy

Introduction

The term 'luxury' has always been associated with bygone splendor in the context of India. Exquisite jewelry, the finest of dress materials, and handcrafted cosmetics are associated with the glorious heritage of India. A sense of nostalgia is intrinsically connected to contemporary luxury products. The past is symbolized by artifacts and monuments that remind one of the grandeur of the monarchy and the aristocratic class. In the words of John Berger, nostalgia is evoked by rediscovering the lost glory of the "ruling class in decline". The Indian luxury fashion industry reiterates the value of this very sense of nostalgia in an age of mass production and consumption. From within the structure of an industrialized, capitalist society, luxury signifies exclusivity. It refers to the craftsmanship and singular attention provided to each and every product that is produced for a single customer. The value of the luxury product is represented through the feeling of envy that the product initiates in the viewer. The terms 'ethnic' and 'traditional' are often used interchangeably to refer to Indian fashion. These terms become significant, as they symbolize the grandeur of the past. As a postcolonial nation, India has a troubled relationship with history and the past, and we find this discomfort reflected in the narratives created for such luxury products meant for Indian consumers. The term 'ethnic,' through its association with the colonial gaze, also "provokes a romantic exoticized image."[1]

The Idea of Luxury and the Contemporary Public Space

In the postmodern age, capitalist society has been replaced by the rise of a consumer society. The products being sold and consumed have lost their sense of utility. Instead products have become signs constructing the identity of consumers. Baudrillard talks about the prevalence of the simulation in place of the reality, what he terms the "hyperreal." The consumer society flourishes on advertisements. The most important role of an advertisement is to make a consumer believe that the only way to access the "good life" is through the consumption of the product it advertises.

The Industrial Revolution created a newer form of consumer market. As a result of the ability to produce goods on a larger scale, all products became affordable. In such a scenario, class distinctions could only be maintained through the lifestyle followed by a particular group of people. This is most apparent in the sphere of clothing, jewelry, and cosmetics. The term 'fashion' cannot be explained in the Indian context, as fashion as an idea is entirely a Western concept. The colonized other has always been inferior in the eyes of the colonizer. In keeping with this thought process, the Indian clothing system was always believed to be unfashionable.

The British Empire found India valuable as a colony for the production of cotton. India was not only used for manufacturing the raw material but also for the dissemination of finished clothes, imported at high rates from Britain. The low cost of producing clothes using power looms meant that the British Empire could make greater profits by selling them in a lucrative market base like India. This greatly affected the Indian handloom industry. Spinners and weavers failed to compete with the finished products being imported from Britain. As a result, there was growing unemployment among them. The Great Exhibition of 1851, which showcased the riches of India, further increased the demand for Indian cotton. This further destroyed the Indian handloom market. During the Indian freedom struggle, Mahatma Gandhi used handwoven 'khadi' as a symbol of Indian nationalism. The 'Swadeshi' movement was centered on the Indian handloom symbolized by the spinning wheel, and textiles became the primary element around which the sense of nationalism was built. The manner of clothing in India was also influenced by the British. The concept of wearing a 'blouse' beneath a sari is a Western idea. The women in precolonial India were in the habit of staying bare breasted, with only a sari used as a covering. This manner of dressing among Indian women was considered vulgar by the British. Gradually Indian women adopted the Western style of a 'blouse' as a part of their costume.

The term *haute couture* has become synonymous with space and temporality. Fashion is always associated with the death of an era. It is the recycling of the retrospective space. It becomes an effective sign that represents a ritual of rebirth, a spectacle, a kind of celebration of the past. The making of fashion has nothing to do with the aesthetic value of the product. Instead it depicts a sense of "wasteful consumption." In the words of Jean Baudrillard,

> What is more anachronistic, more dream-laden than a sailing ship? *Haute Couture*. It discourages the economist, takes up a stance contrary to productivity techniques, it is an affront to democratisation. With superb languor, a maximum number of highly qualified people produce a minimum number of models of complex cut, which will be repeated again with the same languor, twenty times in the best of cases, or not at all in the worst.
>
> (2017)[2]

In the contemporary age, consumption is no longer utilitarian. Instead it is connected to the act of display used to create a spectacle. It is the manner of meaning making related to the image of a product, which is more important than showcasing the utility of a product. The role of the digital space becomes indispensable in this respect. In the world of the Internet, the existence of a finished product is replaced by a process that is furthered by the digital sphere. The contemporary age is the age of information. Therefore it is the digital space that works toward distributing product information in a calculated manner to create meaning associated with the idea of the product. The real product is replaced by a series of images that give meaning to the process of consumption. The models of Sabyasachi against a royal backdrop, staged to portray the essence of royalty, create a dramatized spectacle, which lures consumers not to its value to the user but to its meaning as a commodity.

Similarly the images from Forest Essentials, placing the product within the time and space of the Vedic era, referring to the luxury of the handcrafted cosmetics specially made for consumers of the elite class, adds on to the value of the product. "

> India promotes ayurvedic products and services as an integral part of the process of the new age orientalization where ayurveda has been presented as wellness therapy for rejuvenation or beauty instead of a complete way of life to restore health.[3]

"Commodity fetishism" is an important aspect in the growing relevance of fashion in the contemporary capitalist age, which thrives on spectacle. According to Marx, commodity fetishism describes the veiling of the material conditions under which products are manufactured and consumed. There is a constant friction between the existing codes and the newer codes, often represented by the term 'exotic.' The 'exotic' is always in contention with the familiar. The Western code of fashion is used to define the difference in the codes between the prevalent and accepted, Western codes and the countering codes developed by Eastern cultural artifacts. Sabyasachi Mukherjee talks about saving traditional arts and craft by directly dealing with craftsmen while working on his creations. In his words,

> The country is changing so rapidly, and there's such a wealth of craft and design here that has never been used to its potential. 50 years from now, if all these crafts die out because there is no demand and supply for them, the next generation will have nothing to fall back upon and we will only see it at the Victoria and Albert museum—which is sad. It is vital for us to connect better with our audience to create demand for karigars so that they have a sustainable living.[4]

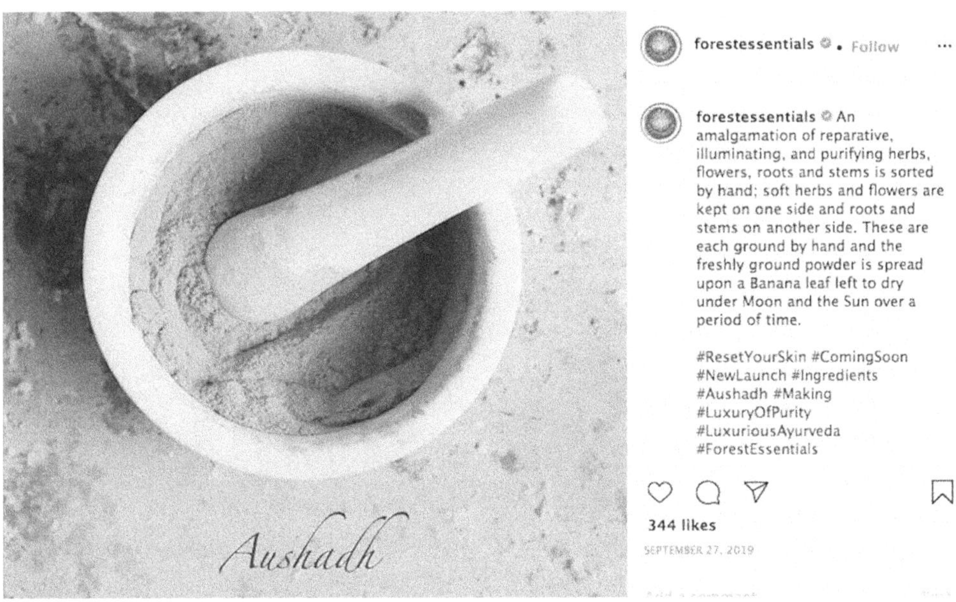

Figure 4.1 An Instagram post from Forest Essentials.[5]

Mukherjee's comment is a reminder of the Great Exhibition of 1851. The British staged their power of imperialism by showcasing expensive products acquired from their colonies. Mukherjee speaks of the dying craftsmanship of India. The 'karigar' has become a part of the colonial past. They were slowly pushed into oblivion with growing trade and industrialization. Specimens of the handwoven cloth 'khadi' can still be found on display in the Victoria and Albert Museum as a remnant of the British Empire. According to Mukherjee, the dying art has to be revived and brought back into the twenty-first century, or else it will just become a form of memorabilia. The brand Sabyasachi portrays itself as working for the upliftment of the 'karigar' and transforms them into a symbol of Indian nationalism, connected to the Gandhian principle of the 'swadeshi.'

The concept of the designer is also a Western one that has been adopted by the East. In the Indian context, the craftsmen or 'karigar' and the tailor referred to by the term 'darzi' were the only two categories associated with the clothing industry. The 'darzi' designed and implemented his ideas through the 'karigar.' The profession of designer is a modern one that in the past was represented by the 'darzi.' Sabyasachi recreates a temporal space to depict the rootedness of the Indian clothing tradition in the idea of nationalism. This space is, however, utopian considering that the images create a dream that persuades potential customers that through the products, they can access the splendor of a bygone era that was extravagant and spectacular. Most Sabyasachi photoshoots are situated in Falaknama Palace in Hyderabad. The allure of a Sabyasachi photoshoot does not portray the hardships of craftsmen during the colonial era. Their living conditions are never brought to the forefront with respect to the past or present and the difficult situations such craftsmen live in. The 'karigars' or craftsmen are always struggling with the pressure and competition of the luxury market.

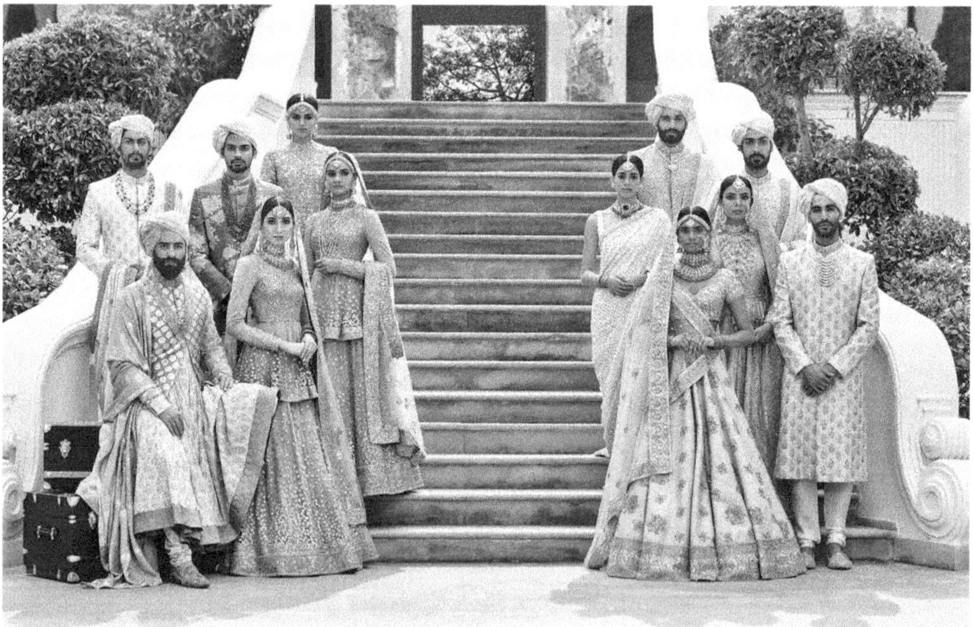

Figure 4.2 Sabyasachi Instagram image shot at Falaknama Palace, Hyderabad.[6]

This image from Sabyasachi's Instagram page was shot at Falaknama Palace, Hyderabad. The open space bordered by a lustrous garden shows the richness of the palace. The marble arches and staircases give the viewer a peek into the royal lifestyle. The exquisite trunks in black and gold also mark the value of the setting. The pastel shades of the costumes inlaid with gold 'zari' paired with precious handcrafted jewelry define the craftsmanship brought into the twenty-first century through years of tradition handed down to the 'karigars.' The models are portrayed at a higher vantage point with a downward gaze toward the viewers, depicting a higher status. This can be explained by referring to the theory of iris eccentricity, which studies the position of the iris with respect to the whites of the eyes to depict the gaze of the looker in an image. The image beautifully captures the splendor of monarchy under the British Empire. However, the reference to the 'karigar' finds an indirect suggestion through the costumes and jewelry. It is the finery of the costumes and jewelry, along with its sense of rarity, that adds value to the image. Going back in time regenerates an idea and association with the glory of the past. The consumerism in the contemporary age is not based on utility but on spectacle.

The Exotic and the Sense of Indianness

The idea of "the west" is required to understand the concept of the 'exotic.' The term 'exotic' is used with reference to the Western viewpoint. It plays the role of the other to 'the west.' The word 'west' does not refer to a mapped-out geographical area. Instead it represents a body of practices and ideologies. The East, associated with the 'exotic,' is always in contrast to the 'west.' Exoticism is a means by which the power politics of British Imperialism was disguised by a sense of aesthetic pleasure. The act of exoticizing a product conceals the negative aspects of the production of goods under the rule of British imperialism.

> Exoticism describes, rather, a particular mode of aesthetic perception—one which renders people, objects and places strange even as it domesticates them, and which effectively manufactures otherness even as it claims to surrender to its immanent mystery.
>
> (Huggan, 2001)[7]

The focal point of luxury goods is to create an 'aura,' a sense of being connected to bygone days. The products are narrativized to transport customers to the time of the "rajas, maharajas, nawabs and mughal rulers." A sense of nostalgia pervades the symbolic meaning of luxury products. It recreates an intangible value associated with the reification of a past temporality. The glorious time and space is recreated and preserved in order to be exchanged as an aesthetically pleasing object. The present age thrives on the commodification of the authentic. Closely related to the idea of luxury is that of heritage. Heritage refers to customs handed down from one generation to the other. In the context of India, genealogical knowledge and craftsmanship of artisans form the base of what is globally known as the heritage of India. The terms 'luxury' and 'heritage,' therefore, are used for the revival and reification of the nationalist fervor of colonial India. British imperialism categorically worked toward destroying the Indian cloth industry, selling expensive garments in India and using the country only as a marketplace.

The traditions and customs of India go back to precolonial India. A plethora of religious and ethnic groups settled in India. Various ages of rules influence the traditions of India. Fashion and clothing in particular underwent enormous changes down the ages. However, the glitter and richness of clothing and attire were restricted to the monarchy and the upper classes. The value of such clothing is born out of the sense of rarity, time, and precision associated with the making of such richly adorned garments. British imperialism paved the way for trade and commercialization. In the face of growing Western influence, the nationalist movement politicized the semiotics of clothing. The *saree* became symbolic of Indian culture, tradition, and rituals. The various regions of India began to be accessed for the craftsmanship of beautifying the saree, along with salwar kameez, sherwani, and lehenga as the national attire.

The nationalist narrative being portrayed in the images of Sabyasachi and Forest Essentials is a retelling of the colonial period. The reconstructed historical period completely disregards the effect of British imperialism on the textile industry of India. The poor state faced by Indian handicrafts finds no mention in the visual narratives. Instead the splendor of nationalism being retold connects to Lord Curzon's theatrical durbars in New Delhi under British rule. David Cannadine uses the term orientalism to refer to the grand style.

> Antiquity and anachronism, tradition and honour, order and subordination; about glory and chivalry, horses and elephants, knights and peers, processions and ceremony, plumed hats and ermine robes; about chiefs and emirs, sultans and nawabs, viceroys and proconsuls; about thrones and crowns, dominion and hierarchy, ostentation and ornamentalism.[8]

Designers such as Sabyasachi Mukherjee have taken a revivalist stance toward Indian fashion.

> As for my design philosophy, it shifts from year to year, but there's one thing that has remained constant—it's the concept of the personalised imperfection of the human hand. Rather than designing 'cookie-cutter' clothes, I'm interested in more personal, handmade ones with a distinctive flavor that cannot be repeated.[9]

Apart from Indian couture, the sense of luxury and heritage has also touched the field of personal care. Ayurveda today no longer has the form of a natural cure but a lifestyle. Its heritage value was constructed during the colonial period, alongside the clothing and jewelry industry.

A form of indigenous medicinal practice, Ayurveda gained popularity during the pre-independence era as a countereffect of the growing market for Western biomedicine. The commodification of Ayurveda derives its meaning not only from its authenticity but also as a marker of Indian nationalism. According to Eric Hobsbawm, most of the traditions considered to have their roots in the faraway past are often 'invented traditions' belonging to the nineteenth and twentieth centuries. The study and development of Ayurveda depend on lineage that forms the basis of the heritage. In the present society, there is a movement toward the revival of the age-old tradition of Ayurveda in order to cope with the complexities of modern life. Most of the remedies are considered to have been derived from important Vedic texts, namely *Charak Samhita*, *Susruta Samhita*, and *Ashtanga Samgraha*. According to Ayurveda philosophy, the body is constructed of five natural elements known as the 'panchamabhuta.' One of the earliest text of Ayurveda, *Susruta Samhita*, mentions two essential functions of the practice of Ayurveda. The two functions are associated with first the cure of diseases and second the methods of leading a healthy lifestyle. It was during the colonial period that India was first perceived as the land of mysticism and spirituality. This is an entirely orientalist viewpoint. According to Edward Said, "The orient was almost a European invention, and had been since antiquity a place of romance, exotic beings, haunting memories and landscapes, remarkable experiences". Ayurveda was initially accepted by the British as an easier form of treatment provided by the 'natives' for the 'natives.' This, however, changed with the setting up of the Calcutta Medical College. With the introduction of the Western medicine in India, Ayurveda was constructed as a form of religious practice surrounded by superstitions. As Hinduism formed the core of this form of medicine, it was considered to be in opposition to western medicine, thereby being viewed as the 'other.' With the rise of western medicine, Ayurveda lost its foothold. In the age of consumerism, however, Ayurveda is viewed as an alternative to the modern mechanized lifestyle. The natural ingredients used in the products provide a welcome escape from harsh chemicals, which come with various side effects. The orientalist belief born during the colonial period has been restructured in the form of a New Age orientalism. The re-orientalist mindset does not challenge the authority of modern medicine. Instead it provides an alternative to it. Ayurveda, in a consumer society, works in sync with western medicine. By tapping into the historical position of Ayurveda, Indian nationalism reached a greater level of achievement. Rare ingredients along with intensive labor transformed Ayurveda into a luxurious affair. The language used by the brand to define its motto enhances the sense of aesthetic pleasure, nostalgia, and good capitalism. The Instagram page of Forest Essentials showcases itself as a part of the luxurious past of India reinvented in the digital age: "Pioneers of Luxurious Ayurveda, our products combine Beauty, Purity and Serenity as a way of life while contributing to the society we live in."[10]

Spectacle, Instagram, and the Digital Flaneur

Baudelaire talks of the figure of the flaneur, who observes and comments on the urban lifestyle. The nineteenth century saw the advent of glass displays that targeted the gaze of the consumer represented by the flaneur. The concept of window shopping developed from the showcasing of goods in large glass displays. A flaneur on a Parisian street observed the clothing on display in the new age department stores and in the process became one with the growing urbanity of the city. In the age of consumerism, the most essential element is that of the development of the spectacle. The aura created by fashion goes back in time to revive the sense of the authentic. This sense of 'originary authentic' is used to add intangible value to commodities. Sabyasachi Mukherjee's photoshoots are designed to capture the gaze of the spectator. John Berger talks about the significance of an image of display. It creates a sense of expectation in the eyes of the consumer. Images used in advertising fashion portray an alternative self of the audience. The opulence captured in the setting of an image advertising Sabyasachi provides access to the nostalgic past and craftsmanship, which has been slowly vanishing in the age of mass production.

Forest Essentials, too, captures an idyllic setting with an orientalist gaze. The images on Instagram depict a pastoral backdrop set in the foothills of Uttarakhand. The

Forest Essentials factory is nothing like the mechanized spaces of the industrialized urban spaces. The separate steps of manufacturing a product are captured to show the care taken to make the products. Each step is individually performed by a single worker or two to three workers together. From collecting the natural ingredients from the heart of a mystical forest to hand-pounding the ingredients to produce exquisite products for personal healthcare, the images successfully depict Ayurveda as an escape from the complexities of modern life. The captions accompanying the images connect the development of the company's ideologies to Vedic rituals: "Our expertise in Ayurveda comes from years of research into Vedic scriptures to bring you exquisite treatments with high performance results."[11] Apart from images, the Instagram page also has videos of testimonials of the workers explaining the various stages of production. The frames focus on the individual attention paid the natural ingredients used in spotless enclosures. The enormous copper utensils used for mixing the various potions add to the value of the product. The videos also show Ayurvedic practitioners referring to yellowing pages of Vedas written in Sanskrit. The captions repeatedly remind the consumers of the ancient knowledge used to prepare the various products:

> Years of painstaking research and testing ensure we create efficacious products that show results with all natural ingredients. Vaids work together with doctors to marry the ancient Ayurvedic scriptures with modern science. This product philosophy is based on Anubhuta Ayurveda: ensuring we adhere to the original scriptures whilst infusing a twist of modernity to suit the present era.[12]

The digital platform becomes a substitute for the urban streets and glass windows. The images and videos transport the spectator to dreamscapes beyond reality. As the consumer travels through different spaces from one link to the other, he or she is presented with myriad options, all catering to the desires of authenticity, rarity, and exquisiteness. Whether it is within the grandeur of the palace walls or the embrace of nature, the digital flaneur can leisurely walk through these spaces away from the horrors of modernity. According to Mike Featherstone, social media platforms have become data cybercities where the consumer walks through the digital space and observes the various goods it puts on display. Instagram images are akin to glass windows with products displayed in the arcades of Paris. The only difference is, unlike the department stores, the Instagram windows are open around the clock. Similarly, there are no temporal restrictions, as were associated with the urban streets of Paris. A consumer no longer needs to physically travel to encounter the desired objects; instead, just a click transports the user to different parts of the world. As a follower travels through the maze of images, s/he looks at India as a space in retrospection. It can be said that a follower is the new face of the digital flaneur.

Semiotics and the Visual Narrative

Instagram originated as a mobile photo-sharing application. Due to its temporal and spatial flexibility, it has become a major social media platform. The images shared on Instagram can be considered a multimodal text. The central focus of Instagram is the images. However, the process of meaning making includes other supporting elements such as captions, comments, and emoticons. The semiotics of the visuals are used by various brands in order to depict the meaning associated with a brand

and its products. Analyzing the various visual tropes portrays the interaction between a brand and its followers. Images have become the driving force in the advertisements of the digital age. In the consumer society, the sign has become much more important than the product itself. The images used in advertisement always project a dream that attracts potential consumers to products. The manner in which an image is constructed narrates a tale connected to the significance of the product being advertised. The most commodified element of human society in the present age is culture. Authenticity and heritage are valued greatly by consumers. There is an intense sense of "missing out" haunting the consumers of society. Consumerism evokes the idea that consuming goods is the only path to a good life. Consumption has become a mode of identity construction.

In the age of social media and consumerism, advertisements no longer sell an object but the emotions attached to and evoked by an object. Advertisements have moved from an object-oriented to a subject-oriented approach. The focus on consumerism has transformed the society into one that is essentially born out of envy, a "society of envy." According to Susan Sontag, a photograph captures a moment or event that aids the construction of identity. Stories and narratives have been intertwined with lives of people from time immemorial. It is human nature to process events in the form of a narrative. Therefore, the role of narratives in advertisement is insurmountable. Raymond Williams discusses narrative advertisements linking emotions to the product being displayed. Abstract emotions that do not have a concrete body are represented through narratives that symbolize different attributes of a product, such as status, gender relationship, and envy. Social media marketing is the most effective form in the digital age. Marketing teams target user engagement to make a brand popular. The different narratives told by images on social media enhance user engagement. The comments of the audience on an image further the process of creating a strong brand narrative that leaves a lasting impression on consumers.

Brands construct a myth of being connected to ancient regimes and knowledge through images. This becomes a part of a larger discourse on nationalism and authenticity. A photograph acquires its meaning by virtue of being considered part of reality. Dubois talks about the role of photographs in the transformation of truth. The intention of the photographer matters greatly in the construction of the truth of an image. Based on the angle, focus of light, and point of view, a photographer manipulates the meaning of an image. Dubois further discuss a photograph as a trace of something that exists or existed even before the photograph.

The photographic discourse represented on Instagram by Sabyasachi and Forest Essentials can be understood through the denotation and connotation of the images. An image has to be studied closely to understand the meaning it chooses to capture. Every element of a photograph, beginning from the background to the foreground, comes together to construct a truth that can only be acquired by studying the image in context. With reference to the construction of meaning on Instagram, two concepts are greatly influential in defining the symbolic significance. The words 'instgrammatics' and 'instagrammism' unite to represent the semiotics of an image. The former concept deals with the structure of an image, whereas the latter defines the aesthetic meaning evoked by an image. A few images will be analyzed in support of images being an essential tool for brand management.

The image in Figure 4.3 captures and freezes a temporal space that signifies grandeur. The frame captures models attired in the various fineries of a bride. Shot inside

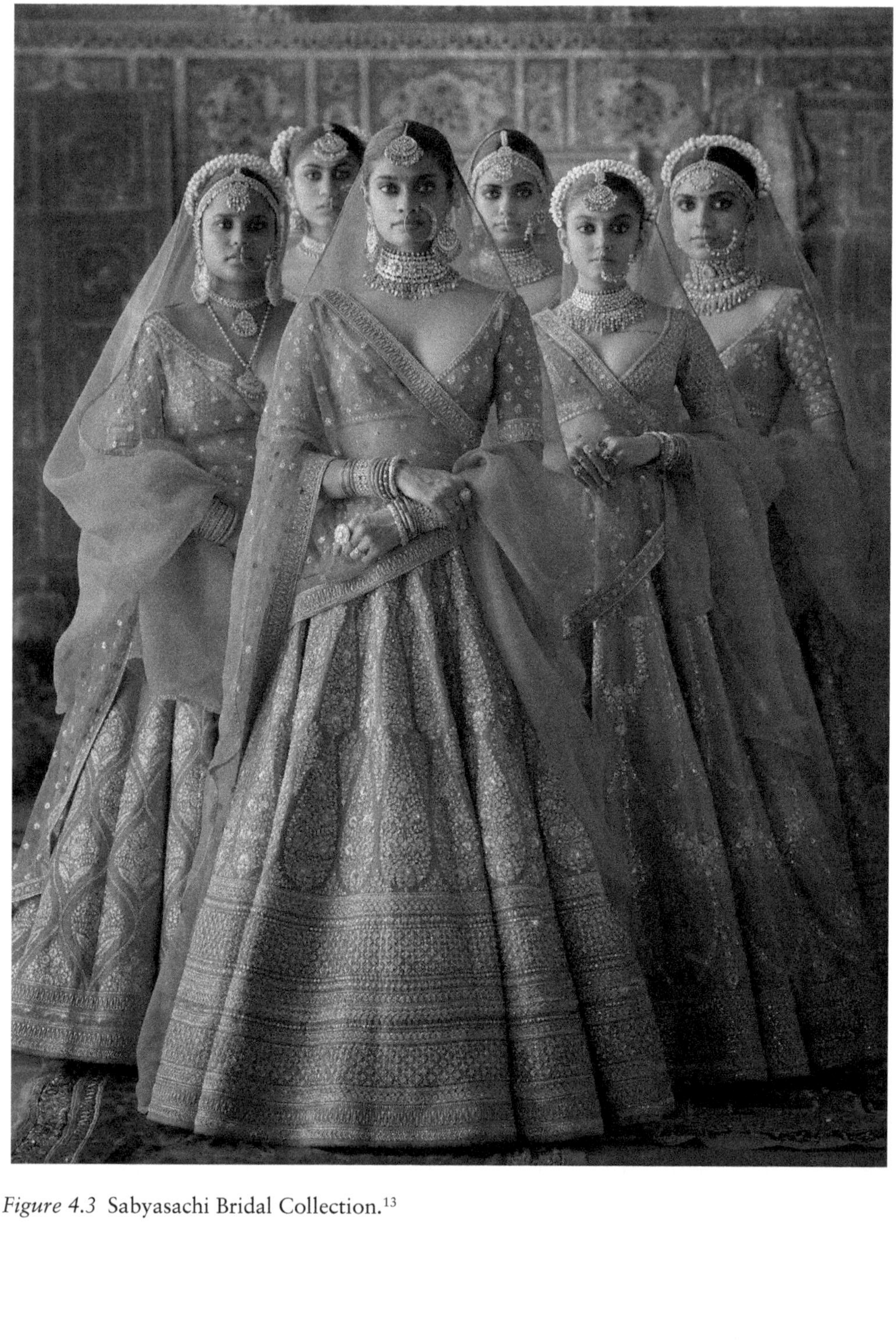

Figure 4.3 Sabyasachi Bridal Collection.[13]

Faluknama Palace, Hyderabad, the photograph focuses on the exquisite costume and jewelry. The dominance of the color red, in unison with the golden zari, woven to form intricate details, is a mark of expensive craftsmanship. The gaze and pose of the models, however, appear anachronistic. The "ghunghat," which is supposed to enhance the docility of a bride, in this photograph becomes just ornamentation. Instead of a demure gaze, the 'brides' in this image look out of the frame with great confidence and a fierce sense of individuality. These are 'brides' of modern India, who are rooted in tradition but at the same time challenge the beliefs of a patriarchal society. The breasts and cleavage of the models are also brought into focus through the play of light and shadow. The body language portrayed through the image could be read as being challenging. The western concept of beauty is also being undermined in this photograph. In contrast to the obsession with fair skin, the image here celebrates dark beauty. In the precolonial era, a dark skin tone was celebrated in Hindu mythology. Lord Krishna and Draupadi were depicted with dark skin tones, which were considered beautiful. Sabyasachi goes back to the ancient belief of the Indian skin tone. Apart from the skin tone, the body type also challenges the western view of a slim body being a symbol of beauty. The image tries to uphold and rewrite the existing notions of beauty and femininity.

Various images use plus-size models for displaying Sabyasachi's products. Dark skin tones are also a very common element in the images. The captions and hashtags add meaning to the images. The signs and meanings used in the context of the images are not arbitrary in nature but manipulated and motivated by the brand's desire to connect with consumers. The comments accompanying the images often praise Sabyasachi for celebrating different Indian body types. The word 'inclusivity' appears in a comment, successfully displaying the brand's intention. The comments also often use words such as 'royal,' 'vintage,' 'heritage,' 'royal,' and 'majestic.' The images magnify the sense of nostalgia, which the consumers easily connect to. However, there are few comments that try to point out the culture portrayed in the images has moved away from its Indian roots. One recurrent criticism is with reference to the models showing skin. The deep plunging necklines, partially exposing the cleavage and the breasts, receive severe criticism in a few comments. The contrast in attitude to the pose and clothing can be clearly understood from the following two comments, which appears alongside the same image.

> Thank you Sabyasachi Sir for celebrating plus size body shape.[heart eyes emoji]. . . . You understand that beauty comes in every shape and sizes. . . . I have always been bullied for my weight. . . . but this photo really inspired me [praise hands emoji] and gave me a hope that life is beyond skinny and thin body. . . . it's actually celebrating yourself and loving yourself [4 x smiling emoji][14]
>
> Good move on the model! But the photo shoot lacks elegance. Show skin, but tastefully. Keeping in mind the culture.[15]

The images are perceived by the followers through cultural filters, which may vary from person to person. This difference in attitude shows class consciousness and the multifaceted culture of India. The modern Indian outlook is constantly in conflict with colonial India. Cultural filters are affected by large-scale globalization.

The second image that will be studied has been taken from a Forest Essentials Instagram post. Figure 4.4 takes the spectator into a pastoral setting that is almost dreamlike. The image frames a burst of myriad colors of plants and flowers. The central

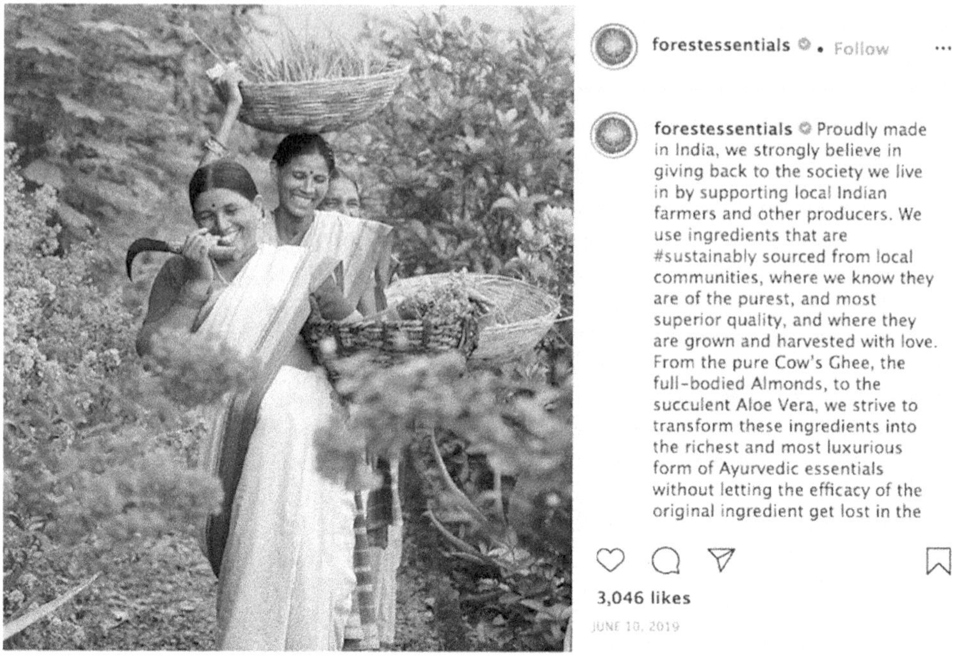

Figure 4.4 Forest Essentials Instagram post.[16]

focus of the image are the three women gathering ingredients from an idyllic space. What captures the attention of the viewer are the happy faces of the women and their laughter. The caption describes the significance of the happy faces. The brand projects itself as one that not only makes world-class products but also behaves responsibly toward its workers. This image is an icon of good capitalism that does not feature exploitation of the workers but the unbridled joy given to them through the company policies. The white color of the sarees might be symbolic of the tranquil atmosphere and the purity of the ingredients. The caption of the image further focuses on the element of luxury symbolized by the purity of the ingredients. The open space is a complete shift from the mechanized and claustrophobic settings of an urban factory.

The comments alongside the images construct a narrative based on the perception of the images. The interaction around the image shown in Figure 4.4 shows that the customers connect to the ideal and principles portrayed by Forest Essentials in order to connect to the consumers. One of the followers comments on Figure 4.4:

> Adorable picture, . . . it captures the beauty and purity of simplicity and nature. Look at those smiles, they get a smile on my face too. The same essence flows into your products too.[17]

This comment depicts that through the image and its composition, Forest Essentials has been able to connect the sense of purity and authenticity that brand associates with itself. The various elements of the photograph capture an instant constructed to produce a desirable meaning for consumers to associate with the brand.

Homogeneity to Heterogeneity: An Exercise in Identity Construction

Cultural identity refers to shared beliefs and attitudes that unite a group through their common practices. Identity is always constructed with reference to another. This dictates the power relationships in the society. In the age of globalization, the networked connections binding different countries together form a 'global village,' which in return creates a homogeneous society. The digital age has sped up the process of globalization. An aspect greatly influencing the move toward heritage and ethnicity is this spread of globalization. Globalization leads to the dissolution of individuality and identity. In the face of loss of this sense of individuality, there is a movement toward relocating by accessing the nationalistic spirit represented by local time-bound traditions that define individuality. However, the local traditions are refurbished in order to be accommodated within the constantly changing stage of globalization. Nationalism helps in distinguishing one nation from the others. Capitalism works toward creating products that are mass produced, thereby dissolving the differences between consumers. As capitalism was slowly taken over by a society of consumerism, national identity became essential for constructing an individual identity. The concept of 'nationalism' is a fictional one. It creates collective memories which bind groups together in the form of an 'imagined community.' What connects such communities is a past remembered by the individuals of the community. The idea of an Indian identity is derived from the imperial gaze, which perceived the natives of India as the other. Globalization leads to a standardization of products. This is why the role of cultural identity becomes essential. Tradition and heritage are concepts associated with quality, rarity, and aesthetic pleasure. The manner of remembering and creating memory affects perception of cultural identity. The movement toward the local in the age of globalization is a response to the sense of loss of individuality due to mass production and technological advancement.

Conclusion

The meaning of consumer products has changed greatly in the digital age. Consumerism is no longer restricted to concrete products; rather, products have been transformed into a process with no definite end. The value of the product has also become extremely mercurial. The system of networks connecting the whole world together has given rise to globalization. The seminal position held by globalization in the age of consumerism affects the construction of identity. Globalization initiates the structuring of a homogeneous identity. The rapid removal of individuality creates a requirement for heterogeneity. For this reason, there has been a shift toward the desire to connect to the root of heredity. Hence, there is a movement toward depicting a national identity through the use of age-old traditions and handcrafts. This is beautifully portrayed through images, as an image becomes a signifier of national identity. Narrative advertisements create a myth in order to connect to a time period of the past, for it is in the sense of nostalgia that the importance of a luxury brand is enhanced. The role of gaze and perception is essential in depicting cultural identity through the use of images. The signs, icons, and symbols come together to form an image. As a viewer, the various elements of an image have to be studied to analyze the message being presented through a single shot by the imagination of a photographer.

This chapter has dealt with the manner in which Indian luxury brands cater to the expectations of consumers through visual narratives by tying the images together.

Each image tells a story of the uniqueness of the brand. They are used to justify the position of the brand as a marker of Indian heritage and culture. Further studies can be conducted to elaborate on the position of local Indian traditions in contrast with global scenarios.

Notes

1. Arti Sandhu, *Indian Fashion: Tradition, Innovation, Style*, New York: Bloomsbury, 2015, 6.
2. Baudrillard, Jean. *Symbolic Exchange and Death*. New Delhi: Sage Publication Ltd. 2017, p. 115.
3. www.researchgate.net/publication/280834881_New_Age_Orientalism_Ayurvedic_'well ness_and_spa_culture'
4. Reflections Kolkata-based fashion designer, Reflections, By: Border&Fall Photography: Sabyasachi Mukherjee, Share this article, Nirupa, Pia Anderson, Ridhi, and Name *. n.d. "Designer Sabyasachi Mukherjee Discusses Craft & Sustainability." *Border&Fall*. Accessed January 17, 2020. www.borderandfall.com/karigar/designer-sabyasachi-mukherjee-craft/.
5. Person and ProfilePage. n.d. "@Forestessentials on Instagram: 'An Amalgamation of Reparative, Illuminating, and Purifying Herbs, Flowers, Roots and Stems Is Sorted by Hand; Soft Herbs and Flowers Are . . .'." *Instagram*. Accessed January 17, 2020. www.instagram.com/p/B26i04RF_JD/.
6. Sabyasachi, *Instagram*.
7. Huggan, Graham. *The Postcolonial Exotic: Marketing the Margins*. London: Routledge. 2001, p. 14.
8. Shashi Tharoor (2016).
9. Rebecca McLaughlin-Duane, "Fashion Designer Sabyasachi Attracts Global Attention." *The National*, January 26, 2012. www.thenational.ae/lifestyle/fashion-designer-sabyasachi-attracts-global-attention-1.394506.
10. Forest Essentials, "@Forestessentials · Instagram Photos and Videos." *Instagram*. Accessed February 10, 2020. www.instagram.com/forestessentials/?hl=en.
11. "@Forestessentials on Instagram: 'Our Expertise in Ayurveda Comes from Years of Research into Vedic Scriptures to Bring You Exquisite Treatments with High Performance . . .'." *Instagram*. 2020. www.instagram.com/p/B8JcgMEFBHX/.
12. Ibid.
13. "Sabyasachi Mukherjee on Instagram: 'The Sabya Edit Classic Sabyasachi Red Wedding Lehengas for Summer 2020 Jewellery Courtesy: Sabyasachi Heritage Jewelry Collection . . .'." *Instagram*, n.d. Accessed January 15, 2020. www.instagram.com/p/B7UynorhbEU/.
14. Sabyasachi Mukherjee. "Sabyasachi Mukherjee on Instagram: 'The New Collection. Winter 2019. Jewellery Courtesy: Sabyasachi Heritage Jewelry Collection @Sabyasachijewelry For All Enquiries, Please . . .'." *Instagram*, 2019. www.instagram.com/p/B4lt0_1hpnV/.
15. Ibid.
16. "@Forestessentials on Instagram: 'Our Expertise in Ayurveda . . . ."
17. Person and ProfilePage. n.d. "@Forestessentials on Instagram: 'Proudly Made in India, We Strongly Believe in Giving Back to the Society We Live in by Supporting Local Indian Farmers and Other Producers . . .'." *Instagram*. Accessed January 10, 2020. www.instagram.com/p/ByhG6Q3lEvr/.

Bibliography

Appadurai, Arjun. *The Future As Cultural Fact: Essays on the Global Condition*. New York: Verso. 2013.

Atwal, Glyn and Bryson, Douglas. *Luxury Brands in China and India*. London: Palgrave Macmillan. 2017.

Barnard, Malcolm. *Fashion: (Critical Concepts in Media and Cultural Studies)*. New York: Routledge. 2009.

Baudrillard, Jean. *Symbolic Exchange and Death*. New Delhi: Sage Publication Ltd. 2017.
BBC News. "Dressing the Indian Woman." www.bbc.com/news/magazine-30330693. 2014.
Berger, Arthur Asa. *The Objects of Affection: Semiotics and Consumer Culture*. New York: Palgrave Macmillan. 2010.
Berger, Arthur Asa. *Applied Discourse Analysis: Popular Culture, Media, and Everyday Life*. San Francisco: Palgrave Macmillan. 2016.
Berger, John. *Ways of Seeing*. London: Penguin Book. 2008.
Berger, John and Dyer, Geoff. *Understanding a Photograph*. Penguin Modern Classic. 2013.
Boccardi, Andrea, Ciappei, Cristiano, Zollo, Lamberto and Laudano, Maria Carmen. "The Role of Heritage and Authenticity in the Value Creation of Fashion Brand." *International Business Research* 9: 135–143. https://flore.unifi.it/retrieve/handle/2158/1050121/147729/Mythopoesis copia.pdf. 2016.
Cannadine, David. *Orientalism: How the British Saw Their Empire*. New York: Oxford University Press. 2002.
Craik, Jennifer. *The Face of Fashion*. New York: Routledge. 1993.
Danesi, Marcel. *Understanding Media Semiotics*. London: Arnold Publishers. 2002.
Harper, Tauel. *Democracy in the Age of New Media: The Politics of the Spectacle*. New York: Peter Lang Publishing Inc. 2011.
Huggan, Graham. *The Postcolonial Exotic: Marketing the Margins*. New York: Taylor & Francis Group. 2008.
Jindal, Abhilasha."Indian Players Going Indigenous to Excel the World."www.researchgate.net/publication/321579180_INDIAN_PLAYERS_GOING_INDIGENOUS_TO_EXCEL_THE_WORLD. 2020.
Kettemann, Bernhard. "Semiotics of Advertising and the Discourse of Consumption." *Arbeiten aus Anglistik und Amerikanistik* 38: 53–67. www.jstor.org/stable/43025841. 2013.
KOÇ, Mustafa. "Cultural Identity Crisis in the Age of Globalization and Technology." *The Turkish Online Journal of Educational Technology* 5: 37–43. Accessed 3 February 2020. https://files.eric.ed.gov/fulltext/EJ1102484.pdf. 2006.
Kuldova, Tereza. *Luxury India Fashion: A Social Critique*. New York: Bloomsbury. 2017. (Langford, 2019).
Lazarus, Neil and Bartolovich, Crystal. *Marxism Modernity Postcolonial Studies*. New York: Cambridge University Press. 2002.
Outka, Elizabeth. *Consuming Traditions: Modernity, Modernism, and the Commodified Authentic*. New York: Oxford University Press. 2009.
Outka, Elizabeth. *Modernism and the Commodified Authentic*. New York: Oxford University Press. 2009.
Popova, Maria. "Aesthetic Consumerism and the Violence of Photography: What Susan Sontag Teaches Us about Visual Culture and the Social Web." Accessed 1 February 2020. www.brainpickings.org/2013/09/16/susan-sontag-on-photography-social-media/. n.d.
Prickett, Sarah Nicole. "Look Out, It's Instagram Envy." *Nytimes.Com*. www.nytimes.com/2013/11/06/t-magazine/sign-of-the-times-look-out-its-instagram-envy.html. 2013.
Raikhan, Sadykova. *The Postcolonial Exotic*. Reprint, Jean. Fluent Bodies. Reprint,
Raikhan, Sadykova, Moldakhmetb, Myrzabekov, Ryskeldyc, Myrzabekova and Aluad, Moldakhmetkyzy. "The Interaction of Globalization and Culture in the Modern World." *Science Direct*. Accessed 10 February 2020. https://s100.copyright.com/AppDispatchServlet?publisherName=ELS&contentID=S1877042814013111&orderBeanReset=true. March 19, 2014.
Rubinstein, Daniel and Sluis, Katrina. "A Life More Photographic." *Photographies* 1: 9–28. 2008.
Said, Edward W. *Orientalism: Western Conceptions of the Orient*. New York: Penguin. 2001.
Sandhu, Arti. *Indian Fashion: Tradition, Innovation, Style*. London: Bloomsbury. 2015.
Serafinelli, Elisa and Karatzogianni, Athina. *Digital Life on Instagram: New Social Communication of Photography*. Bingley: Emerald Publishing. 2018.

Seyfi, Murat and Soydaş, Ayda Uzunçarşılı. "Instagram Stories from the Perspective of Narrative Transportation Theory." *The Turkish Online Journal of Design, Art and Communication* 7: 47–60. Accessed 3 February 2020. www.tojdac.org/tojdac/VOLUME7-ISSUE1_files/tojdac_v07i1105.pdf. 2017.

Srivastav, Gaurav and Singh, Pankaj. "Indian Handicraft & Globalization: In Context of Export. *Researchgate*. Accessed 12 February 2020. www.researchgate.net/publication/283009715_INDIAN_HANDICRAFT_GLOBALIZATION_IN_CONTEXT_OF_EXPOR. January 2016.

Tharoor, Sashi. *An Era of Darkness*. India: Aleph Book Company. 2016.

Victoria and Albert Museum. "The Fabric of India: Textiles in a Changing World." *Vam.Ac.Uk*. Accessed 24 January 2020. www.vam.ac.uk/content/exhibitions/the-fabric-of-india/textiles-in-a-changing-world/.

Weiss, Julian. "The Flânerie of Instagram: Studying the Photography-Based Social Network as a Self-Curated Newspaper within the Modern Cityscape of the Internet." http://writing.rochester.edu/celebrating/2017/HUMhonorable.pdf. Accessed 7 January 2020.

Wheeler, Rebecca. "Local History as Productive Nostalgia? Change, Continuity and Sense of Place in Rural England." *Social & Cultural Geography* 18: 466–486. https://core.ac.uk/download/pdf/80788379.pdf. 2016.

5 "Terrain of Every Hue"

Locating the Luxury Knitwear Trade in Scotland's Landscapes

Marina Moskowitz

In 1924, Edward, Prince of Wales (later to become Edward VIII, king of the United Kingdom for his short stay on the throne before abdicating) was vacationing in Biarritz, France, recovering from a steeplechase accident, when he was photographed by Alfieri image service for the *Illustrated London News*.[1] The photograph depicted him on the Biarritz golf course, staring into the camera, while holding his "great favourite," a Cairn terrier, and accompanied by General Gerald Trotter. He was wearing a flat cap, collared shirt, tie, long trousers, and Fair Isle pullover. Even in the black and white photograph, the characteristic features of the allover patterned sweater from one of Scotland's Shetland Isles are very apparent: horizontal bands of small motifs (such as x's and o's and small medallions) in contrasting colors and multicolored ribbing, known as corrugated, around the waist, collar, and cuffs. Though not identified in any way, the sweater was likely already recognizable to many readers as having originated in Scotland or at least having been modeled on Scottish knitwear designs. Indeed, two years earlier, Edward had "played in" to mark his new role as Captain of the Royal and Ancient Golf Club at St. Andrews, Scotland and had been widely reported to have worn a sweater from Fair Isle, though in photographs, it was mostly covered by his jacket.[2] The Prince was credited in the contemporary popular press with reviving this style of knitwear, transferring it from an everyday garment in the northern isles of Scotland to sportswear for the British elite, and his sartorial influence is still discussed by historians of fashion and design.[3]

The 1924 Alfieri photograph, showing the knitwear in full, took on a life of its own; though perhaps not at the pace we would today associate with "going viral" in the digital sphere, it had several incarnations, leading to widespread circulation. The photographic image was adapted by the British painter John St. Helier Lander, known at the time for his portrayals of elite British society, into a more focused portrait of the Prince, still with his beloved terrier but without General Trotter, in an image titled *Royal Friends*. In cropping Edward's body from the thigh up, the painted portrait emphasizes the Fair Isle sweater, which dominates the center of the painting. On November 23, 1925, in its "Christmas Number," the *Illustrated London News* published a color photogravure of the Lander painting, bringing the cropped color image to a broad audience.[4] At least one publisher of "knitting and handicraft" patterns, Leach's, incorporated the figure of the Prince into the cover design for "Leach's Sportswear for Men . . . New Designs in Knitting with Simple Directions," although a closer look at this image shows that while the cropping is similar to the Lander portrait, it is actually a copy of the original photograph (in which the Prince has slightly different hand positions and a visible wristwatch), with some added color to the motifs on the original sweater, whereas Lander and the *Illustrated London News* have retained the essence of the Fair Isle design without replicating it precisely.[5] Using the recognizable characteristics of this particular style of Scottish knitwear, Lander was able to feature a convincing version of a Fair Isle sweater while taking the artistic license that painting allows.

The narrative that the Prince of Wales served as a catalyst in popularizing the Fair Isle sweater for British and even international elites obviously predates the digital era. But it is relevant to digital storytelling in two ways: first in the persistence of the story and second in its emphasis on that story's setting. Over the years from the 1920s until the present day, the familiar image of Edward, Prince of Wales, in a Fair Isle sweater has moved from the sphere of paint and print into the digital realm. The image still appears today on numerous websites selling men's knitwear, often accompanying a Fair Isle sweater inspired by the portrait, blog posts and Pinterest boards detailing historic fashion influences, and even the Wikipedia page for the Fair Isle stranded knitting technique exemplified by the Prince's sweater.[6] The ways in which royalty, social elites, movie stars, and today's "internet influencers" have acted as trendsetters and endorsers of particular commodities has a long and varied history that continues to hold resonance.[7] While portraits such as Lander's were not intended to promote commercial products, they nonetheless helped to establish links between cultural representation and commerce.[8]

However, in this chapter, I want to look beyond the subject of Lander's portrait to the carefully constructed landscape that the painter has inserted and argue that the broader precedent that this painting establishes is not only in the representation of its subject, which today is taken often as the sweater as much as its royal wearer, but also the crafting of its background. For today's purveyors of luxury Scottish knitwear, heritage is often rooted not just in iconic historic figures but in the landscape itself. Lander's alterations to this image were not only in the cropping, patterning, and color, but also in the backdrop. Where the setting for the original photograph was only identifiable from its caption, showing just a small patch of grass in front of a large fence, Lander has placed the Prince of Wales in front of an expansive landscape. About four-fifths of the backdrop on the canvas depicts a leaden gray sky, below which a narrow band of blue water lies in the distance beyond an undulating ground of earth tones: browns, greens, golds, and warm russet red highlights. With this color scheme, Lander cleverly ties the Prince to the setting, inverting in his clothing the position of the same colors used for the landscape; the gray trousers in the bottom of the painting are reminiscent of the dominant background color of the sky, while the Fair Isle sweater uses small bands of blue and red to highlight the shades of brown, tan, and dull yellow that make up most of the pullover's pattern. Lander even replicated from the original photograph the informal, slightly rolled and partially inside-out appearance of the waistband, here shown in a blue and tan representation of corrugated ribbing, making the bottom of the sweater into a wavy blue band that sits in the painting just at the horizon point above the wavy blue sea. In this painting, the Prince of Wales' Fair Isle pullover rises from the landscape. Though the original photograph was taken in Biarritz, and the painting does not reference a specific location, I would argue that Lander transposed the setting to generalized representation of a Scottish landscape, recognizable not only because of the association with the sweater. Lander's palette, and the elements of landscape shown, accord to numerous landscape paintings of the Scottish Highlands and Islands in the late nineteenth and early twentieth centuries, images that constructed what the art historian Martin Halliwell calls "a romantic cultivated wildness."[9]

The landscapes that provide the backdrop for luxury knitwear suggest varied, and even conflicting, images of Scottish national heritage. On the one hand, there is a long tradition of knitwear production rooted in small-scale factories now portrayed as picturesque in the face of later and more intrusive industrial manufacturing. On the other hand, there is a *seemingly* more natural heritage, rooting knitwear in a landscape tradition that encompasses sheep husbandry, baronial estates, and elite sporting wear (as we see in Lander's painting), all of which wrought change to Scotland's environment.[10] Both of these landscapes are referenced in the visual imagery on the websites and digital marketing campaigns of many Scottish knitwear brands; the chapter will examine two case studies of Johnstons of Elgin and Pringle of Scotland. In real ways, contemporary knitwear might draw in terms of palette and pattern on images of the past. But perhaps as important to the marketing of Scottish knitwear are the imaginaries of the past that these landscapes—of production and consumption—evoke. In marketing their own wares drawing upon tropes of a heritage landscape, Scottish knitwear companies may also—intentionally or not—take part in "place marketing" for the nation.[11] At the same time, they both draw upon and reinforce the tropes of Scotland's landscapes, adopting the sense of deep time rooted in natural history to extend their company heritage.

"The Unique Blend of Color, Romance, and History"

Johnstons of Elgin was founded in 1797 as a weaving mill but is now a producer and purveyor of a range of luxury textiles, including knitwear. Since the nineteenth century, Johnstons has been associated with the Scottish landscape through its production of "estate tweeds" and continues to produce woven textiles but is now equally known for fine-gauge knitwear in luxury fibers such as cashmere.[12] While Johnstons alludes to its heritage in a variety of ways in its digital marketing, the company's use of film, with canny juxtapositions of sound and image, is a particularly effective tool for presenting the company's heritage. Johnstons provides "Our History" on a discrete webpage that features a "video discovery" of the company, with a choice of seven different languages for the film's voiceover, suggesting the geographic reach of the firm's products.[13] The film also sits at the bottom of a recently added page detailing a company timeline, offering two forms of heritage storytelling on the website.[14]

The video opens with a panoramic view of the Scottish countryside; the top third of the screen shows leaden gray clouds almost identical in color to Lander's expansive sky. The horizon line sits above a landscape of rolling hills (with just one peak catching light), a middle ground of forested terrain, and a foreground with an undulating greensward bordered by deciduous trees and a rocky track leading off the frame of the screen. This landscape is greener than that depicted by Lander but has the same basic palette of earth tones. Though it is not easy to spot a building in the five seconds of film footage that this landscape is on the screen, there is one—in the middle distance toward the right of the screen—but it is almost entirely masked in this image by the surrounding vista. That the very first words of narration are "Nestled deep in the Scottish countryside"—coupled with the first strains of a guitar playing traditional Celtic music—demonstrating that whatever the subject of this sentence, and this film, turns out to be, its place in the Scottish landscape is foremost in consideration.[15]

After detailed images of flowing water identified as the River Lossie and the bough of an evergreen tree, that subject is revealed as "a majestic mill," the home of Johnstons of Elgin.[16] While the company is said to be "known the world over as *the* experts in cashmere and fine woollens," the mill is described as "one of the best kept secrets in Scottish textiles," as if the mill is not only "nestled" in the Scottish landscape but protected by it.[17] That protective landscape is linked to the company's heritage in a montage of the historic mill buildings, including various dated signage that travels back in time, from 1958 to 1911 to 1867, and finally to a label on a new product that simply but proudly states "Johnstons of Elgin Since 1797" while the voiceover states that the firm has "stood strong for over two centuries and will stand strong for many more."[18] The combination of image, spoken word, music, and design of the webpage in which the film is embedded indicates that Johnstons' authority in textile production derives from its history but also that its history is rooted in that specific place and its resources.

The implication is that the company incorporates the chosen characteristics of the natural setting into its products, for example, describing the River Lossie as having the "softest Scottish waters."[19] The film's narrator states that Johnstons has learned "how to weave the beauty of the Scottish landscape into each and every one of our products" as an image of fine reeds and grasses along the river bank blends into an image of spun fibers within the factory.[20] Of course, the fibers we see are likely wool (or possibly cashmere) as opposed to plant-based fibers, so the company is not weaving that particular "beauty" into its products, but the metaphor nonetheless ties together the timelessness of nature, the industrial heritage of the company, and the luxury products it sends out into the broader world. Stating "every piece is made to last," Johnstons' film draws on the history of the sites of production as part of a continuum between past, present, and future, implying that both the quality of workmanship and the classic design aesthetic of its textiles will endure.[21]

Though nature is depicted as timeless, it is specific in place, incorporating production sites across Scotland. While Johnstons claims its Scottish heritage as the basis of its authority as a purveyor of knitted and woven cashmere and fine woollens, it also supports the political economy of that place. The film enumerates "lessons learned" since the company's founding in 1797; among them is "Why we choose not to export our manufacturing away from its Scottish roots . . . whether it be from our mills in Elgin in the Highlands or Hawick in the Borders." As these words are being said, the camera focuses on still-robust, though worn by years of manufacture, metal machinery, centering on the words "Elgin," and then "Scottish," inscribed on the machinery, the latter image perfectly timed to coincide with the words "Scottish roots" in the voiceover. The screen then immediately shifts to a different type of roots: while showing the Elgin mill, the building recedes between the branches of a large tree that dominates the screen.[22] The winter-time image shows the tree with no leaves but with an elaborate system of branches stemming from a gnarled trunk in the middle of a green lawn that implies a parallel, if invisible, root structure under the ground. The broader implication is that Johnstons' industrial history is rooted in, and adds to rather than interfering with, the natural history of Scotland.

Having focused on the namesake town of Elgin for the first minute of the film, this commitment to Scottish production offers the first glimpse in the film of the company's knitwear manufacturing site of Hawick in the Scottish Borders region south of the capital city of Edinburgh. Though this initial representation of Hawick is far more built up than the landscape with which the film begins, the town is directly in the middle of the screen, seemingly situated within a small bowl in the gently undulating grassy landscape that is shown circling the town.[23] The colors of Hawick's architecture are muted earth tones that seem enveloped by this landscape. The sky stretching across the top third of the screen contains some heavy cloud against a watery light blue, but here the sun pierces those clouds, almost as if rewarding Johnstons' investment in this place. The narrator intones another of the firm's lessons: "that you can't buy heritage or provenance," underscoring the company's history with a visual of large leather-bound, gilt-lettered books, presumably order books or account books, with dates from the 1880s.[24] Although Johnstons began working with Hawick manufacturers as recently as the 1970s and opened its own knitwear factory in 1980, it is claiming its much longer corporate history, of centuries rather than decades, to extend across its manufacturing sites and across its product range.[25]

The crucial message is Johnstons' situation in Scotland, from which the company appears to draw both the grounding and inspiration of the Scottish landscape and the history of industrial innovation. However, what also seems to set Johnstons apart is its staying power, in remaining "the only vertical mill still standing in Scotland."[26] The film then quickly surveys all the processes, across the two factory sites, that contribute to this vertical integration, again grounding these processes in place:

> From raw fiber in the wool store, to perfected garment on the showroom floor, from dyeing to blending, carding to spinning, winding to weaving, knitting to scouring, milling to teaseling, cutting to folding, it all happens in our own mills on Scottish soil.[27]

An expanded version of this production process is included on a separate page dedicated to "Our Craftsmanship." It is noteworthy that in an array of photographs that primarily feature fibers being worked by both hand and machine, there is one photograph of a rushing river surrounded by autumnal trees to remind the viewer of the importance of the natural setting to this production process: "We use only the softest, natural Scottish water to scour our fabric, ensuring that it is gently restored to its natural, super-soft state." Echoing the message of the heritage film, Johnstons links this image of nature to the company's heritage, explaining that the processes that create "a luxurious finished product . . . have remained unchanged for hundreds of years."[28]

While the firm makes both woven and knitted fabric in a wide array of colors, and these are highlighted throughout the heritage film, it is also striking that as the narrator mentions "the colors stacked from floor to ceiling," there is a sequence of images of spun fiber in shades of green and brown and then two shades of gray, the latter with a cast of blue, showing the same combinations of earth and sky tones that are so in evidence in the earlier footage of the landscape around Elgin and Hawick, and indeed the palette of Lander's painting.[29] While the company states that "It's the unique blend of color, romance, and history in our cloth that sets it apart," the colors featured are reminiscent of the Scottish landscape.[30] "Color, romance, and history" also characterize the corporate story that Johnstons presents in its digital marketing.

Even as the heritage film pivots to discuss the importance of family heritage and human relations in the enduring legacy of the company, stating "That it's not just mortar that keeps these walls standing strong," the accompanying visual of the Eastfield Mills factory in Hawick, where Johnstons knitwear is produced, nonetheless highlights the architectural heritage, with the façade of the solid sandstone building filling the screen.[31] Though Johnstons' investment in knitwear production in Hawick may be a relatively recent event in the company's history, it did in this case "buy heritage" in the sense of buying this historic mill building, with the year 1882 carved into the sandstone, in which to situate its operations. Here, Johnstons is both tapping into Scotland's industrial heritage in textile—and particularly knitted textile—production and also supporting the continuing regional participation in the political economy of Scotland against the backdrop of a common narrative of deindustrialization. Here the company's heritage is rooted in the architecture, but that architecture itself is composed of local sandstone, so that these few seconds of film message the layering of natural, architectural, industrial, family, and labor history as underpinning the success of the company. At another point in the film, Johnstons subtly shows the ways in which, in addition to its own brand, its own heritage of textile production now underpins a variety of British luxury brands. While the narrator states simply "From accessories to fabrics, our products define luxury," the accompanying visuals depict products similar to others shown in the film but with different labels, for the firms Gant (on a tartan scarf or throw), Brora (on a fine-gauge cardigan sweater), Burberry (on a gray woollen fabric that appears destined for a coat), and ending back with its own label.[32] In just a few seconds of film footage, Johnstons is revealed as the maker, or one of the makers, behind these iconic brands. This visual messaging establishes Johnstons within a cohort of luxury purveyors and ties all of them to these sites of production in Scotland.

From this multistrand legacy, the firm remains forward looking, claiming both the traditions of handicraft and a history of technological innovation, wherever each is most appropriate to each specific phase of textile manufacture. As the narrator states that the company is "harnessing the wisdom gained in over 200 years in textile manufacturing," the images again survey different processes of the vertically integrated production, highlighting industrial-scale machinery, hand work, and, interestingly, a close-up of teasels—the dried spiky heads of the thistle-like *Dipsacus* plant that were traditionally used in the finishing of woollen cloth to raise the nap and soften the fabric.[33] Johnstons' continued use of this natural tool (often today replaced by metal teeth similar to that used for wool carding but still preferred for excellent results that cannot mar the fabric's finish) as one of its array of processes shows the blend of tradition and innovation that underpins its luxury product. The voiceover ties both historic sites of production, at Elgin and Hawick, with this balance of technology and craft in both the labor systems of the factories and the commodities that are produced: "These walls, steeped in history, cloak the cutting-edge technology held within."[34]

The film uses metaphors of the landscape and its natural vistas even in its more basic descriptions of the company's aims and commodities: "Our mastery of fabrics means we can explore new horizons in luxury."[35] Here Johnstons links the craftsmanship that comes from a collective attainment of skill with a luxury product. It matters not whether that product is crafted by hand or using "cutting-edge technology"—or indeed both. "Mastery" implies the lengthy process of practice and achievement of both skill and knowledge that is rooted in the company's history; only from this heritage can these "new horizons" be achieved. The company's emphasis on heritage, Johnstons explains, is not about looking backward and replicating textile traditions for their own sake but about harnessing that expertise for new products. As the film states, "For us, heritage is not about nostalgia, it is the heartbeat which drives us into the future"; the digital platform reinforces this message.[36] Interestingly, Johnstons' emphasis on the Scottish landscape serves not only as an expression of its company heritage but also as a way of capturing the forward-looking qualities of the business today. There is another story, not captured on film, but on a different page of the website, which situates the company's present-day interests in sustainable manufacturing in a new image of the Scottish landscape as a source of alternative energy solutions.

Johnstons' heritage film closes, "We've learned a lot since 1797, but we always have been and always will be, made in Scotland."[37] In the case of Johnstons' knitwear, the raw materials of cashmere and merino wool that become many of its products are not native to the company's home nation. But the process of transforming those materials into woven or knitted fabric can nonetheless be rooted in the Scottish landscape. But, interestingly, in this final statement of the film, it is not just the company's products that are made in Scotland, but "we"—that is, Johnstons itself as a corporate entity and as a community of production—that is forged from this place.

"Pringle Has Always Told Stories"

Unlike Johnstons, for whom the production of luxury knitwear was an extension of its well-established weaving mill, Pringle of Scotland always produced knitted goods. The company followed a trajectory from the more utilitarian commodities of hosiery, beginning in 1815, into a broader range of knitted undergarments and then eventually into elegant leisure clothing knitted from fine fibers. Indeed, Pringle claims to have coined the term "knitwear" as its mastery and production of fine-gauge knitted fabric expanded across different sectors of the clothing industry.[38] Pringle now sells some woven products as well, reversing Johnstons' history in the Scottish textile trade, but is most associated with knitwear. The two companies share the home town of their knitwear production in Hawick and, to a degree, the representation of their corporate histories is similar. Pringle is forthright in the way it uses its company website for digital storytelling, and, indeed, the structure of the site with links across its main sections creates repetition of those stories, with an overall message emerging about the importance of heritage as design inspiration for the present and future.

The advantage of such a long heritage is that the back catalogue can continue to provide reference points for contemporary fashions. As one of a series of "Pringle Moments" enumerated on its website, the company demonstrates the recurring cycles of fashion: "Many of Pringle's designs are referenced by today's Design Directors." They note that a "contrast striped cardigan" from 1972 has "origins in the early 20th century Pringle sportswear," while also influencing styles in current collections.[39] Further moments show archive designs ranging from undergarments and bathing suits to sweaters, a trajectory that reveals the history of the company's production. With a 1907 image of a union suit, the company writes "Pringle of Scotland was established firstly as manufacturers of knitted undergarments and hosiery, and was later responsible for turning 'knitwear' into a clothing category of its own."[40] Its experience of fine-gauge knitwear in increasingly fine fibers led to shifting the company's fortunes from undergarments to luxury sportswear.

Although it produces a range of knitwear in terms of both material and design, much of Pringle's brand heritage rests on a particular fiber, cashmere, and a particular design motif, the interlocking diamond patterning known as argyle. Pringle notes that it is "proud to protect and evolve our cashmere manufacturing legacy since 1815."[41]

However, it also states that while it used cashmere for the production of some knitted undergarments early in their history, its stronger reputation for cashmere knitwear as "integral and iconic" to the company developed after World War II, in particular through export to the United States. Cashmere fiber is derived from a breed of goats that are certainly not native to Scotland but rather the Middle East and Central Asia. The company nonetheless claims that its treatment of these fibers, drawing upon local resources and knitting traditions, is at least equally important to the quality of this luxury knitted fabric: "The fibre is harsh to the hand in its raw state. It is only after we have knitted it in the perfect tension and washed in the pure, clear, beautiful Scottish water that it becomes very soft."[42] Thus, even when using materials that are not native to Scotland, Pringle stakes this claim on the Scottish landscape by highlighting its role in processing these fibers.

Pringle's association with the argyle pattern, produced by using the intarsia knitting technique to interlink diamond-shaped motifs of different colors, began at the turn of the twentieth century but harks back to earlier Scottish traditions of woven textiles.[43] The company states that the diamond pattern now familiar on socks and sweaters was inspired by a particular woven tartan pattern of the Clan Campbell of Argyll: "Originally designed in 1897 after experiments with the Tartan pattern, Argyle moved from socks to outerwear during the 1920s with the evolution of Pringle's signature intarsia pattern."[44] An early draft of the design with the unassuming name "Jacquard Design II" is included in several places on the Pringle website, showing the diamonds as a more square, overlapping, motif, perhaps closer to the original tartan design, en route to becoming the more recognizable argyle pattern.[45] A more elongated diamond, with the shape used for both solid knitted panels, and a diagonally oriented grid of knitted lines seemingly overlay one another, but through the methods of intarsia knitting, the individual fiber strands are interlinked but not overlapped. The Pringle argyle sweater derived its warmth from its cashmere fiber, as opposed to the double layer of stranded knitting commonly made from wool in, for example, the traditional Shetland Fair Isle designs discussed previously. While claiming the lineage of textile design in Scotland "since at least the 17th century," Pringle also sets the development and evolution of its recognizable design in its manufacturing base in Hawick.[46]

As with Johnstons, the setting of production becomes a key element grounding Pringle's history, as well as the contemporary marketing of its luxury knitwear. On the Pringle of Scotland website homepage, one of the available options for further detail, besides the various garment collections, is a photograph corresponding to the words "Our Story"—the photo is a hazy, yet seemingly sunlit, landscape in which shades of green are dominant.[47] The foreground of the image shows a gorse-covered hill and rolling grassy field, with the roofs of a few buildings in the middle distance silhouetted against the pale blue and cloud-strewn sky. Although the buildings appear to be more domestic in scale than manufacturing sites, and there is no attribution of place, the image clearly associates landscape with the company's "story." (This same photograph is also seen in thumbnail size as part of a dropdown menu under the header "Our World.") Upon following the link embedded in this photograph to an entire page devoted to "Our Story" (also accessible by following a link titled "Heritage" from a dropdown menu entitled "Discover"), the place depicted is made clear in an opening paragraph that introduces "this knitwear company, whose origins lie in the unassuming town of Hawick, Scotland, United Kingdom."[48] While the Pringle "story" is told on this page almost solely in words, a similar photograph serves as the top banner for the page: there is actually very little color differentiation across the earth tones of greens and browns in this panoramic image, which shows the rooflines of similar sandstone buildings melding into the trees around them.

While Pringle of Scotland's recounting of its heritage is far less grounded in imagery of the Scottish landscape than this dominant theme in Johnstons' storytelling, at each key site on its webpage in which it signals a focus on the company's history, it deploys these similar moody pictures of the Hawick landscape, subtly reminding the reader that the company's global reach and glamorous clientele are grounded in this "unassuming town" in Scotland. The focus on Hawick continues in the "Bulletin" section of the company website—in its new digital format, the "Bulletin" is now outward facing, but in its title is an homage to a print publication that began in 1949 as "an in-house magazine . . . a lovely, friendly, personal communication that had people at its heart." It now functions as an online magazine sharing "narratives" of the company's history and contemporary collections primarily through photo essays: commissions by photographers ranging from recent art school graduates to established fashion photographers. The introduction explains that "Pringle has always told stories, and we are delighted to add new ones by Pringle friends and family from across the industry."[49] The company's digital presence allows this history of storytelling to incorporate these visual forms in profusion from the "articles" in the Bulletin; to the aforementioned series of "Pringle Moments"; to features on production, design, and advertising, both historic and contemporary.

One of the "stories" in the new "Bulletin" is entitled "Welcome to Hawick" and features photographs by William Scarborough, a 2017 graduate of Central St. Martins, and text by fashion editor Ben Reardon. Prior to a series of what might be considered portraits—of both Pringle employees and machines—there are a few more landscape images, the largest of which carries through the theme of the "unassuming" landscape of Hawick, with its focus on a single evergreen tree growing from the wooden-fenced back courts of anonymous stucco buildings with the now familiar wooded hills and watery sky of Hawick in the background. Another image of a part forested and part gorse-covered hill against a cloudy sky is accompanied by key text that explains the situation of Pringle's headquarters in Hawick:

> The Scottish countryside with its panoramic scenery, rolling hills, moors, mountains and terrain of every hue is hard to describe to someone who hasn't experienced this wonderful part of the world. It is in no small part why that 'of Scotland' is stitched into every garment produced by Pringle.[50]

This text suggests that beyond simply the company name, Pringle of Scotland, there is reason to identify these garments with this landscape, making them "of Scotland."

Pringle's roots in Hawick are also lauded in the narrative of "Pringle Moments" in which one of the images is a printed black and white map of Hawick, on which someone appears to have noted the location of the Pringle headquarters handwritten with a blue pen. The accompanying text echoes what becomes throughout the website a common refrain about Pringle's originating town: "Pringle is proudly 'of Scotland'—it was founded in the unassuming town of Hawick, now considered the iconic home of the British knitwear industry." Here Pringle claims not only its own corporate history as redolent of this 'unassuming' place, but also discreetly claims credit for starting the industrial trend that would turn Hawick from "unassuming" to "iconic."[51] The claim that the company and its knitwear are "of Scotland" seems to go a step beyond the "Made *in* Scotland" tag that many Scottish knitwear companies use. While "*in* Scotland" does stress the importance of the place and heritage, of origin and manufacture (if not always materials), "*of* Scotland" suggests that there is a particular quality associated with the nation—whether design, craftsmanship, or even a quality of life—that is rooted in the Scottish landscape and adheres to the garment regardless of where it travels.

While the firm's commercial aim is to distribute its knitwear to a global market, it also seems to be claiming that each piece of clothing holds the essence of the Scottish countryside. Furthermore, the experience of landscape that can be embodied in the knitwear is tied to the company's heritage:

> To fill your lungs with the cleanest air and to drink the natural spring water on tap is to be at one with nature in its purest undiluted form; this is God's Own Country and has served as a constant never-ending inspiration to Pringle for over 200 years and counting.[52]

The reference to Scotland as "God's Own Country" is reprised as the title of another photo essay—this one drawing on images from Pringle's Autumn/Winter 2018 advertising campaign—featured in the Bulletin section of the company's website.[53] This series of advertising photographs, in the words of the company,

> showcase[d] the famous patterns, textures and stitches pioneered by Pringle and made famous over our 200 years of history. . . . Argyle, Fair Isle and classic cashmere are highlights of the collection and campaign, inspired by our rich archives and long-time favourites of our customers.

Fashion photographer Harley Weir took these images, and by pairing the patterns and palettes inspired by the company's archive with "the site of Blackness Castle—a fifteenth-century fortress," on the rugged, rocky shoreline of the Firth of Forth at Linlithgow, Scotland—she places the 2018 collection not only in the framework of the company's heritage but a deeper history associated with the nation's landscape.[54]

This reference to different historical scales also evokes the nature of Pringle's storytelling: the company refers to Weir's photographs as telling "a beautiful and poetic story of Pringle life—celebrating the iconic facets, patterns, knits, and textures of our heritage." This wording is echoed later on the page, as the company explains the aim of the advertising campaign, to "showcase the famous patterns, textures and stitches pioneered by Pringle and made famous over our 200 years of history." While the "knits" and "stitches" of these phrases refer specifically to Pringle knitwear, the broader features of "patterns" and "textures" might apply equally well to the landscapes in which Pringle situates their heritage. When the copy describes the setting for the photographs "as if captured in a faraway land" that "faraway" space seems to refer to time as much as space, as the "scenery, light and natural landscapes," while described as "mysterious," are also quintessentially Scottish and revive in photography the tropes of Scottish landscape painting of a century earlier. In one of the photographs, the two models, Jamily Meurer and Henry Kitcher, are draped in and also hold aloft a plethora of knitwear in different patterns in poses that seem almost reminiscent of modern dance, but they occupy only the right half of the image. The left half of the image depicts an allover

Fair Isle patterned sweater—one of the sleeves is tied to another sweater that is held by Kitcher, while the other sleeve reaches beyond the left-hand frame of the image, so that the sweater is stretched across the foreground, against the blue of the Firth of Forth, with lighter blue sky above and the rocky beach below. The earth-tone colors of the sweater match the tans and browns of the beach exactly, and even the bands of X and O motifs seem to echo the texture of the crags, so that the sweater parallels the landscape in both orientation and composition. The models, in contrast, wear a range of modern interpretations of classic Scottish knitwear motifs and patterns, such as contrasting scales of argyle diamonds and the incorporation of bands of animal print into the horizontal motifs of a Fair Isle cardigan. The verticality of the models—taking up almost the entire vertical axis of the right half of the image—also contrasts with the stretched horizontality of the more traditional earth-tone sweater on the left half of the image. "Reading" the photograph from left to right suggests a narrative in which the more traditional Fair Isle sweater depicted has emerged from the aesthetics of the Scottish coastal landscape, and then the more modern interpretations have emerged from that heritage knitwear. This trajectory visualizes the company's "design philosophy: reinterpreting iconic knitwear for modern lives."

Other images in this campaign more subtly associate the heritage of Pringle's designs and fibers with the Scottish environment. A photograph featuring Meurer and Kitcher in a variety of argyle knitwear depicts them lying on the ground with arms intertwined so that the varied colors, scales, and textures of the argyle diamonds merge together almost as part of the dark landscape of dried seaweed and rocks. Two other photographs of the company's "contemporary approach to 'all-knit dressing'" show Meurer in layers of amorphous knitwear. In one image, she is dressed from cowl neck to mid-calf leggings in a light blue that mediates between the paler blue sky and darker blue water that she is silhouetted against; in the other, the layers of purple, blue, red, and gray suggest the colors of sunrise or sunset—the model is indeed shown against the backdrop of a low sun, which she appears to catch in her hand, reflecting on the water. Harley Weir's campaign, preserved on the Pringle website, demonstrates how the company's contemporary knitwear is inspired by its design archive, as well as the natural history of the Scottish landscape.[55] Weir also contributes to a section of the website called "Postcards from Scotland," part of the "Bulletin" section listed under "Our World." These six landscape photographs, from a mundane telephone pole to an almost glowing yellow field of rapeseed, capture images of Scotland today but do not directly reference Pringle knitwear. Rather their subjects speak to Pringle's interest in projecting this landscape as home to both the company and by extension its knitwear. As that knitwear is exported around the globe, those pieces, too, can act as "postcards," or souvenirs of their place of origin.[56]

While the "Pringle Moments" reinforce and even repeat messages from other parts of the company's website, taken together, they show the ways in which the company's history intersected with broader histories of fashion, industry, community, and even the nation. Many of the images are advertisements or promotional photographs, showing the outward-facing stories that the company has told over the years, like earlier versions of Weir's "postcards." Although not organized chronologically as a timeline, they do range from the early years of the company to the present day so, pulled together in this way, they now document the company's 200-year heritage and contribute to its status as a luxury brand. There is a noticeable trajectory toward featuring Pringle knitwear within the Scottish landscape. Earlier twentieth-century images feature cropped photographs that read more like celebrity portraits, for example, the ballerina Margot Fonteyn and actress Grace Kelly, noted as "one of Pringle's most iconic fans," each wearing a Pringle cashmere cardigan; "action shots" such as brand ambassador Nick Faldo on a distinctly un-Scottish miniature golf course or full-length shots of posed models in Pringle's London showroom on Savile Row.[57] By contrast, more recent promotional photos, particularly those taken around the time of the company's 200th anniversary, situate the knitwear within the Scottish landscape. For example, photographer Ryan McGinley's 2010 promotional campaign is exemplified by an image of "Scottish actress Tilda Swinton . . . against backdrops from Scotland's scenic landscapes," in this case a moss and lichen-covered dry stone wall that fills the frame behind Swinton.[58]

Further "moments" feature this same campaign, for example, a print advertisement in which Swinton is pictured in gray knitted dress and coat against a full-frame backdrop of copper-brown bracken, photographed in the Woodland Garden at Ardingklas House on Loch Fyne. In contrast to these tightly framed images showing particular textures of the landscape is a still from a film McGinley made as part of this campaign, where Swinton, wearing a flowing black dress, is silhouetted against an expansive landscape; while she walks across rocks that appear to make up the retaining wall of a grass-covered parterre in the foreground of the image, behind her we see fields separated by clusters of shrubs and trees, with a dramatic sky of swirling clouds that seem to be echoed in the movement of the dress.[59] As some of the most recent images in this series of Pringle "moments," these recurring images of Swinton show how Pringle is now framing, visually as well as metaphorically, its varied history of design, production, and commerce in the Scottish landscape.

Another cluster of "moments" explicitly carries through this interest in presenting Pringle as "of Scotland" by again linking its product to the Scottish landscape. The tightly cropped image, which appears to be red-leaved trees growing out of a moss-covered outcrop of rocks, has no reference point such as a horizon line to orient the viewer, so the focus is very much on the colors and textures of the landscape. No knitwear is depicted in this image, but the purpose of featuring the landscape is clear from the caption, which states, "To celebrate 200 years, Pringle collaborated with photographer Albert Watson for a campaign shot on the Isle of Skye, contrasting the textures of the Scottish landscape with the textures of the collections."[60] This more recent generation of Pringle storytelling seems more focused on the setting of its story than previous generations. Watson's work for the company's 200th anniversary also features in a dramatic framing of craggy hills in shades of brown—peat, bracken, umber—reaching toward the sky, their peaks obscured by a cloud formation that appears to reach down to the ground in almost a mirror image of the hills. The cloud formation has paler and more translucent echoes of these same rust colors, edged in gray. Again, there is no representation of knitwear, but the caption explains that "Pringle fell in love" with this image when the British Broadcasting Corporation featured Watson's photographs of the Isle of Skye.[61] Even the southernmost tip of the Isle of Skye is approximately 300 miles away from Pringle's headquarters in Hawick, so in this case, the company is not focusing on local landscapes, as with the images of Hawick discussed earlier, but rather on broader evocations of the Scottish nation and longer natural histories in which the company's heritage sits.

As part of the company's "Reissued" campaign, adapting argyle patterning in new scales to new garments such as hoodies, there is an explanation of the "story" of argyle, showing how the company consistently uses its base in the Scottish landscape as the origin of its production and of its products:

> It's not just the people who've worn our argyle knitwear over the years that we're proud of—the story behind it is pretty amazing too. We've always loved telling stories, and this one's too good not to share. Allow us to set the scene. Nestled amongst the rolling hills, lush green planes and soaring peaks of the Scottish countryside, you'll find our home and birthplace, Hawick. A place that inspires us, drives us and defines us. We are Pringle 'of Scotland', after all. It's here where our story began, and where—in the 1920s—we created one of the most iconic patterns of all time.[62]

This "story" shows the ways in which the company's heritage is intertwined with its setting in the Scottish landscape—both industrial and natural—and how both are used to promote Pringle's luxury knitwear.

* * *

Both Johnstons of Elgin and Pringle of Scotland were founded during the Industrial Revolution and played their part in the rapid growth of textile manufacturing in Scotland. In persisting to the present day, these firms are understandably proud of the roles they took in transforming towns such as Elgin and Hawick from "unassuming" to "iconic" and grounding their company histories in these specific places. At the same time, the changes that textile manufacturing brought to these landscapes, whether through sheep husbandry, harnessing the power of local waterways, or creating new concentrations of workers, also spurred romanticized and even imagined cultural representations of landscape as a form of preservation, in paint, print, and other media. Throughout the twentieth, and into the twenty-first, centuries, purveyors of Scottish knitwear have drawn on both of these landscape traditions: the vibrancy of the manufacturing sites they helped establish and the "romantic cultivated wildness" where their products were consumed. The first strand grounds the company's heritage in a specific place, while the second allows that heritage to be extended by allusions to natural history. Although the palette and patterns of artists such as Lander have been largely replaced by the framing and filters of photographers and videographers to produce contemporary digital storytelling, the message that luxury textiles are "of Scotland" remains.

Acknowledgments

This chapter was written as part of the project "Fleece to Fashion: Economies and Cultures of Knitting in Modern Scotland," generously funded by the Arts and Humanities Research Council, UK (Grant Ref: AH/S011528/1). It was also informed by research undertaken for the project "Knitting in the Round: Hand-Knitted Textiles and the Economies of Craft in Scotland," supported by the Royal Society of Edinburgh. I would like to thank Lynn Abrams, Simon Newman, and Amanda Thatch for their assistance and inspiration.

Notes

1. "The Prince of Wales; Fall at Army Race Meeting," *Times*, March 17, 1924, Times Digital Archive; "On Holiday at Biarritz, After His Accident . . .," *Illustrated London News*, April 12, 1924, 631, Gale Primary Sources, Illustrated London News Archive.
2. "The Prince Plays Himself in at St. Andrews," *Daily Mail*, September 28, 1922, Daily Mail Historical Archive, 1896–2004; "Prince's Golf Sweater: A New Fashion," *Daily Mail*, September 19, 1922, Daily Mail Historical Archive, 1896–2004.
3. Claire Price, "He Is the World's Most Dressed Man," *New York Times*, October 27, 1929, 2, ProQuest Historical Newspapers; Philip Long and Joanna Norman, eds., *The Story of Scottish Design* (London: Thames and Hudson for the Victoria and Albert Museum, 2018) 119.
4. John St. Helier Lander, "Royal Friends," *Illustrated London News*, November 23, 1925, n.p., Gale Primary Sources, Illustrated London News Archive.
5. *Leach's Sportswear for Men*, pictured in "Prep Craze: The Fair Isle Sweater," *New England Classic Beauty*, accessed April 30, 2020, https://newenglandclassicbeauty.com/2015/11/05/prep-craze-the-fair-isle-sweater/.
6. See, for example, "The Prince of Wales Mens Fair Isle V Neck Jumper," *The Great English Outdoors*, accessed April 30, 2020, www.greatenglish.co.uk/product/the-prince-of-wales-mens-fair-isle-v-neck-jumper/; Joan Fraser, "Influences on Fair Isle Knitwear Design in the 1920s and 1930s," *Fraser Knitwear*, accessed April 30, 2020, www.fraserknitwear.com/influences-on-fair-isle-knitwear-design-in-the-1920s-and-1930s; "Origins of Fair Isle Knitwear," *WoolOvers*, accessed April 30, 2020, www.woolovers.us/blog/origins-of-fair-isle-knitwear-209; "Fair Isle (technique)," *Wikipedia*, accessed April 30, 2020, https://en.wikipedia.org/wiki/Fair_Isle_(technique).
7. Marina Moskowitz and Marlis Schweitzer, eds., *Testimonial Advertising in the American Marketplace: Emulation, Identity, Community* (New York: Palgrave Macmillan, 2009).
8. See, for example, Advertisement, Macdougall and Co., Ltd, *Times*, October 20, 1922, Times Digital Archive; Advertisement, Best and Co., *New York Times*, September 9, 1929, 4, ProQuest Historical Newspapers.
9. Marcus Halliwell, *Highland Landscapes: Paintings of Scotland in the 19th Century* (London: Garamond Publishers, 1990), 5. See also John Morrison, *Painting the Nation: Identity and Nationalism in Scottish Painting* (Edinburgh: Edinburgh University Press, 2003).
10. The work of "cultivating" or romanticizing the Scottish landscape through art as discussed in Halliwell, *Highland Landscapes*, and Morrison, *Painting the Nation*, are of course part of a broader cultural "invention of tradition" surrounding the Scottish Highlands, as discussed by Hugh Trevor-Roper in "The Invention of Tradition: The Highland Tradition of Scotland," in *The Invention of Tradition*, ed. Eric Hobsbawm and Terence Ranger (Cambridge: Cambridge University Press, 1983).
11. Gary Warnaby and Dominic Medway, "What About the 'Place' in Place Marketing?," *Marketing Theory* 13, no. 3 (September 2013): 345–363.
12. E.P. Harrison, *Scottish Estate Tweeds* (Elgin: Johnstons of Elgin, 1995).
13. "Our History," *Johnstons of Elgin*, accessed April 30, 2020, www.johnstonsofelgin.com/us/about-johnstons-of-elgin/our-story-johnstons-of-elgin/. Johnstons' heritage film is also available on YouTube, which both broadens the audience for this work of digital storytelling and, important for the purposes of this chapter, allows for locating specific timestamps, which is not possible on the company's own website: "Our Story—Celebrating 215 Years," *YouTube*, accessed April 30, 2020, www.youtube.com/watch?v=SEyeWsoISLM. Subsequent references to this film will be drawn from this YouTube location in order to allow direct reference to specific moments of the film; subsequent references will be in the form, "Our Story," x:xx [timestamp].
14. "Our Timeline," *Johnstons of Elgin*, accessed April 30, 2020, www.johnstonsofelgin.com/us/about-johnstons-of-elgin/our-story-history-timeline/.
15. "Our Story," 0:06–0:12.
16. Ibid, 0:12–0:18.
17. Ibid, 0:19–0:28.
18. Ibid, 0:29–0:36.

19. Ibid, 0:43–0:45.
20. Ibid, 0:46–0:51.
21. Ibid, 3:24–3:26.
22. Ibid, 0:58–1:05.
23. Ibid, 1:05–1:07.
24. Ibid, 1:08–1:13.
25. "Our Timeline."
26. "Our Story," 2:02–2:05.
27. Ibid, 2:09–2:32.
28. "Our Craftsmanship," *Johnstons of Elgin*, accessed April 30, 2020, www.johnstonsofelgin.com/us/our-story/our-craftsmanship/.
29. "Our Story," 2:40–2:44.
30. Ibid, 3:00–3:05.
31. Ibid, 3:46–3:51.
32. Ibid, 3:27–3:33.
33. Ibid, 4:38–4:43.
34. Ibid, 4:47–4:52.
35. Ibid, 5:01–5:05.
36. Ibid, 4:30–4:36.
37. Ibid, 5:22–5:32.
38. "Our Story," *Pringle of Scotland*, accessed April 30, 2020, https://pringlescotland.com/pages/our-story.
39. "Pringle Moments," no. 38, *Pringle of Scotland*, accessed April 30, 2020, https://pringlescotland.com/pages/pringle-moments. "Pringle Moments" is a series of 47 images with captions telling anecdotes from the company's history. All of the individual "moments" share the same URL, so subsequent references will state "Pringle Moments" with the relevant number.
40. "Pringle Moments," nos. 42–44.
41. "Why Pringle Cashmere," *Pringle of Scotland*, accessed April 30, 2020, https://pringlescotland.com/pages/why-cashmere.
42. "Starts with a Goat," *Pringle of Scotland*, accessed April 30, 2020, https://pringlescotland.com/pages/introduction.
43. "Iconic Argyle," *Pringle of Scotland*, accessed April 30, 2020, https://pringlescotland.com/pages/iconic-argyle.
44. "Pringle Moments," no. 31.
45. "Iconic Argyle;" "Pringle Moments," no. 31; "Pringle the Argyle," *Pringle of Scotland*, accessed April 30, 2020, https://pringlescotland.com/pages/pringle-the-argyle.
46. "Iconic Argyle."
47. *Pringle of Scotland* (homepage), accessed April 30, 2020, https://pringlescotland.com/.
48. "Our Story," *Pringle of Scotland*.
49. "The Bulletin," *Pringle of Scotland*, accessed April 30, 2020, https://pringlescotland.com/pages/bulletin-introduction.
50. "Welcome to Hawick," *Pringle of Scotland*, accessed April 30, 2020, https://pringlescotland.com/pages/welcome-to-hawick.
51. "Pringle Moments," no. 32.
52. "Welcome to Hawick."
53. "The Bulletin."
54. "The Autumn/Winter '18 Campaign," *Pringle of Scotland*, accessed April 30, 2020, https://pringlescotland.com/pages/autumn-winter-18-campaign.
55. Ibid.
56. "Postcards from Scotland," *Pringle of Scotland*, accessed April 30, 2020, https://pringlescotland.com/pages/postcards-from-scotland.
57. "Pringle Moments," nos. 1, 4, 9, 11, 14.
58. Ibid, no. 15.
59. Ibid, no. 21, 27.
60. Ibid, no. 16.
61. Ibid, no. 28.
62. "Pringle the Argyle."

Bibliography

Best and Co. Advertisement. *New York Times*, September 9, 1929. ProQuest Historical Newspapers.

Fraser, Joan. "Influences on Fair Isle Knitwear Design in the 1920s and 1930s." Accessed April 30, 2020. www.fraserknitwear.com/influences-on-fair-isle-knitwear-design-in-the-1920s-and-1930s.

Halliwell, Marcus. *Highland Landscapes: Paintings of Scotland in the 19th Century*. London: Garamond Publishers, 1990.

Harrison, E.P. *Scottish Estate Tweeds*. Elgin: Johnstons of Elgin, 1995.

Johnstons of Elgin. "Our Story—Celebrating 215 Years." Accessed April 30, 2020. www.youtube.com/watch?v=SEyeWsoISLM.

Johnstons of Elgin. Accessed April 30, 2020. www.johnstonsofelgin.com/.

Lander, John St. Helier. "Royal Friends." *Illustrated London News*, November 23, 1925. Gale Primary Sources, Illustrated London News Archive.

Long, Philip and Joanna Norman, eds. *The Story of Scottish Design*. London: Thames and Hudson for the Victoria and Albert Museum, 2018.

Macdougall and Co., Ltd. Advertisement. *Times*, October 20, 1922. Times Digital Archive.

Morrison, John. *Painting the Nation: Identity and Nationalism in Scottish Painting*. Edinburgh: Edinburgh University Press, 2003.

Moskowitz, Marina and Marlis Schweitzer, eds. *Testimonial Advertising in the American Marketplace: Emulation, Identity, Community*. New York: Palgrave Macmillan, 2009.

New England Classic Beauty. "Prep Craze: The Fair Isle Sweater." Accessed April 30, 2020. https://newenglandclassicbeauty.com/2015/11/05/prep-craze-the-fair-isle-sweater/.

"On Holiday at Biarritz, After His Accident . . ." *Illustrated London News*, April 12, 1924. Gale Primary Sources, Illustrated London News Archive.

Price, Claire. "He Is the World's Most Dressed Man." *New York Times*, October 27, 1929. ProQuest Historical Newspapers.

"Prince's Golf Sweater: A New Fashion." *Daily Mail*, September 19, 1922. Daily Mail Historical Archive, 1896–2004.

Pringle of Scotland. Accessed April 30, 2020. https://pringlescotland.com/.

The Great English Outdoors. "The Prince of Wales Mens Fair Isle V Neck Jumper." Accessed April 30, 2020. www.greatenglish.co.uk/product/the-prince-of-wales-mens-fair-isle-v-neck-jumper/.

"The Prince of Wales; Fall at Army Race Meeting." *Times*, March 17, 1924. Times Digital Archive.

"The Prince Plays Himself in at St. Andrews." *Daily Mail*, September 28, 1922. Daily Mail Historical Archive, 1896–2004.

Trevor-Roper, Hugh. "The Invention of Tradition: The Highland Tradition of Scotland." In *The Invention of Tradition*, edited by Eric Hobsbawm and Terence Ranger. Cambridge: Cambridge University Press, 1983.

Warnaby, Gary and Dominic Medway. "What About the 'Place' in Place Marketing?" *Marketing Theory* 13, no. 3 (September 2013): 345–363.

WoolOvers. "Origins of Fair Isle Knitwear." Accessed April 30, 2020. www.woolovers.us/blog/origins-of-fair-isle-knitwear-209.

6 Stories of Turkish Cultural Heritage Motifs Subject to Digital Marketing in Fashion

Zaliha İnci Karabacak and Ayşe Aslı Sezgin

Introduction

The first examples contained in the international legislation for the protection of works of art that belong to cultural heritage appeared in Europe in the fifteenth century. After the term "cultural heritage" was addressed in international law in 1907, international treaties and drafts have been developed in this regard with the initiatives of UNESCO and several states since the 1950s. It is noteworthy that concerns about the protection of cultural heritage especially increased during World War II.[1] The worry during the war was then replaced by discussions about the content of the concept of cultural heritage.

Within the context of discussions on cultural heritage, a variety of approaches stand out pertaining to tangible and intangible cultural heritage. Toward the end of the twentieth century, the concept of "heritage" began to be regarded within a wider framework. As a result of that perspective, it became possible to say that the limits were expanded in terms of the semantic interpretation of the concept of "cultural heritage." Frequently used in descriptions of monuments and cultural property, this concept has required the implementation of a number of practices for the protection of intangible cultural heritage, along with new approaches and more awareness.[2] The changes observed in approaches toward cultural heritage in the period from the beginning to the end of the twentieth century have appeared in a different aspect in the twenty-first century. The impact of developing technologies is not only observed on daily life but also in the re-examination, revelation, and protection of the values of the past.

The digital platform of new media offers some technology-oriented solutions to the protection of cultural heritage. Individual researchers, as well as professional associations, universities, and governments, use computer-based modeling and visualization techniques to protect cultural heritage that is under threat or is completely lost.[3] The use of such new technologies provides important opportunities for the preservation of tangible or intangible cultural heritage and its introduction to new generations. In time, people have been attracted to digital environments, especially by symbols and motifs that are among the elements related to cultural heritage. The revitalization of motifs and symbols as part of cultural heritage in digital environments has made it possible to involve them in daily life as well as protecting them. Especially with the effect of digital marketing, such motifs, which are also used in fashion-related content, quickly spread by crossing geographical boundaries.

There are many different consequences of the digitality of such cultural heritage collections. As an example, different segments of society are now aware of these motifs. The motifs belonging to the past and cultural backgrounds have now been discovered and made accessible.[4] This chapter examines some motifs dating back to the past, describing a certain cultural accumulation, symbolizing different elements through their stories, and drawing attention to Turkish cultural heritage. The story of such motifs used in different product segments in digital marketing, especially in fashion-related content, in recent years is explained in this chapter based on historical sources. However, before that, the concept of "cultural heritage" is first examined specifically for Turkish society under the heading of Turkish cultural heritage.

Evaluating digital marketing in regard to fashion-related content, this chapter presents the appearances of the motifs, along with their stories told, through descriptive analysis considering the transition from traditional culture to popular culture. Such motifs are reinterpreted through fashion-related content by comparing past stories with the way they are told in the twenty-first century.

Turkish Cultural Heritage

In the period after UNESCO's Convention for the Protection of the World Cultural and Natural Heritage of 1972, such concepts as "folklore, popular and traditional culture, non-material culture, oral and intangible heritage" stood out in UNESCO documents. Although the term "intangible" has different meanings in Turkish, in the UNESCO Convention of 2003, it referred to the protection of all aspects of knowledge, tradition, and background that enable the production of cultural heritage, as well as sustaining and transferring them to other generations in every sense.[5] Today, the process of transferring these cultural elements to new generations is experienced in a different dimension. Sharing and interpreting different cultural elements in digital media has led to coming across such elements in daily life. The symbols of Turkish cultural heritage draw attention to relevant content shared on digital platforms.

The traces and expressions of the communicative elements and behaviors of human beings, to which meaning is attributed through individual or existing social values and which are protected accordingly and came from the past, are regarded as cultural heritage. Cultural heritage is not only part of a common heritage but also the reflection of the creative strength and lifestyle of that society. Each detail of the heritage is part of the data collected by the members of that society through living.[6] Turkish cultural heritage possesses the characteristics of a deep-rooted history and rich cultural background. This heritage also has reflections of cultural identity.[7] Cultural heritage is composed of reflections of human life. It represents a certain historical background as well as witnessing its evolution in time. It can be embodied as an expression of culture or proof of a lifestyle. Cultural heritage does not only describe immovable elements. All kinds of works of art such as paintings, drawings, moving objects, and important historical figures are also included in this definition of cultural heritage. These elements, which are notable representatives of life at a certain time, are crucial due to their roles as historical records.[8]

Cultural heritage is also evidence of cultural diversity. Designs based on the traditions of different cultures existing in a society are transmitted through the elements of such cultural heritage. Among the cultural heritage elements that define the social identity of that culture are many different forms, from literature to games and from architecture to handicrafts. The elements of cultural heritage are continually recreated in line with the social environment, history, and cultural interaction in which they exist and thus gain continuity by representing a social identity.[9]

With a style unique to the Turkish social structure, cultural elements created different branches of art as they migrated from Central Asia to Anatolia. These arts, such as illumination, calligraphy, miniature drawing, tiling, and weaving, took shape according to the Turkish traditions, beliefs, culture, and lifestyle, spreading over lands far and wide.[10] Representing significant values in Turkish culture, these elements also serve as a means to carry values from the past to the future. Each element has been influenced by the daily life and traditions of the region in which it was born.[11]

An analysis of the appreciation of culture and art in Turkish cultural heritage clearly reveals that many different Turkish states had their own rules. In other words, motifs in Turkish cultural heritage are of particular importance and considered a reflection of the Turkish sense of art. Among the first examples, especially within the decorative arts, are the stylized interpretation of animals, Rumi motifs, and supernatural creatures, as well as motifs shaped by the different beliefs developed in Central Asia. Following the influence of Manichaeism, Shamanism, and Buddhism in these motifs, traces of Islamic culture are distinctly apparent.[12]

Motifs have been used in many domains of Turkish culture. Traces of these motifs have been found in many fields, from clothing to making everyday tools, from architecture to mining, and from carpet weaving to making weapons. Such motifs often symbolize certain stories about life. The stories behind the motifs narrate significant phenomena such as birth, death, long life, fertility, truthfulness, and beauty. These motifs have survived along with art and culture during migrations and wars from Central Asia to Anatolia and Europe.[13]

UNESCO adopted the Convention for the Safeguarding of the Intangible Cultural Heritage at its 32nd General Conference held between September 29 and October 17, 2003. This treaty was adopted in the Grand National Assembly of Turkey, published in the Official Gazette and entered into force as of January 21, 2006. As of December 2019, Turkey has 18 cultural elements[14] inscribed in the Intangible Cultural Heritage list.[15] By taking this list into consideration, this chapter uses a descriptive analysis method to compare the historical background of the motifs in the aforementioned list with the present-day stories associated with such motifs, which are now regarded as cultural elements used for digital marketing products. Each motif has its own unique story. These stories have traces of the history of the societies in which they were born. Accordingly, the traditional Turkish motifs selected to be examined in this chapter have their own stories.

Turkish Motifs and Their Stories in Cultural Heritage

This chapter investigates the historical background of the motifs to be analyzed comparatively in Turkish culture in particular. The stories of how such motifs are used in fashion-related content for digital marketing will be explained in the comparative descriptive analysis in the "Methodology and Results" section of the chapter. The motifs in the chapter were selected from among the elements inscribed in Turkish Intangible Cultural Heritage List as of December 2019. For the purposes of this chapter, the items in this list that are widely used in fashion-related content include Mevlevi Sama ceremonies, marbling art, and ceramic tile art. In the following section, the historical background of each element will be presented.

Motifs of Mevlevi Whirling Ceremonies

Living in the thirteenth century, Mevlâna was a great thinker of Sufi and Mevlevi philosophy, and his thoughts on tolerance and love have always drawn attention. Located in the Central Anatolia region and hosting members of many religions every year, the city of Konya still continues to present the traces of that period. "Turning dervishes," or particularly "whirling dervishes," who symbolize this philosophy and are mainly called "whirling" because of their figures in their dances called "Sama," are still represented in different forms and platforms. Mevlâna's mysticism based on love and tolerance without discriminating between culture and religion is conveyed by the dances of the whirling dervishes. The whirling movement in these dances expresses deep meanings with respect to Sufism. The basic condition of existence is explained by the metaphor of whirling. Created by God, every being is in this action of whirling. Thus, whirling dervishes consciously participate in this vortex-like turn. The Sama ceremony represents a spiritual journey. Anyone who searches will ultimately return to God and truth, love, and self.[16]

Mevlâna Celaleddin Rumi was an Islamic scholar, jurist, and poet. According to historical data, he migrated to Konya, the center of the Seljuk Sultanate of its time, with his family. One of the most influential sheikhs of all time, Mevlâna explained the values of Mevlevi philosophy in his great work, called Mesnevi. After his death, the Mevlevi Sufi sect was established in Konya. After the Seljuk Empire, many statesmen were inspired by that philosophy during the reign of the Ottoman Empire. In that period, the discipline of the Mevlevi Order symbolized an urban and distinguished character. Art and culture centers in urban settings especially developed under the influence of this philosophy. Great works of art emerged in the field of music and literature. The Mevlevi philosophy, which represented "high-elite culture," also gained an important position in the Ottoman Empire[17]. Rituals of the Mevlevi philosophy, especially symbols of this system of thinking in culture and art life, attracted the attention of the whole world in time. Often depicted as the subjects of painters, Mevlevi dervishes also inspired European artists using a variety of means, especially photographs.[18] The analysis of the historical process of Mevlâna, Sufi dervishes, and Sama ceremonies shows that some themes have come to the fore more than others in the narrative of symbols and motifs used by different media contents today to represent the Mevlevi philosophy in general. Such themes as love, tolerance, return to God, high culture, and exclusivity are used to convey the stories of Mevlevi motifs.

The Motifs of Turkish Marbling Art

There are no exact dates in the literature for the history of marbling art. Its first examples were found in China and then in Japan (artistic products using techniques similar to Turkish marbling art) from the eighteenth century onward. However, the examples in Japan draw attention to uniform motifs, unlike those of Turkish marbling art. Today, examples of Turkish marbling art found in the library of the Topkapı Palace Museum in Istanbul date back to the fifteenth and sixteenth centuries. Examples specific to marbling art spread all over the world in time. In each example, traces of the cultural characteristics and traditions of the society to which it belongs are found.[19] Turkish marbling art was included in the Turkish Intangible Cultural Heritage List in December 2019. Many sources show that the origin of the word *marbling* is derived from the Persian word "eb," meaning "cloud." In the definition of marbling art, a poetic approach is generally adopted in Turkish culture. It is stated that artists are often in a spiritually different mood when making marbling art. In shaping the marbling, it is believed that one is oriented to sensing the creation of the universe and leading people to think about and understand this creation.[20] Marbling motifs are thus evaluated as a reflection of the artist's spiritual characteristics. By using special materials, marbling motifs are formed as a result of sprinkling color pigments on a tray of oily water and carefully transferring them to paper. In this transfer, sometimes the artist does not interfere with the paint in the water and can sometimes shape the paints by using materials such as rods.[21]

The process of change in motifs in marbling art can be explained through historical development. Some of these motifs are the tidal motif; heart and star motifs; sand grain motifs; nightingale's nest motifs; motifs with pastel-colored flooring with inscriptions; and floral motifs such as tulips, carnations, roses and poppies. Marbling art is an art branch that can have different applications due to its range of use. Today, examples of this art can be seen on different surfaces such as fabric, leather, and glass.[22] Each of the motifs for marbling art has a distinct story. If we are to specify the themes in the stories of these motifs in general, themes such as nature, love, and the universe come to the fore. Indeed, each motif also reflects the characteristics of the marbling artist.

Tile Art Motifs

Tile art has an important place in traditional Turkish arts. Information about its origin is often associated with ceramic art in many sources, but it is known to have a history dating back to Central Asia. Tile art showed its main development in Anatolia and experienced its most successful period in the Ottoman Empire period during its expansion in popularity that started during the time of the Anatolian Seljuk dynasty. The motifs in Turkish tile art mostly reveal the traces of the period when it was born and the Turkish tribes living in Asia at that time. In that period, animal figures were an especially important element in Turkish tile art. In the Ottoman period, on the other hand, the use of animal figures is observed to have decreased.[23]

Two cities that stood out for tile art in the Ottoman Empire were İznik and Kütahya. The works of Ottoman tile art produced in the sixteenth and seventeenth centuries are generally considered to have been produced in İznik. It is noteworthy that those produced in Kütahya often involved productions suitable for daily life. The effect of the Ottoman palace is mostly observed in the tiles of Iznik, while there is an approach reflecting the art taste of the people in the tiles made in Kütahya, especially in the eighteenth century. In Kütahya tiles, there are motifs that are maintained with a linear painting tradition with inspirations from everyday life. In Iznik tiles, motifs including human figures, architectural structures, ships, and Ottoman palace depictions are striking.[24]

Tile art developed mainly within ceramic art. It is known that some drawings were made on ceramic surfaces at different times in history. The motifs on ceramics also reflect the culture-specific setting in which they flourished. Many techniques that increase the attractiveness of floor materials used in ceramic art have also increased interest in these products. In the context of ceramic art, tile art can also be considered a special domain where intensive brush decor and painting meet. Especially with the influence of the religion of Islam, the pictorial descriptions on tiles made in the period of the Ottoman Empire are also very rich in composition, theme, and color.[25]

With its significance in Turkish cultural heritage, tile art and its motifs have been evaluated from different perspectives when compared to other kinds of art. Especially in the Ottoman period, the class distinction in tile art motifs attracts attention. On the one hand, the daily life of the street is narrated in the motifs, and on the other, the motifs depict palace life, which should be considered an important example to reflect social attributes.

Digital Marketing, Fashion, and Turkish Cultural Heritage Motifs

Today, developing communication technologies have moved their marketing activities to digital platforms. Knox[26] stated that many retailers have both online shopping sites and physical stores, but generally online stores sell more than the "brick-and-mortar" ones. Thanks to the Internet, traditional cultural memory can be transferred to members of different communities. For example, patterns of traditional clothing, makeup, or motifs available on the Internet can inspire a contemporary fashion designer.[27]

In an era in which the human body is surrounded by prestigious logos and fashion brands, models (Gisele Bündchen, Kate Moss, etc.) have become indispensable elements of fashion.[28] The growing power of social media has enabled fashion blogs and fashion bloggers to become important players in fashion brand marketing strategy.[29] Outfits can become part of fashion, which desires to use elements of various cultures and different periods, and can reflect the aesthetic understanding of the time only when they are incorporated in social, political, and economic culture.[30] According to Baudrillard,[31] fashion repeats the dead and stocked forms it keeps in an out-of-time warehouse by transforming them into signs. In this context, fashion is never up to date. Mangani[32] emphasized that rituals became stable cultural references by nature. Rook[33] listed four components related to ritual experience: "ritual artifacts," "a ritual script," "ritual performance role(s)," and "a ritual audience." According to Gruendl,[34] consumption has become a new religion for consumers in a world where rituals are the new weapons of marketing. Kowinski[35] described shopping malls as "cathedrals of consumption," where people go to fulfill their religion of consumption.

Ritzer treats new means of consumption and cathedrals of consumption in the same sense. He argued that cathedrals of consumption, like religious cathedrals, are magical, but they are also rationalized. He further asserted that such cathedrals of consumption need to reproduce their enchantment systematically to meet growing consumer demand. Ritzer's views on new means of consumption are mainly based on the opinions of two scholars, Karl Marx (for the concept of means of consumption) and Max Weber (for the concepts of rationalism-enchantment and disenchantment). Weber argued that the process of capitalism and modern rationalization in the West was destroying the once magical (mysterious, mystical) world. Ritzer listed various structures such as fast food restaurants, chain stores, catalogs, shopping malls, online shopping malls, discount stores, supermarkets, cruise ships, casinos, sports centers, museums, charities, and so on as new means of consumption[36].

Emphasizing the importance of consumer goods in the culturally created world, McCracken[37] stated that the fashion system is also part of this construction.

Baudrillard[38] emphasized that beauty was created by means of various items and accessories (tattoos, waxing, foundation, mascaras, necklaces, jewelry, etc.) since the existing cultural order was reorganized by making use of the human body, which was replaced by certain signs. According to Barthes,[39] system of signs for clothing, fashion,

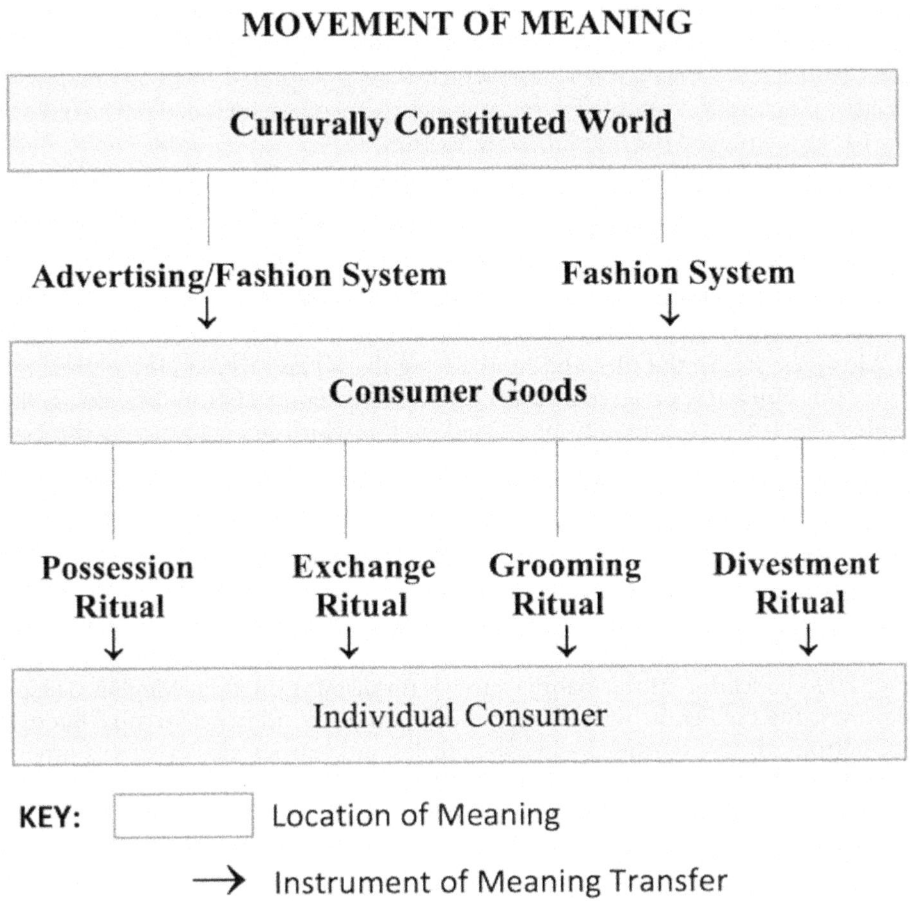

Figure 6.1 Movement of meaning.

nutrition, and so on are managed by the myth, which is a signification system that contains many connotations.

One of the prominent practices in fashion marketing is the use of stories. A Turkish brand, Silk & Cashmere, which has spread to different parts of the world over time, effectively uses the component of storytelling in marketing. Silk & Cashmere reaches its consumers through stories that are renewed every month. This is seen in the stories that, in addition to the raw materials, patterns, and accessories used by the brand, give particular attention to special days in the current month (Mother's Day, Father's Day, etc.) as well.[40] Barthes lists the main references of fashion as nature, geography, history, and art. In this respect, artistic references are apparently predominant.[41] In the national and international world of fashion, we encounter important events where there are a variety of designs that carry the motifs included in the Turkish Intangible Cultural Heritage List and that meet with fashion lovers.

In 2016, during New York Fashion Week, Turkish fashion designers presented their Spring–Summer 2017 collections with the theme of "Fashion Istanbul." Fashion designer Nilüfer Satorius showed her collection with Turkish marbling patterns designed by a marbling artist, Bingül Tatlı, who lives in New York.[42] In the 2015 Spring/Summer season of Vakko Home, the pillow collection called "Bosphorus" included patterns of Ottoman heritage, which were interpreted from a contemporary perspective. The motifs suitable for the summer theme were included in the collection in a way that referenced the formula of Iznik tiles.[43]

An international Japanese brand, Issey Miyake, set its theme for Spring–Summer 2010 collection as "Turkey." The motifs of a tile pattern, tulip pattern, and Seljuk sun particularly inspired the brand's design team. For the purpose of research, prior to the creation of the collection, the heads of Issey Miyake brand's design team, Shugo Moritani and Yoshiyuki Miyamae, visited Istanbul. The team visited the Topkapı Palace, the Archeology Museum, the Tiled Kiosk, the Museum of Islamic Art, and the Rüstem Pasha Mosques, where the tiles and motifs were dense, and took many photos there. Later on, Dai Fujiwara, creative director and chief designer of Issey Miyake, came to Istanbul. Fujiwara was especially impressed by the whirling ceremony at the Galata Mevlevi House.[44]

Fashion designer Nedret Taciroğlu's collection "Ebruli," inspired by Turkish marbling art, was shown at New York Haute Couture Fashion Week in 2009. Taciroğlu stated that the fabrics used in his Autumn–Winter 2010 collection of thirty-five pieces were prepared in three months with important teachers of marbling art.[45] A world-renowned Turkish fashion designer, Atıl Kutoğlu, organized a fashion show in Times Square Studios during New York Fashion Week in 2003. Kutoğlu presented his Spring/Summer 2003 collection at the fashion show with inspiration from Mevlâna. Inspired by Mevlevis, the collection was dominated by white. In addition to silk, linen, and natural cotton fabrics, synthetic—Lycra—fabrics and leather also attracted attention in the collection.[46]

Methodology and Results

A descriptive analysis method was used to analyze cultural motifs that are included in digital marketing strategies. The steps that the researchers should follow for descriptive analysis are listed as follows:[47]

- Creating a framework for descriptive analysis
- Processing the data in compliance with the framework
- Identifying the findings
- Interpreting the findings

In this part of the descriptive analysis, the data were processed according to the thematic framework, and the findings were identified and interpreted under the three main headings given subsequently.

Tile Art Motifs in Jewelry

Rooted in China, the "Çintemani" figure is also called the "Timuçin Stamp." "Çintemani" was brought from Chinese art to Turkish art by Turkish artists from Tabriz in the sixteenth century. It was used as a symbol of power in the Ottoman Empire. In Ottoman culture, it was also used in different areas such as royal clothes,

Problem Statements	Themes
Turkish motifs from the cultural heritage continue to exist in different fields of use in fashion-related content.	-Adaptation of Turkish motifs of the cultural heritage to fashion-related content for the marketing of necklaces, pendants, shawls and scarves.
Turkish motifs of cultural heritage have become the object of the consumption ritual in fashion-related content in digital marketing.	-Using Mevlevi figures on pieces of jewelry -Using Tile Art for accessories -Using motifs of Turkish Marbling Art in clothing accessories -Using Mevlevi motifs in home accessories -Using motifs of Turkish Marbling Art in home accessories
Turkish motifs of the cultural heritage, which have become the object of consumption ritual in fashion-related content in digital marketing, present a hybrid appearance by gaining meanings that combine traditional and contemporary stories.	- Turkish motifs of the cultural heritage have become indicators to decorate the human body and the house as a personal living space. - Turkish motifs of the cultural heritage stand out as the objects of the consumption ritual, making a difference and offering privileges.

Figure 6.2 Problem statements and themes.

tile embroidery, carpet-rug patterns, and stonework. The "Çintemani" figure is a single crescent-shaped figure consisting of a combination of circles of different sizes lined up together or the use of three round motifs, two at the bottom and one at the top. The "cloud motif" (Chinese cloud), which consists of "Çintemani" and two wavy lines lying side to side, is generally used together.[48] In the second half of the sixteenth century in tile art, the style with "four flowers" was born and named after four important flowers (tulips, hyacinths, roses, and carnations)[49]. The "Tulip" motif, which is one of the prominent figures in Turkish cultural heritage, can be transformed into the

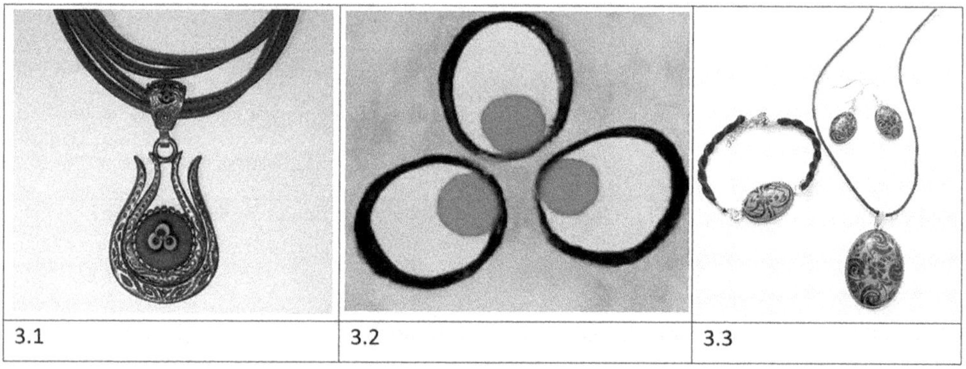

Figure 6.3 Tile art motifs in jewelry.

word "Allah" by replacing the Turkish letters used in the spelling with the Arabic letters.[50] A tulip blooming on a single branch is seen as a representation of the uniqueness of God. In this context, this plant has been regarded as valuable for Islamic belief and gave its name to a period, the "Tulip Era," of the Ottoman Empire.

The "Çintemani" motif placed in the bronze tulip figure brings together the representation of belief in God and power in Turkish culture in a single design in this jewelry (Figure 6.3.1). Likewise, the "Haliç work" design is used in the turquoise-colored tile jewelry set (Figure 6.3.3). Spiral branches consisting of small leaves and flowers are used in the pattern of tiles called "Haliç work."[51] Seen from the examples discussed in this chapter, tile motifs appear in fashion-related content in today's digital marketing as an indicator that decorates the human body with jewelry.

Motifs of Mevlevi Whirling Ceremonies in Jewelry and Home Accessories

As a tradition, the sheikh of the Galata Mevlevi House always guided the ceremonies held by the palace for almost all Ottoman sultans when they first came to the throne. In the ceremony, the ritual that the sultan was girt with the sword of Islam by the sheikh of the Galata Mevlevi House shows the belief to spiritually reinforce the sultan's office[52]. The word "Sama" means *to hear* and the *sky* in Arabic. The meaning of *sky* in the origin of the word brings to mind the dances of shamans, with movements signifying their way up to the sky. The traditional white garment worn during the whirling dance in the Mevlevi Order is called *tennure*. This garment, which is wide below the waist, flares during the turn and helps the *Semazen* find his balance.[53]

Mevlevi clothes and Sama have a number of symbolic meanings. The headgear, called *sikke*, represents the tombstone, the cloak represents the tomb, and the *tennure* represents the shroud. The right side of the Sama square represents the visible realm, while the left represents the invisible spiritual realm. The Sama ritual is performed by whirling from right to left in harmony with the music. Each of these turns is called spinning. In the Sama ritual, the Mevlevi dervish, who takes off his cloak and begins whirling in his *tennure*, with his right hand up and left hand facing down.[54] Whirling during the Sama ceremony represents watching God from everywhere and all directions. During the Sama, the arms are wide open, with the right hand up and the left hand down, symbolizing taking power from God with the right hand and turning away from everyone but Him and allowing the grace of God to flow with the left hand.[55]

One of the most important elements in the garment of the sheikh (*Sama Dede*), who is the person who manages the Sama ceremony from the beginning to the end is the traditional headgear called *Destar*. It is fabric headgear wrapped around the head made of felt called *sikke*. This fabric is usually green. The person who has the authority to wear the *Destar* represents someone who can carry a message between the spiritual world and the material world.[56] Combining the stylized *Destar* and the aesthetics of Islamic calligraphy, the pendant (Figure 6.4.1) is like a spiritual shield designed as an accessory for today's consumers. It also symbolizes the bond that someone establishes between the spiritual world and the material world. *Destar* (Figure 6.4.2), one of the symbols of the Mevlevi tradition, is presented to contemporary consumers as an accessory with a new form in this necklace design.

In another figure, a frame (Figure 6.4.3) with the motif made of metal representing a Mevlevi performing the Sama ritual has been designed as a home accessory to become a trend in fashion design. In the design, it is striking that the headgear (*sikke*) and the garment (*tennure*), which form the outfit of the Mevlevi motif, are decorated with tiny stones. The ornamentation of these garments, which are very plain in their original form (Figure 6.4.4), with ornamental stones shows that this traditional cultural motif has been made more attractive and alluring to appeal to today's consumers. This way, it has become an symbol that decorates homes, which are personal living spaces. In this context, the story of the Mevlevi motif gains a hybrid appearance to form a bridge between the past and the present and is taken to a new dimension adapted to our age by adding elements that reflect the materialist trend of our contemporary sense of consumption on the spiritual values in the traditional story of the Mevlevi motif. The Mevlevi motif (Figure 6.4.5) engraved on a table spoon handle and placed on the top of a decorative hand bell (Figure 6.4.6) are other examples of this traditional cultural motif in fashion-related content as home accessories with functionality.

Turkish Marbling Art Motifs in Home Accessories and Clothing Accessories

Today, Turkish marbling art is applied on different surfaces and objects, such as fabric, felt, wood, metal, ceramics, glass, and leather by going beyond the compositions and

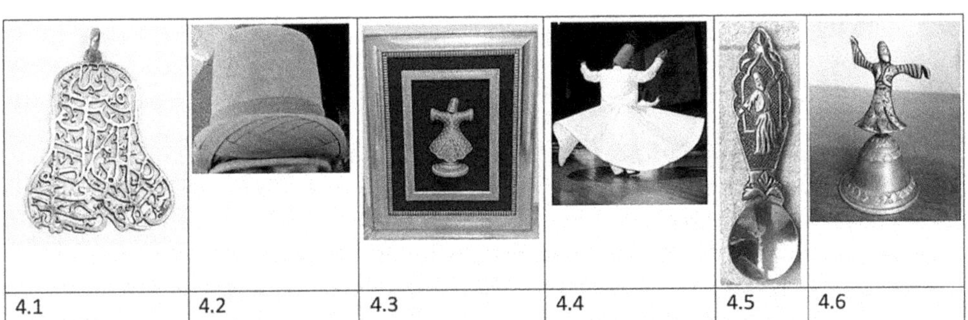

Figure 6.4 Motifs of Mevlevi whirling ceremonies in jewelry and home accessories.

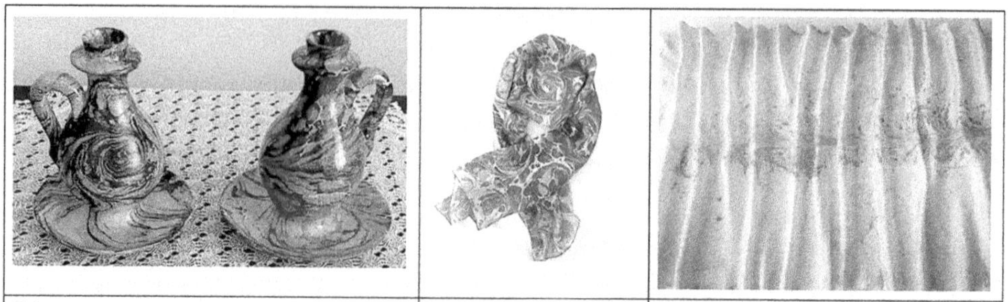

5.1 | 5.2 | 5.3

Figure 6.5 Marbling art motifs in home and clothing accessories.

classical applications created on paper. These contemporary practices contribute to increasing the recognition and sustainability of Turkish marbling art.[57] Three important features that are seen in all Islamic arts are also valid for marbling art: infinity, harmony and anonymity. Turkish marbling art has motifs that are similar but never repeated like a copy. In other words, it is a "fractal" art. Although marbling artworks do not present symmetrical images, they have a hidden aesthetic and color harmony. Anonymity, which is a common practice in Islamic Sufi art, means that the marbling artist does not sign his/her work. A marbling artist is understood from the style, not from the signature.[58]

In the subsequent figures, marbling is applied on ceramic for a candle holder design (Figure 6.5.1),[59] on silk fabric for a scarf design (Figure 6.5.2),[60] and also on silk fabric for a shawl design (Figure 6.5.3)[61]. The patterns and color harmony in such handmade home and clothing accessories are unique, as they are specific to the piece of work and cannot be repeated in the same way. In this context, these accessories made with marbling are tailor made. In addition to the references such as divine love, nature, and universe in its traditional culture, Turkish marbling art stands out as a representation of a tradition of art as well as a privileged product for its current consumer, as contained in its contemporary narrative. Given the increasing importance of features such as feeling different and being privileged for contemporary consumers, Turkish marbling art offers attractive product alternatives for today's fashion lovers. In this respect, it appears as a symbol to decorate personal living spaces through home accessories and the human body through clothing accessories.

Conclusion

People have many expectations from fashion, such as mirroring certain ideas, showing belongingness, contributing to the reflection of individuality, and disguising oneself. Fashion has continued to exist as a ritual feast of aesthetic creativity throughout the ages.[62] In this feast, the products in the current range of fashion items (clothes, shoes, jewelry, accessories, home decorations, etc.), which are the objects of consumption that has become a ritual in our age, are embellished with cultural symbols that mark the history of societies. These cultural symbols, which derive their power from myths, rituals, legends, and stories, seem to have inspired fashion throughout history.

In particular, the possibilities offered by digital communication technologies make this collaboration between fashion and cultural symbols visible through the Internet and a large number of fashion products in the virtual world today. Examining the representation of Turkish cultural heritage motifs in fashion products subject to digital marketing, this chapter sought to make a contemporary study of the footsteps of traditional Turkish culture in our age through descriptive analysis. It is seen that the stories of cultural motifs, which are an important part of the cultural identity of countries, are also significant for the fashion products that are the subject of fashion-related content in digital marketing in an era where brands are present in the market with their stories. In this regard, the motifs of Mevlevi whirling ceremonies, marbling art, and tile art inscribed in the Turkish Intangible Cultural Heritage List appear to be influential in Turkish fashion and even in world fashion through cultural interactions and digital marketing. The examples analyzed with the descriptive analysis method in this chapter show that the figures (Mevlevi), art (marbling art—creation, divine love), and objects (*destar, tennure*) used for religious rituals in the past are now used for home decoration and clothing as the objects and figures of today's consumption ritual. As a result, it is noteworthy that the motifs in the Turkish Intangible Cultural Heritage List used for the purposes of digital marketing, as discussed in this chapter, carry references to religion, culture, and traditional art to the contemporary world with the use of hybrid stories that combine the past and the present in the fashion system. Consequently, the Turkish cultural heritage motifs examined within the scope of this chapter have not only become symbols to decorate the human body, as well as houses as personal living spaces, but also objects of the consumption ritual that expose the distinguished features of the motifs, such as making a difference and offering privileges for those who are interested.

Notes

1. Janet Blake. "On Defining the Cultural Heritage." *International and Comparative Law Quarterly*, 49.1, (2000), p. 61. doi:10.1017/S002058930006396X.
2. Marilena Vecco. "A Definition of Cultural Heritage: From the Tangible to the Intangible." *Journal of Cultural Heritage*, 11.3, (2010), p. 321.
3. Yehuda Kalay, Thomas Kvan and Janice Affleck. *New Heritage: New Media and Cultural Heritage*, London: Routledge, 2007, p. 2.
4. Trevor Owens. "Digital Cultural Heritage and the Crowd." *Curator: The Museum Journal*, 56.1, (2013), p. 127.
5. M.Öcal Oğuz. "Intangible Cultural Heritage as a Term." *Milli Folklor*, 25.100, (2013), p. 11.
6. Özlem Köroğlu. Hasret Ulusoy Yildirim and Cevdet Avcikurt. "Examining the Perceptions of the Concept of Cultural Heritage through Metaphor Analysis." *Tourism Academic Journal*, 5.1, (2018), p. 99.
7. Yüksel Sayan. "On The Protection of Turkish Cultural Heritage and the Consciousness of Historical Environment." *Journal of Turkish World Studies*, 9.1, (2009), p. 153.
8. Lyndel V. Prott and Patrick J. O'Keefe. "Cultural Heritage' or 'Cultural Property?" *International Journal of Cultural Property*, 1.2, (1992), p. 308.
9. Federico Lenzerini. "Intangible Cultural Heritage: The Living Culture of Peoples." *European Journal of International Law*, 22.1, (2011), p. 105.
10. Münevver Üçer. "Tradition Is the Future" in the Context of Cultural Heritage Awareness." *Journal of Art-e*, 12, (2019), p. 87.
11. Sinan Çakmak. "With Cultural Heritage Approach 'Symbolic Analysis of the Turkey: Explore Potential Logo'." *İdil*, 65, (2020), p. 156.

12. Kaya Üçer. "Readings of "Motif" in the Context of Traditional Turkish Arts in Our Cultural Heritage." *Journal of Art-e*, 12, (2019), p. 77.
13. Ibid, pp. 77–78.
14. Arts of the Meddah (public storytellers), Mevlevi Sama Ceremony, Aşıklık (Minstrelsy) Tradition, Karagöz, Nevruz, Traditional Sohbet Meetings, Semah-Alevi-Bektaşi ritual, Kırkpınar Oil Wrestling Festival, Ceremonial Keşkek Tradition, Mesir Macunu Festival, Turkish Coffee Culture and Tradition, Ebru- Turkish Art of Marbling, Flatbread Making and Sharing Culture, Traditional Craftsmanship of Tile Art (Çini) Making, Spring Celebration Hıdırellez, Dede Korkut- Heritage of Korkut Ata, Traditional Turkish Archery, Whistled Language (UNESCO National Commission of Turkey. "The Intangible Cultural Heritage Representative List of Humanity," accessed April 8, 2020, www.unesco.org.tr/?page=15:64:1:turkce).
15. UNESCO National Commission of Turkey. "The Intangible Cultural Heritage Representative List of Humanity."
16. Ikrame Selkani. "The Whirling Dervishes: An Old Heritage Recognized at Last." *Annals of Social Sciences & Management Studies*, 1.4, (2018), p. 71.
17. Burcu Sağlam. "A Discussion on the Myth of Mevlânâ in Modern Turkey." *Journal of Intercultural Studies*, 38.4, (2017), p. 417.
18. Jamal J. Elias "Mevlevi Sufis and the Representation of Emotion in the Arts of the Ottoman World." *Affect, Emotion, and Subjectivity in Early Modern Muslim Empires: New Studies in Ottoman, Safavid, and Mughal Art and Culture*. Brill, 2017, p. 185.
19. Osman Mutluel. "Art Marbling in Terms of Aesthetic Object Analysis in the Philosophy of Art." *Electronic Turkish Studies*, 9.11, (2014), p. 421.
20. Aynur Maktal and Süreyya Uyan. "The New Approaches to the Designing of Marbling (Ebru) with Calligraphy and Illumination Disciplines in Turkish Arts." *Turkish Journal of Fashion Design and Management*, 1.1, (2019), p. 50.
21. Ibid.
22. Hacer Nurgül Begiç. "New Interpretations in Traditional Turkish Marbling Art Which Appears in UNESCO World Cultural Heritage List." *Selçuk Üniversitesi Türkiyat Araştırmaları Dergisi*, 1.37, (2015), pp. 594–596.
23. Nuran Ocakoğlu. "Animal Patterns Used on the Turkish Tile and Ceramics and Their Reflection on Clothing Design." *Kalemişi-Turkish Arts Journal*, 6.13, (2018), p. 409.
24. Vedat Kaçar. "Evaluation and Advices of Kütahya Tile Art from Past to Present." *İdil*, 7.48, (2018), p. 986.
25. Semih Kaplan. "Contemporary Painting with Traditional Tile." *İdil*, 6.31, (2017), pp. 1113–1114.
26. Alistair Knox. "E-Ticaretin Yükselişi." In *Fashion: The Whole Story*, Edited by Marnie Fogg, Translated by Emre Gözgü, İstanbul: Hayalperest, 2014, p. 545.
27. Nebi Özdemir. "ICH, Media and New Technology." In *The Future of Intangible Cultural Heritage Turkey's Experience, Turkish National Commission for UNESCO*, 2013, pp. 53–66.
28. Harold Koda and Kohle Yohannan. *The Model as Muse: Embodying Fashion*, Metropolitan Museum of Art, 2009, p. 206.
29. Akvilė Mickevičiūtė and Daiva Siudikienė. "The Role of Fashion Bloggers in Fashion Marketing Communication." *Informacijos Mokslai*, 85, (2019), pp. 8–50.
30. Marnie Fogg. Ed. *Fashion: The Whole Story*, Translated by Emre Gözgü, İstanbul: Hayalperest, 2014.
31. Jean Baudrillard. *L'échange symbolique et la mort*. Éditions Gallimard, 1976.
32. Lorenzo Magnani. "Ritual Artifacts as Symbolic Habits." *Open Information Science*, 2(1), (2018), p. 154. https://doi.org/10.1515/opis-2018-0011.
33. Dennis W. Rook. "The Ritual Dimension of Consumer Behavior." *Journal of Consumer Research*, 12(3), (1985), p. 253.
34. Harald Gruendl. *The Death of Fashion: The Passage Rite of Fashion in the Show Window*, Wien: Springer, 2007, p. 198.
35. William Severini Kowinski. *The Mailing of America: An Inside Look at the Great Consumer Paradise*. New York: William Morrow, 1985.
36. George Ritzer. *Enchanting a Disenchanted World: Revolutionizing the Means of Consumption*, Pine Forge Press, 1999.

37. Grant McCracken. "Culture and Consumption: A Theoretical Account of the Structure and Movement of Cultural Meaning of Consumer Goods." *Journal of Consumer Research*, 13, (1986), p. 72. https://doi.org/10.1086/209048.
38. Jean Baudrillard. *Pour Une Critique de l'économie Politique du Signe*. Éditions Gallimard, 1972.
39. Roland Barthes. *Mythologies*, Translated by Annette Lavers. Farrar, Straus and Giroux, 1972.
40. Evrim Kabukcu. "The Use of Story in Fashion Marketing: Case of Silk & Cashmere." *International Journal of Academic Value Studies (Javstudies)*, 3.16, (2017), pp. 1–6.
41. Kubilay Aktulum. "Textual Genericity and Fashion: Intertextuality-Intervestimentality-Archivestimentality." *Modern Turkish Literature Researches*, 11.21, (2019), pp. 1–37.
42. http://turkishlifenews.com/turk-cariklari-new-york-moda-haftasinda-podyuma-cikti/, Accessed May 19, 2020.
43. Vakko Magazine. https://img.vakko.com/files/corporate/documents/magazine-1.pdf, 2015, Accessed April 20, 2020.
44. www.sabah.com.tr/cumartesi/yasamadair/2009/07/18/moda_dunyasi_turk_mozaiklerini_konusuyor, Accessed May 10, 2020.
45. www.cumhuriyet.com.tr/haber/new-yorkta-ebruli-buyuk-begeni-topladi-42318, Accessed May 19, 2020.
46. www.hurriyet.com.tr/gundem/new-yorkta-mevlevi-modasi-124838, Accessed May 10, 2020.
47. Ali Yıldırım and Hasan Şimşek. *Sosyal Bilimlerde Nitel Araştırma Yöntemleri*, Ankara: Seçkin Yayıncılık, 2013, p. 256.
48. Hacer Sönmez. *Yeni Başlayanlar İçin Tezhip—1*, İstanbul: İnkılâb Yayınları, 2018, p. 31.
49. Sevgi Çekinmez. Tulip in Turkish Tile and Ceramic Arts, Master Thesis, Anadolu University Fine Arts Institute, 2010, p. 19.
50. Lale Görünür and Semra Ögel. "The Differences between Ottoman "Kaftan" and "Entari" with Their Usage." *İTÜDERGİSİ/b*, *3*(1), (2006), p. 65.
51. Seda Dilay. "Artistic and Cultural Aspect of Fish Motifs." *Türk Bilimsel Derlemeler Dergisi*, 4(1), (2011), p. 56.
52. Nilgün Açık Önkaş. "The Relationships of Mawlawism with Government." *Akademik Bakış Dergisi*, 23, (2011), p. 4.
53. Erkan Ergin. "Türklerde Dini Danslar." *Ankara Üniversitesi, Dil, Tarih ve Coğrafya Fakültesi, Tiyatro Araştırmaları Dergisi*, (1995), Sayı: 12.
54. Özdemir, "ICH, Media and New Technology," p. 56.
55. www.kulturportali.gov.tr/portal/mevlevisematoreni, Accessed May 10, 2020.
56. Melih Ümit Menteş. *Sema Ayini: Semboller ve Anlamlar*, Cinius Yayınları, 2011, p. 39–40.
57. Begiç, "New Interpretations in Traditional Turkish Marbling Art Which Appears in UNESCO World Cultural Heritage List," pp. 587–605.
58. Haluk Berkmen. *Bir Sufi Sanatı: Ebru*, 2014, http://halukberkmen.net/pdf/109.pdf.
59. Designer, Ziynet Yıldırım.
60. Designer, Lütfiye Konuk.
61. Designer, Ziynet Yıldırım.
62. Fogg, *Fashion*, p. 12.

Bibliography

Aktulum, Kubilay. "Textual Genericity and Fashion: Intertextuality-Intervestimentality-Archivestimentality." *Modern Turkish Literature Researches* 11(21), 1–37, 2019.

Baudrillard, Jean. *Pour Une Critique de l'économie Politique du Signe*. Paris: Éditions Gallimard, 1972.

Baudrillard, Jean. *L'échange symbolique et la mort*. Paris: Éditions Gallimard, 1976.

Barthes, Roland. *Mythologies*, translated by Annette Lavers. New York: Farrar, Straus and Giroux, 1972.

Begiç, Hacer Nurgül. "New Interpretations in Traditional Turkish Marbling Art Which Appears in UNESCO World Cultural Heritage List." *Selçuk Üniversitesi Türkiyat Araştırmaları Dergisi* 1(37), 587–605, 2015.

Berkmen, Haluk. *Bir Sufi Sanatı: Ebru*, http://halukberkmen.net/pdf/109.pdf, 2014.

Blake, Janet. "On Defining the Cultural Heritage." *International and Comparative Law Quarterly* 49(1), 61–85. doi:10.1017/S002058930006396X, 2000.

Çakmak, Sinan. "With Cultural Heritage Approach 'Symbolic Analysis of the Turkey: Explore Potential Logo'." *İdil* 65, s. 155–164. doi: 10.7816/idil-09-65-14, 2020.

Çekinmez, Sevgi. Tulip in Turkish Tile and Ceramic Arts, Master Thesis, Anadolu University Fine Arts Institute, 2010.

Dilay, Seda. "Artistic and Cultural Aspect of Fish Motifs." *Türk Bilimsel Derlemeler Dergisi* 4(1), 53–56, 2011.

Elias, Jamal J. "Mevlevi Sufis and the Representation of Emotion in the Arts of the Ottoman World." *Affect, Emotion, and Subjectivity in Early Modern Muslim Empires: New Studies in Ottoman, Safavid, and Mughal Art and Culture*. Brill, 185–209, 2017.

Ergin, Erkan. "Türklerde Dini Danslar." *Ankara Üniversitesi, Dil, Tarih ve Coğrafya Fakültesi, Tiyatro Araştırmaları Dergisi*, 1995. Sayı: 12.

Fogg, Marnie. Ed. *Fashion: The Whole Story*, translated by Emre Gözgü. İstanbul: Hayalperest, 2014.

Görünür, Lale and Ögel, Semra. "The Differences between Ottoman "Kaftan" and "Entari" with Their Usage." *İTÜDERGİSİ/b* 3(1), 59–68, 2006.

Gruendl, Harald. *The Death of Fashion: The Passage Rite of Fashion in the Show Window*. Wien: Springer, 2007.

Kabukcu, Evrim. "The Use of Story in Fashion Marketing: Case of Silk & Cashmere." *International Journal of Academic Value Studies (Javstudies)* 3(16), 1–6, 2017.

Kaçar, Vedat. "Evaluation and Advices of Kütahya Tile Art from Past to Present." *İdil* 7(48), 985–989, 2018.

Kalay Yehuda, Thomas Kvan and Janice Affleck. *New Heritage: New Media and Cultural Heritage*. London: Routledge, 2007.

Kaplan, Semih. "Contemporary Painting with Traditional Tile." *İdil* 6(31), 1111–1123, 2017.

Koda, Harold and Kohle Yohannan. *The Model As Muse: Embodying Fashion*. New York: Metropolitan Museum of Art, 2009.

Knox, Alistair. "Rise of E-Commerce." In *Fashion: The Whole Story*, edited by Marnie Fogg, translated by Emre Gözgü. İstanbul: Hayalperest, 544–545, 2014.

Köroğlu, Özlem, Hasret Ulusoy Yildirim and Cevdet Avcikurt. "Examining the Perceptions of the Concept of Cultural Heritage through Metaphor Analysis." *Tourism Academic Journal* 5(1), 98–113, 2018.

Kowinski, William Severini. *The Mailing of America: An Inside Look at the Great Consumer Paradise*. New York: William Morrow, 1985.

Lenzerini, Federico. "Intangible Cultural Heritage: The Living Culture of Peoples." *European Journal of International Law* 22(1), 101–120, 2011.

Magnani, Lorenzo. "Ritual Artifacts as Symbolic Habits." *Open Information Science* 2(1), 147–155, https://doi.org/10.1515/opis-2018-0011, 2018.

Maktal, Aynur and Süreyya Uyan. "The New Approaches to the Designing of Marbling (Ebru) With Calligraphy and Illumination Disciplines in Turkish Arts." *Turkish Journal of Fashion Design and Management* 1(1), 33–46, 2019.

McCracken, Grant. "Culture and Consumption: A Theoretical Account of the Structure and Movement of Cultural Meaning of Consumer Goods." *Journal of Consumer Research* 13, 71–84, https://doi.org/10.1086/209048, 1986.

Menteş, Melih Ümit. *Sema Ayini: Semboller ve Anlamlar*. Istanbul: Cinius Yayınları, 2011.

Mickevičiūtė, Akvilė and Daiva Siudikienė. "The Role of Fashion Bloggers in Fashion Marketing Communication." *Informacijos Mokslai* 85, 8–50, 2019.

Mutluel, Osman. "Art Marbling in Terms of Aesthetic Object Analysis in the Philosophy of Art." *Electronic Turkish Studies* 9(11), 419–428, 2014.

Ocakoğlu, Nuran. "Animal Patterns Used on the Turkish Tile and Ceramics and Their Reflection on Clothing Design." *Kalemişi-Turkish Arts Journal* 6(13), 409–425, 2018.

Oğuz, M.Öcal. "Intangible Cultural Heritage as a Term." *Milli Folklor* 25(100), 5–13, 2013.

Owens, Trevor. "Digital Cultural Heritage and the Crowd." *Curator: The Museum Journal* 56(1), 121–130, 2013.

Önkaş, Nilgün Açık. "The Relationships of Mawlawism with Government." *Akademik Bakış Dergisi* 23, 1–8, 2011.

Özdemir, Nebi. "ICH, Media and New Technology." In *The Future of Intangible Cultural Heritage Turkey's Experience*. Ankara: *Turkish National Commission for UNESCO*, 53–66, 2013.

Özdemir, Yavuz. *Galta Mawlawi Lodge Museum*. İstanbul: Touring and Automobile Club of Turkey, 2018.

Prott, Lyndel V. and Patrick J. O'Keefe. "Cultural Heritage' or 'Cultural Property?" *International Journal of Cultural Property* 1(2), 307–320, 1992.

Ritzer, George. *Enchanting a Disenchanted World: Revolutionizing the Means of Consumption*. London: Pine Forge Press, 1999.

Rook, Dennis W. "The Ritual Dimension of Consumer Behavior." *Journal of Consumer Research* 12(3), 251–264, 1985.

Sağlam, Burcu. "A Discussion on the Myth of Mevlânâ in Modern Turkey." *Journal of Intercultural Studies* 38(4), 412–428, 2017.

Sayan, Yüksel. "On the Protection of Turkish Cultural Heritage and the Consciousness of Historical Environment." *Journal of Turkish World Studies* 9(1), 153–156, 2009.

Selkani, Ikrame. "The Whirling Dervishes: An Old Heritage Recognized at Last." *Annals of Social Sciences & Management Studies* 1(4), 70–72, 2018.

Sönmez, Hacer. *Yeni Başlayanlar İçin Tezhip—1*. İstanbul: İnkılâb Yayınları, 2018.

Üçer, Kaya. "Readings of "Motif" in the Context of Traditional Turkish Arts in Our Cultural Heritage." *Journal of Art-e* 12, 77–85, 2019.

Üçer, Münevver. "Tradition Is the Future" in the Context of Cultural Heritage Awareness." *Journal of Art-e* 12, 86–97, 2019.

Unesco National Commission of Turkey. "The Intangible Cultural Heritage Representative List of Humanity," Accessed April 8, 2020, www.unesco.org.tr/?page=15:64:1:turkce.

Vakko Magazine. https://img.vakko.com/files/corporate/documents/magazine-1.pdf, 2015. Accessed April 20, 2020.

Vecco, Marilena. "A Definition of Cultural Heritage: From the Tangible to the Intangible." Journal *of Cultural Heritage* 11(3), 321–324, doi:10.1016/j.culher.2010.01.006, 2010.

Yıldırım, Ali and Şimşek, Hasan. *Sosyal Bilimlerde Nitel Araştırma Yöntemleri*. Ankara: Seçkin Yayıncılık, 2013. http://turkishlifenews.com/turk-cariklari-new-york-moda-haftasinda-podyuma-cikti/, Accessed May 19, 2020.

www.cumhuriyet.com.tr/haber/new-yorkta-ebruli-buyuk-begeni-topladi-42318, Accessed May 19, 2020.

www.sabah.com.tr/cumartesi/yasamadair/2009/07/18/moda_dunyasi_turk_mozaiklerini_konusuyor, Accessed May 10, 2020.

www.hurriyet.com.tr/gundem/new-yorkta-mevlevi-modasi-124838, Accessed May 10, 2020.

www.kulturportali.gov.tr/portal/mevlevisematoreni, Accessed May 10, 2020. https://pixabay.com/tr/, Accessed May 10, 2020.

7 Louboutin's Red

Using Color to Connect France's Past and Present

Alexandra Jordan Thelin

Luxury goods exude a certain aura, and being associated with them provides a distinct level of taste and exclusivity. The consumer identifies an elevated level of quality, expensive cost, well-designed features, limited production, and the acquisition of an item that is coveted by others. A luxury item encompasses all of these categories, making it stand out from other purchases.

In addition to these quality standards, luxury brands also have a rich history that sets them apart from other goods on the market. It is this rooted past that raises luxury brands above others. Fast fashion and its associated brands are inexpensive and allow consumers to be on trend for a short period of time. However, purchasing these types of goods may bring one joy in the moment, but when the item is out of fashion or degrading due to poor quality, the consumer is left with an unusable product. So although it may be appealing on the surface to buy cheap, popular items, there are also multiple aspects that should warn the consumer to avoid them. These can include abusive labor practices, harmful environmental materials, and wasteful consumption. By supporting brands with ethical standards of production and a commitment to quality and embracing the powerful symbolism with which they are associated, consumers are supporting a legacy of historical connections. Despite having high price points, buyers feel the acquisition of these articles invites them into a unique group, to which entrance can only be earned by the purchase of high-end goods. Additionally, since these brands do have rich histories, the consumer is empowered once again with exclusivity and becomes associated with the class, distinction, and elite connotations that the brand symbolizes. This strong foundation from the past was built upon, with enduring traditions, a commitment to quality and standout designs that rise above the rest. One of these is Christian Louboutin, a French designer, who is well known for his trademark use of red on the soles and back of the heels of his footwear. The use of this color as a signature aspect of his shoes connects Christian Louboutin and his brand with France's extensive history with this color.

Christian Louboutin

It is not just Louboutin's innovative designs and attractive shoe silhouettes that make him stand out as a shoe designer. In addition to these aspects, Louboutin recalls past royalty, public usage, and other appearances of the color in French history. This connection forms a deep tie between the country's cultural usage of the color and the shoes of one designer. Thus, in addition to an aesthetically beautiful product, his work is categorized as luxury with this cultural connection.

Louboutin's lacquered cherry-red soles make others stop and take notice. This trademark evolved organically with his design process. Louboutin began his career working for shoe designer Charles Jourdan in the early 1980s,[1] then began his own line of shoe designs in the early 1990s, added the red soles in 1993, and ultimately expanded his brand to include women's handbags in 2003 and men's shoes in 2011.[2] Louboutin knew there was an element of sex appeal and uniqueness with his brightly colored soles and has played with this association within his designs. Additionally, he spent some of his early years as a designer making shoes for the showgirls for Paris' Folies Bergère, so shoes that attract have been a priority and necessity in his work since the beginning. In a 2003 interview with *People*, Louboutin explained that his shoes make the wearer stand out and draw attention. As the wearer walks, others are drawn to the color and take notice in an almost voyeuristic manner, and he told the magazine that this combination of shoes and color have "the 'follow me, young man' effect—the modern equivalent of dropping your handkerchief."[3] He believed that these shoes are not for the faint of heart, and wearing them would definitely get one noticed.

Tales of his early work now hold great interest, as it is compelling to hear about his humble beginnings, knowing his talent ultimately led him to sell over one million pairs of shoes a year.[4] In his early days, Louboutin created custom shoes for customers. One story claims a client visited him desiring shoes for her large feet, since they were sized 13.5. Louboutin made her a pair, yet the client ended up not purchasing them, so Louboutin gave them to a friend, who passed the shoes along to her husband.[5] Giving up a pair of custom-made Louboutins would be unheard of now, knowing the designer's success and commitment to his work.

Other anecdotes explain the beginnings of the red sole. Originally, Louboutin did not plan for his shoes to utilize this pop of color but instead introduced the design element after not being pleased with his previous work. What was a quick fix after many design applications ultimately became the designer's go-to signature style. While creating his first shoe collection, Louboutin felt his shoes needed something extra and noticed an assistant painting her nails red. Louboutin originally sketched designs on paper yet was unhappy with the three-dimensional resulting shoes and felt they lacked a certain pizzazz. So, according to the story, he spontaneously grabbed his assistant's nail polish and covered the sole with the red lacquer.[6] This instantly changed the overall look of the shoe, and Louboutin's signature standout hallmark was born.

After deciding upon this unique sole, Louboutin was fortunate enough to launch his career with celebrity clients such as Princess Caroline and Princess Diana. Additionally, Princess Diana inspired Louboutin to create one of his early designs. The princess visited India in 1992, corresponding to the time when the designer was working on his first individual creations, and she was photographed looking down at her feet sadly. Louboutin used this imagery of the melancholy royal and designed an early pair flat suede pumps for his brand spelling out the word 'LOVE' with the letters 'L' and one half of 'O' on one foot and the other half of 'O' as well as 'VE' on the other. Louboutin explained his design in the 2015 Channel 4 documentary, stating that the photos of Princess Diana from her trip inspired him to create a shoe that would make her grin as she glanced down. He noted, "She was looking at her feet, and I thought she looked sad. I thought it would be nice for her to have something to make her smile when she looked at her feet."[7] This inspirational shoe concept was later rereleased in 2018, when Louboutin offered an updated take on his original design, and in addition to a patent leather version of the iconic flat pumps displaying the word 'LOVE,' his collection featured handbags, wallets, totes, and sneakers with graffiti-style iterations in a myriad of colors set against a solid background.

As will be shown, the usage of the color red is a deep-rooted connection to France's history. In addition, Louboutin embodies other associations that are also distinctly French. As he spent his early years creating shoes for showgirls, this association with panache and sex appeal continued in his later designs. Louboutin's ties to burlesque enabled him to find inspiration in music-hall dancers, noting that the cabaret is "an iconic Parisian monument, a monument to dance, a modern and dreamlike conceptualization, celebrating women in honor of women."[8] He ultimately collaborated with Crazy Horse Paris, a cabaret establishment, in the spring of 2012,[9] to design a unique theatrical experience through the show *Feu*, which played for three months on the Crazy Horse stage. Of the collaboration, Andrée Deissenberg, general manager of Crazy Horse Paris, noted: "

> Christian Louboutin and Crazy Horse Paris are symbols of Parisian nightlife, whose universes cross borders. Symbols of the realms of creation, of astonishment and modernity, they share the same sources of inspiration—Women, of course, but also the world that surrounds them—and have the exceptional know-how to produce hitherto and breath-taking creations. It was therefore a matter of course that we called upon Christian Louboutin.[10]

Louboutin's distinctly French aesthetic, celebration of the female form, and commitment to innovative designs make him a unique choice for French entertainment combinations.

Louboutin's Logo and Digital Marketing

It is not just the actual shoe designs that tie Louboutin with France's rich history. Elements of his logo and digital marketing also highlight the luxury branding and fit in with his overall appeal.

In addition to the signature red soles that distinguish Louboutin's shoes, the logo is used on the instep of formal shoes, as well as other products such as sneakers, purses, and nail polish. This icon is a well-designed combination of a Roman serif font displaying the designer's first name and a handwritten iteration of the last name. The uppercase C from 'Christian' and L of 'Louboutin' are one swooping character that emulates the silhouette of one of the designer's high-heeled shoes. Originally, the logo was just black on a white background[11] but underwent multiple iterations, including the addition of the signature red color, and ultimately placing the white logo in a red circle with a white border. An eye-catching logo such as this instills a noticeable commitment to quality, associating all products from the brand as superior. Independent brand consultant Rebecca Battman stated: "A logo is a simple and functional signpost to help people find and identify your business."[12] Also, a study on corporate logos noted:

> Various authors state that the design can influence consumers' degree of recognition, clear meaning, subject familiarity, and effect . . . [the] corporate logo perception as an aesthetic response . . . creates an essential component of stimulus that can draw the attention and emotional reaction of consumers.[13]

The branding of the company goes beyond the red soles and recognizable logo. The tan-colored boxes that hold each pair of shoes are made of high-quality cardboard, with the logo printed in white. The shoes inside are wrapped in tissue paper, with a red cotton drawstring dust bag stamped with a black version of the logo. Additionally, Louboutin's logo design fits in well with his product designs:

> The Christian Louboutin logo is just as bold and provocative as the designer's design. Attractive colors and a graceful script combine to display the brand's devotion to comfort, class, and audacity. Just like the designer's famous shoes, the red shade of the logo is instantly recognizable as a status symbol. It serves as an excellent brand representative, so the Louboutin logo will most likely remain the same in the future.[14]

However, this type of logo design and packaging is one of the first steps needed for a brand to differentiate itself. Beyond logo design, the products must speak for themselves and embody the elements of style and quality promised by the logo. Business journalist Peter Shadbolt explained, "But for a logo to be successful, the company behind it must be a respected and trusted brand. A logo won't allow a company to build a respected brand on its own."[15] Louboutin has certainly proved over time that his designs fit the luxury market with his innovative styles and well-made goods.

The company's digital marketing and social media postings are also innovative and unique approaches to showcasing their products. As the brand established itself as a luxurious style setter with a slightly quirky side, some of the marketing materials play into this fun aspect of the brand's personality.

First, the photographs of Louboutin's products stand out from other editorial images of footwear. Louboutin's pictures of his products have an interesting tie to the art history of France. During the Post-Impressionism period of the late nineteenth and early twentieth centuries, artists of the era reacted against the naturalistic style that was dominant during the Impressionist period of the late 1800s. Instead of using a painterly style of brushstrokes to loosely apply color depicting natural forms, the Post-Impressionists utilized color, line, symbolism, optics, and form to create a distinctly different style of artwork. Their work also displayed a clear emotional response of the subjects, showing unique character and tone.

Some of the French artists that excelled in this style were Henri de Toulouse-Lautrec, Paul Cézanne, and Paul Gauguin. Each of these artists experimented with ways of expressing form, and some of these aspects are loosely applied to the marketing photography materials used to promote Louboutin's products. For example, Toulouse-Lautrec experimented with different line qualities, coupled with irregular areas of color. Some of the forms are filled with solid color, while others are patchy and rough, with the background still visible. However, there is a unifying usage of bright pops of color that is intertwined between his works. Although Louboutin's marketing images are created by the use of photography and not paint on a canvas, there is a similar theme of blurring some areas, like applying sparse color, and keeping some in focus, just as Toulouse-Lautrec made some areas more prominent through his use of solid color. Additionally, browsing through Louboutin's Instagram feed, the viewer is hit with pops of color. Besides the obvious red that is used, other hues such as hot pink, yellow, and bright blue stand out among dark backgrounds or blurred environments. Also, the point of view of the images varies from frame to frame. The same angle is not used repeatedly; there is diverse usage of the subjects, providing a varied, non-stagnant view of the designer's products. One image may show a full figure with the shoes visible by just a pop of red from the sole, while the image next to it may be a close-up of one accessory, photographed from above. Another accompanying image could be photographed from below, again providing a different point of view of the designs. Overall, the viewing experience shows that all of his works look artistic and attractive from every angle, and it pulls the viewer in to want these products in their life to recreate this lively, artistic, ever-changing beauty.

The Louboutin website showcases the designer's goods, and, as to be expected, there are pops of red throughout. As most websites selling goods feature the brand's logo, some promotional photography, and separate product pages organized by categories leading to pages for each item with an online shopping cart, the Louboutin site differs in that the site itself can be seen as an artistic expression. Although the site's design and layout do change over time, there are some basic elements that remain constant. Multiple artistic photographs display the products, all shot from varying angles and utilizing different models. Some of these photos feature footwear, while others highlight accessories. Interactive elements such as a custom shoe finder, categorization of the shoes by heel height, and grouping by product color have also been available. As the Louboutin brand is active in philanthropy, travel, and new products, the site features a section labeled 'LouboutinWorld,' displaying a news feed of important updates for the company and Christian Louboutin himself. This gives a distinct personal view to the brand, which is an aspect that is not always visible on retailer sites.

The architectural design of the designer's stores also pays homage to a rich cultural history, creating a one-of-a-kind visual and shopping experience. For example, the brand's flagship store in Miami, Florida was created by the design firm 212box, and used a mixture of natural and vintage materials to create an eye-catching space. The exterior of the building is covered in peeled tree panels, harvested by hand in such a way that the trees remain intact.[16] Additionally, recycled materials also form the interior of the space:

> I-shaped columns originally used for a 1970s Parisian office building are re-used in the shop, to form a dark colonnade around the mezzanine level. This detail is among a number that draw on Louboutin's Parisian heritage—the brand was established in the city in 1992.[17]

In keeping with a luxurious experience that remains synonymous with the upscale level of Louboutin's products, it was necessary that this be a decadent vision with exclusive touches. 212box founder Eric Clough noted,

> We tried to keep the use of the materials simple by puzzling various patterns of bark or relentlessly coating entire surfaces to create a new painting of nature as a backdrop to the elegant sculptures of each of Christian's shoes,[18]

referring to the infusion of pale bark, agate, keystone, coral, and travertine materials that encompass the space. An opulent brand such as Louboutin deserves this attention to detail, forming an elevated shopping experience that fits in beautifully with the high-end brand.

Red in France's History

The color red has appeared in many iterations throughout France's past, becoming a bright flash of color, trailblazing and weaving throughout important moments in France's narrative. Although Louboutin is now synonymous with the color red on shoe soles, he was not the first French figure to incorporate this design element into footwear. Other figures in France's history utilized the same color as well. Louis XIV, King of France from 1643 through 1715, limited the usage of the color red on the heels of footwear to his court, ensuring that the wearer would stand out and that only his favored court members would have the privilege of wearing such a bright color on their feet:

> Red was a very important color for the monarchy: Sumptuary laws, as well as the high cost of red dyes, meant that you had to be rich and powerful to wear it, and red heels were worn by the monarch since the early 1600s. But they were especially dear to Louis XIV: He passed an edict claiming that only nobility could wear them. According to historian Philip Mansel, the painted heels showed that nobles did not dirty their shoes. They also demonstrated that their wearers were "always ready to crush the enemies of the state at their feet."[19]

Moreover, the red-heeled shoes worn by Louis XIV were an aristocratic privilege, as "red heels in seventeenth- and eighteenth-century European courts were also considered a symbol of nobility and status."[20] By utilizing the color red on the soles of his shoes, Louboutin again creates an illusion of status and wealth, as his creations usually hover around the $1,000 mark. Louboutin's red soles and their earlier counterparts are examples of how a single characteristic in footwear, such as color, symbolized many attributes for a culture.

In this manner, color acts as a way to unify a group. Anthropologist Ted Polhemus noted: "Just as adornment allows us to assert ourselves as individuals, it also allows us to identify ourselves as part of a social collective . . . dress and adornment may communicate 'I'm one of us.' "[21] Whether a French royal or a consumer with the ability to purchase designer footwear, wearing the red sole signifies a particular level of status and its accompanied meanings.

There was also an element of vanity associated with the usage of the color red in the case of Louis XIV. French history expert Joan DeJean reported that Louis XIV was a man who was proud of his gorgeously shaped legs, and he chose fashionable garments that would specifically show them off, including knee-length tight pants and stockings.[22] Similarly, the high heels seen in many of Louboutin's designs elongate and show off the leg. As such, the usage of the color red places the wearer in a specific group in both France's past and the present era.

Louboutin was aware of the historic connection in relation to his designs:

> Louboutin has drawn inspiration from the intersections of fashion, art, and history throughout his career. He considers himself to be outside the influence of current fashion and chooses instead to make innovative use of elements from historical styles. Perhaps the most conspicuous example of this is his use of red soles. Although this idea did not come directly from a historical source, he is not the first to notice the power of red on the bottom of shoes. In the late seventeenth century,

> Louis XIV famously wore red-heeled shoes to bring attention to his shapely calves and dancing skills. He dictated that red soles could be worn only by members of his court, thereby making them a sign of aristocratic privilege.[23]

In other areas of French textile and fashion history, the color red also held important meaning. Extremely skilled artisans, known as *brodeur ordinaire*, were official embroiderers working with royalty to provide extravagantly decorated clothing. One example was the merchant Jean Magoulet, whose shop in the late sixteenth century produced luxury embroidered garments for clients such as royalty, bishops, and cavalry officers, who all had the means to pay for the custom pieces.[24] Additionally, craftsmen such as Magoulet incorporated distinctly colored ribbons in their embroidery symbolizing different events. For instance, a red or pink color-coded ribbon worked into the embroidery represented marriage, which differed from the standard straightforward stitches often used to decorate clothing.[25]

Approximately thirty years after Louis XIV's reign, the color red was still a favorite to French culture and royals. Madame de Pompadour, the mistress of Louis XV, favored the color but desired its application in a different manner than had previously been seen. She changed the aesthetic of Versailles from sumptuous red velvets to more simple red fabrics such as cotton and chintz.[26] The new textiles featured designs like stripes and small-scale prints, and her upholstered furniture such as chairs and beds displayed the fabric. She even kept her interior design style until the end of her life, as DeJean noted that she died comfortably in a red-and-white striped chair.[27]

As Louis XIV and Madame de Pompadour utilized red as an exclusive color enjoyed by the monarchy, the color took on a different meaning by the end of the eighteenth century. During the French Revolution, marked from May 5, 1789 through November 9, 1799, the French public disapproved of absolute monarchy and the country's feudal system and instead wanted to reshape how France was run. Ultimately, liberty and freedom for the commoner were achieved, as well as the abolishment of slavery and more rights for women. However, during this ten-year period of great turmoil, the color red was reappropriated by the people as a symbol of unification. This exemplifies how the associations of a color can change and its symbolism can be reclaimed and repurposed.

One garment worn by the revolutionary public was the Phrygian bonnet, also known as the Phrygian cap (in French, *bonnet Phrygian*), Liberty cap (*bonnet de la Liberté*), or red cap (*bonnet rouge*). Originating in ancient Greece around 500 B.C.E., which is now modern-day Turkey, the bonnet was a tight-fitting, conical, hood-like hat with a pointed top that angled at the front, also known as a cap.[28] Made from stiffened fabric or leather with the pointed top curving toward the front of the head, the Phrygian cap did not have a brim but sometimes had flaps that covered the ears or a flap in the back to protect the neck.[29] There were also examples made from soft wool felt, where the natural, plant-based fiber did not provide the same stiff support as the leather examples, causing the point to hang to one side of the head, become flat, or tentatively stand up straight.[30]

As historical analysis in the early modern period of European history states that this form of headwear was worn by liberated slaves in the Anatolian region,[31] there is a poignant connection between the newly freed slaves and the disheartened French population choosing the same style of headwear. In reality, this connection was probably not a conscious choice but is rather a fanciful anecdote established by the modern era. However it came to be, the red version was utilized by resisters and ultimately became a symbol of the French Revolution.

More likely, however, is the connection between red hats and social unrest, as a similar style of headwear was also a symbol of the American Revolution in the mid- to late eighteenth century. Just as the red cap was used during a time of political and social upheaval in France, the American Colonies also experienced similar employment of red hats as part of their revolutionary symbolism. For France, during the Estates General meeting in 1780, the Phrygian cap in red appeared as a symbol for freedom for France's public,[32] reclaiming the usage of the previously seen royal color. By 1790 and 1791, the hat was "an essential symbol of the *sans-culottes*, whose legwear (after which they were named) and their headwear (the *bonnet rouge*) was a quasi-uniform showing the class and revolutionary fervor of working Parisians."[33] As a crowd stormed the Palace of Tuileries on June 20, 1792, King Louis XVI was forced to wear a liberty cap despite his royal status, and the Archbishop of Paris had to replace his mitre with a Liberty cap when compelled to resign.[34] Additionally,

> it had become *de rigueur* for *sans-culotte* militants to wear one to show their loyalty and was widely used in propaganda. By 1792, it had been adopted by the government as an official symbol of the revolutionary state and has been resurrected at various moments of tension in French political history, right into the twentieth century.[35]

By 1793, members of the Assemblies of Paris were obliged to wear a Liberty cap.[36] Although Napoleon is reported to have detested the Phrygian cap,[37] it was most common after the fall of the French monarchy[38] and continued as a symbol of freedom for France.

Throughout the twentieth century, the hat still acted as an emblem of freedom:

> The liberty cap is one of the generally recognised symbols of sovereignty not mentioned in article 2 of the French Constitution of 1958, which refers only to *le drapeau tricolore*, bleu, blanc, rouge: The French Flag, *L'hymne national*, the national anthem, The Marseillaise and *la devise de la République*; the motto: "Liberté, Égalité, Fraternité."[39]

This explanation, although not official, explains important beliefs of the French, creating a believable and respectable understanding of the power of color. Additionally, recognizable French figures such as Liberty, Marianne, and renditions of French revolutionary army figures often wear Liberty caps in artistic representations.[40] Also, the creation of France's flag followed the same color meaning. The French flag displays three equal vertical bands of color in blue, white, and red. At the time of its creation on February 15, 1794, the revolution was still a current event for the people of France, and representation of the king through the color white, as it was the traditional color of the House of Bourbon,[41] is seen in the middle of the flag design. The blue and red sections embodied the colors adopted by the people of Paris in support of the revolution, as they flew red and blue, and wore red and blue ribbons formed into a cockade while storming the Bastille in 1789.[42]

As such, the Liberty cap was an important icon for France, denoting the existence of extreme revolution.[43] Louboutin's shoes with their red soles playfully tap into this same symbolism, exuding a hint of rebellion and differentiating themselves from other footwear.

The color red has also been associated with the uniforms worn by the French Army. Known as *Le Pantalon Rouge*, the uniform had a distinct sentiment of French pride as Eugène Etienne, former minister of war, exclaimed how the color red was essential as a symbol for France[44] in response to the uniforms being changed to a more drab, easily camouflaged color. Red pants were a part of the nation's military history, and they were worn by soldiers in the Balkans War of 1912–13. Adolphe Méssimy, the minister of war in 1911 through 1912 as well as for some time during the outbreak of World War I, noticed that the red was not allowing the soldiers to blend in with their surroundings but made them highly visible. As a result, many were killed.[45] As the French believed their army was the greatest in all of Europe, hearing that something needed to be changed just did not seem possible. In a way, they also felt their success in battle was associated with the boldness of their uniforms. It was noted:

> Visiting the Balkan front in 1912, Messimy saw the advantages gained by the dull-colored Bulgarians and came home determined to make the French soldier less visible. His project to clothe him in gray-blue or gray-green raised a howl of protest. Army pride was as intransigent about giving up its red trousers as it was about adopting heavy guns. Army prestige was once again felt to be at stake. To clothe the French soldier in some muddy, inglorious color, declared the army's champions, would be to realize the fondest hopes of Dreyfusards and Freemasons. To banish "all that is colorful, all that vies the soldier his vivid aspect," wrote the Echo de Paris, "is to go contrary both to French taste and military function." Messimy pointed out that the two might no longer be synonymous, but his opponents proved immmovable [sic]. At a parliamentary hearing a former War Minister, M. Etienne, spoke for France. "Eliminate the red trousers?" he cried. "Never! *Le pantalon rouge c'est la France*!" "That blind and imbecile attachment to the most visible of all colors," wrote Messimy afterward, "was to have cruel consequences."[46]

The red uniforms, however, stood for much more and created a sense of national pride, despite their ineffectiveness in war:

> When [Messimy] tried to change the uniforms, the popular press whipped up a storm of outrage at his undermining of good taste and national pride, and so the French marched into World War One in their red trousers. It was only after thousands of more deaths that they accepted change.[47]

Historic Red Dyes

The attainment of the color red as a pigment itself holds its own unique history. What seems like a standard color that is readily attainable to the modern consumer actually has a deep association as a favored commodity and a secret, powerful, natural dyestuff. Throughout time, colors take on particular associations, as each causes different psychological reactions. One early dye used to create the color red from as early as the second century B.C.E. was cochineal, derived from insects. Belonging to the substantial red color family, cochineal is full of symbols and meanings. Textile conservator Elena Phipps noted: "Red—associated with fire, fertility, and life force in many cultures throughout the world—has always been one of the most highly prized colors, in part because it is among the most difficult to achieve."[48] Red causes a visceral effect, creating a demand for goods containing this hue and making them desirable objects, and it has been this way for centuries.

Cochineal is not native to Europe but rather originated in North America. An advanced system of trading placed great value on the dye. Cochineal has a venerable appearance throughout history, with an extensive past. Historian of ink David Carvalho remarked: "The term scarlet as employed in the Old Testament was used to designate the blood-red color procured from an insect somewhat resembling cochineal, found in great qualities in Armenia and other eastern countries."[49] Designer and author Amy Butler Greenfield noted:

> No one knows when humans began using cochineal to dye fabric, but archaeologists have found cochineal-saturated textiles that date back two thousand years. The oldest samples come from a great necropolis in Peru, leading some scholars to speculate that the Peruvians discovered cochineal dyeing and introduced it to Central America. Others argue that the people of ancient Mexico discovered the dye first, or at any rate independently.[50]

As a result, the usage of dried bugs producing red dye has been around for ages.

Provided by Carvalho, a succinct definition for *Dactylopius coccus* can be concluded as:

> Cochineal: a 'grain color,' similar to kermes . . . consisting of the dried bodies of an insect known as *coccus cacti*, because it lives upon certain kind of cactus which are native to Mexico and Central America. This dyestuff was largely used for dyeing wool and silk goods, and produced fairly fast shades of crimson or scarlet, according to the mordant employed. But it has been replaced almost entirely now by the various acid dyes."[51]

There is, however, some confusion surrounding the different categories and types of cochineal, as the term is used to define other similar types of red dye. Phipps noted:

> The most brilliant crimson red dye, however, was obtained from a group of scale insects of the superfamily Coccoidea. The group includes several genera of dye-producing insects, called kermes, lac, and cochineal, that have been used since antiquity. Throughout history, there has been confusion regarding the identification of the different insects and the name of the different dyes they produce.[52]

Additionally, the *Pigment Handbook* edited by scientist Temple C. Patton stated:

> These three dyestuffs—kermes, cochineal, and lac—come to the market in the form of little dark colored grains, which, when ground up with hot water, give a bright red solution called carmine, which contains a considerable amount of a coloring known as carminic acid.[53]

This results in a collection of akin dye sources, all containing common elements and dyeing processes. Narrowing down the categorizations, there are two forms of cochineal red dyes that are very close to the Mexican version. The first is St. John's blood, also known as Polish cochineal, which lives on the roots of knawel in Eastern Europe,[54] the scientific name of which is *Porphyrophora polonica*.[55] The other is Armenian cochineal, also called *Porphyrophora hamelii*,[56] found on the roots of a plant in Armenia.[57] However, cochineal had advantageous attributes over St. John's blood and Polish cochineal. First, cochineal had a lower percentage of lipids, resulting in less fat. As a result, the carminic acids contained by the bug's bodies adhered nicely to textiles such as silk, as the abundance of a presence of lipids coated the fibers and caused the dye not to stick.[58] Second, cochineal was more prolific and could be harvested multiple times a year,[59] providing an abundance of material. And cochineal produced a more vibrant, bright red than St. John's blood or Polish cochineal.[60] In short, "cochineal, in other words, was the closest thing Europe had ever seen to a perfect red."[61] This sentiment is repeated by historians, who studied how the introduction of cochineal affected the European market:

> None of the beautiful red dyes produced from the Old World parasitic insects, however, could match the deep crimson color, ease of use, and abundant supply of the dye extracted from the *Dactylopius coccus*, an American species of the same superfamily, Coccoidea, that yields more red colorant than any of them.[62]

It is fascinating to think such a revered colorant was the result of an insect, as it was not obvious: "Only the dyer know that, through his chemical manipulations, brilliant and hardy colors can be derived from the often unattractive natural materials."[63]

In addition to the usage of cochineal, other natural dyestuffs produced brilliant reds. As mentioned, kermes and lac are similar to cochineal but are different, as they are all part of the same genera, or taxonomic rank that determines the biological classification of living things.

Although the American cochineal was favored, another similar natural dye was kermes. Despite coming from a different insect, the dyes produced by the two were very similar, and it is often difficult to tell at first glance if the color was produced from cochineal or kermes. Modern textile scientists can use advanced technology to determine the source of red dyestuffs from surviving textiles and find that cochineal was often used. Scientific analysis of dyes on surviving textiles noted:

> Contemporary historical publications have been systematically affirming that, within a few decades after first shipments of American dyestuff started to arrive in Europe, this was swiftly adopted by textile manufacturers, replacing other insect sources of red, by the end of the 16th century.[64]

One of the other insect sources of red that was previously used included kermes.

In the late nineteenth century, a dyeing handbook named *A Practical Handbook of Dyeing and Calico-Printing* identified oak kermes as living on the green oak with prickly leaves (*Quercus coccifera*), which was native to the south of France, Spain, Italy, the Greek island, and Candia in large quantities,[65] and also stated the natural dye source was used more frequently in France rather than England.[66] Similar to the late twentieth-century published research on cochineal, kermes was established in the late nineteenth century as having a prolific history:

> No colouring substance or other material used in dyeing possesses so great an antiquity; it was known in the time of Moses, and is mentioned by its Hebrew

> name *Tola*. Its name, *Coccus*, frequently occurs in the Greek and Latin writers. Kermes, like cochineal, was supposed to be berries or grains, and colours dyed with them were said to be *grained* or *engrained*, and since the kermes colours were fast and durable the term 'grained' expanded in its signification, and meant a fast colour whether dyed with kermes or not. Nevertheless, kermes are insects, and the word is Arabic, signifying 'little worm,' and in the middle ages they were called *Vermiculi*, and the cloth dyed with them *Vermiculata*. Through the French we have vermillion, a word now employed as the name for one of the compounds of sulphur and mercury. The term crimson is also derived from kermes through the Italian and French languages.[67]

Just as cochineal grows on cacti, kermes also relies on a plant source for its food and shelter. Kermes attaches itself to evergreen oaks and eats the sap:

> Kermes when alive on the trees is fixed to the twigs either in groups or alone. It appears as if forming bluish berries, covered with a whitish powder; it occurs in commerce as pale reddish brown grains, which colouration is due to the vinegar used for killing them.[68]

However, cochineal is still being used today as a dye for products such as food and makeup, but by 1874, kermes was considered archaic: "Kermes may now be considered as having merely a historical interest, and need not, therefore, further occupy our attention."[69]

Another insect which produced red dye similar to cochineal and kermes was lac, indigenous to southeast Asia.[70] Found often on banyan and juniper trees, the lac insect excretes shellac resin, and a deep red colorant is extracted from this.[71] Due to its natural location, areas such as India, Indonesia, Nepal, Burma, Cambodia, Laos, and Thailand, as well as Tibet, Persia, Japan, and China used the colorant.[72] In addition to dyeing silk and leather, the shellac resin was also used as a protective covering for wood, and these usages were seen as early as 250 A.D.[73] The color significance varies from culture to culture, but lac and its resulting red dye have associations in Laos, as red, black, and white threads were tied around the neck or wrist, and a shaman empowered the threads to keep bad spirits away.[74] The colorant has also been used as a substitute for henna, and its application to the body had religious connotations in addition to being used as an insect repellant.[75]

Despite the different natural dyestuffs and their varied ability to produce red goods for different uses, it is clear that the color red they produced was considered special and was not something always easily attainable by the general public.

Conclusions

Whether the color red exemplifies power, healing, money, or sex appeal, it is still a strong hue that sets aside the wearer, and owners of red goods become members of particular, exclusive groups. The ties with France's history, the reiteration of the color red as a main design point, and association with thematically French themes in art history all establish Christian Louboutin and his footwear company as having a rich history with close ties to France. All design choices for footwear styles and accessories, as well as photography and marketing, are well thought out, with hints of historic elements and materials. Luxury brands have high standards to uphold, and these strong connections ensure that these standards are met. It is evident that Louboutin is honoring the past of his nation while making innovative and stylish fashion for consumers today. This is above and beyond the duty of a clothing or accessory designer, solidifying the brand as a company that continually produces heirloom goods.

Since Louboutin formed these strong bonds, the consumer of these goods is also associated with the brand's characteristics. The brand a consumer purchases is synonymous with associations of class, membership, and gender and brings up other connections. Additionally, anthropologist Karen Tranberg Hansen noted this importance, as it had been ignored in the past: "Anthropology contributes to this growing body of research by giving new life to the study of clothing, which for a long time received only passing attention."[76] The shoes on one's feet can speak volumes on culture. Louboutin's work today highlights the rich symbolism and connection that spans three centuries.

Notes

1. Jill Di Donato, "The Inspiration behind Christian Louboutin's Red-Bottomed Soles," *Medium*, August 18, 2017, https://medium.com/the-omnivore/the-inspiration-behind-christian-louboutins-red-bottomed-soles-99985dcdaa3e.
2. "Christian Louboutin Biography," *Biography.com*, April 2, 2014; last modified July 23, 2019, www.biography.com/fashion-designer/christian-louboutin.
3. Allison Adato, "Heel de France: For the Red Carpet or the Wedding Aisle, Stars Are High on Christian Louboutin's Sexy Stilettos," *People Weekly*, February 10, 2003, 88.
4. "Christian Louboutin," *Business of Fashion*, accessed October 4, 2019, www.businessoffashion.com/community/people/christian-louboutin.
5. Tiffany Yannetta, "Christian Louboutin's New Men's Store Includes a Tattoo Parlor," *Racked*, August 30, 2012, https://ny.racked.com/2012/8/30/7712557/christian-louboutin-new-mens-store-does-include-a-tattoo-parlor.
6. Alexia Antsakli Vardinoyanni, "Wildflowers: Interview with Christian Louboutin," *Art Flyer*, September 25, 2015, https://artflyer.net/christian-louboutin-exclusive-interview-factory-nerviano-italy/.
7. "Channel 4 to Meet Christian Louboutin in New Documentary," *Channel 4*, July 27, 2015, www.channel4.com/press/news/channel-4-meet-christian-louboutin-new-documentary.
8. "Christian Louboutin: First Guest Creator of Crazy Horse Paris," *Crazy Horse Paris*, accessed September 15, 2019, www.lecrazyhorseparis.com/en/createur/christian-louboutin-en/.
9. "Feu, The Movie," *Crazy Horse Paris*, accessed September 15, 2019, www.lecrazyhorseparis.com/en/collaboration/feu-the-movie-by-christian-louboutin/.
10. "Christian Louboutin: First Guest Creator of Crazy Horse Paris."
11. Tanya O'Donnell, "Christian Louboutin Logo Design History and Evolution," *Logo Realm*, accessed September 21, 2019, https://logorealm.com/christian-louboutin-logo/.
12. Peter Shadbolt, "How Important Is It for a Company to Have a Great Logo?" *BBC*, May 7, 2015, www.bbc.com/news/business-32495854.
13. Pantea Foroudi, T.C. Melewar, and Suraksha Gupta, "Corporate Logo: History, Definition, and Components," *International Studies of Management & Organization* 47, no. 2 (Summer 2017): 187.
14. O'Donnell, "Christian Louboutin Logo Design History and Evolution."
15. Shadbolt, "How Important Is It for a Company to Have a Great Logo?"
16. Eleanor Gibson, "Tree Bark Covers Christian Louboutin Boutique in Miami Design District," *Dezeen*, December 21, 2018, www.dezeen.com/2018/12/21/christian-louboutin-flagship-miami-design-district/.
17. Ibid.
18. Ibid.
19. "From Louis XIV to Christian Louboutin: A History of Red-Soled Shoes," *Forbes*, accessed December 20, 2016, www.forbes.com/pictures/emjl45ghf/louis-xiv-of-france-posing-in-red-heeled-shoes/#203503751893.

20. Yuniya Kawamura, *Sneakers: Fashion, Gender, and Subculture* (New York: Bloomsbury Academic, 2016), 52.
21. Ted Polhemus, *Fashion and Anti-Fashion: Anthropology of Clothing and Adornment* (London: Thames & Hudson, 1978), 11.
22. Susan Stamberg, "The Color Red: A History in Textiles," *NPR*, February 13, 2007, www.npr.org/2007/02/13/7366503/the-color-red-a-history-in-textiles.
23. Whitney A. Jones and Julie Ann Orsini, *Sole Desire: The Shoes of Christian Louboutin, Exhibition Catalogue* (New York: Fashion Institute of Technology, 2008).
24. Joan DeJean, *The Queen's Embroiderer: A True Story of Paris, Lovers, Swindlers and the First Stock Market Crisis* (Bloomsbury: Bloomsbury Publishing, 2018), 8.
25. Ibid.
26. Stamberg, "The Color Red: A History in Textiles."
27. Ibid.
28. Bronwyn Cosgrave, *The Complete History of Costume and Fashion: From Ancient Egypt to the Present Day* (New York: Checkmark Books, 2000).
29. Ibid.
30. Ibid.
31. Robert Wilde, "Phrygian Cap/Bonnet Rouge," *Thought Co.*, April 2, 2018, www.thoughtco.com/phrygian-cap-bonnet-rouge-1221893.
32. Ibid.
33. Ibid.
34. "French National Symbols: The Liberty Cap or Phrygian Cap," *Languedoc*, accessed September 27, 2019, www.languedoc-france.info/06141204_libertycap.htm.
35. Wilde, "Phrygian Cap/Bonnet Rouge."
36. Ibid.
37. Ibid.
38. Ibid.
39. "French National Symbols: The Liberty Cap or Phrygian Cap."
40. Ibid.
41. "Why Is the French Flag Blue, White, Red?" *Institut Linguistique Adenet*, July 14, 2015, www.ila-france.com/blog/why-is-the-french-flag-blue-white-red.
42. Ibid.
43. "French National Symbols: The Liberty Cap or Phrygian Cap."
44. Barbara W. Tuchman, *The Guns of August* (New York: Ballantine Books, 1962), 45.
45. Andrew Knighton, "11 Military Uniforms That Got Soldiers Killed," *War History Online*, August 7, 2016, www.warhistoryonline.com/history/11-military-uniforms-got-soldiers_killed.html.
46. Tuchman, *The Guns of August*, 45–46.
47. Knighton, "11 Military Uniforms That Got Soldiers Killed."
48. Elena Phipps, *Cochineal Red: The Art History of a Color* (New York: Metropolitan Museum of Art, 2010), 5.
49. David N. Carvalho, *Forty Centuries of Ink* (New York: Burt Franklin, 1971), 7.
50. Amy Butler Greenfield, *A Perfect Red: Empire, Espionage, and the Quest for the Color of Desire* (New York: HarperCollins Publishers, 2005), 36.
51. Temple C. Patton, *Pigment Handbook, Volume I Properties and Economics* (New York: John Wiley & Sons, 1973), 18–19.
52. Phipps, *Cochineal Red: The Art History of a Color*, 7–8.
53. Patton, *Pigment Handbook*, 11.
54. Lorenza Smith, "The Red Craze," *Fashion History Timeline of the Fashion Institute of Technology*, accessed September 19, 2019, https://fashionhistory.fitnyc.edu/the-red-craze/.
55. "Polish Cochineal," *The Craft Atlas*, accessed October 10, 2019, https://craftatlas.co/natural-dyes/polish-cochineal.
56. "Armenian Cochineal," *WikiVisually*, accessed October 10, 2019, https://wikivisually.com/wiki/Armenian_cochineal.
57. Smith, "The Red Craze."
58. Greenfield, *A Perfect Red*, 75.
59. Ibid, 76.
60. Ibid.
61. Ibid.

62. Phipps, *Cochineal Red: The Art History of a Color*, 9–10.
63. Gösta Sandberg, *The Red Dyes: Cochineal, Madder, and Murex Purple: A World Tour of Textile Techniques* (Asheville: Lark Books, 1997), 43.
64. Ana Serrano, Andrew van den Doel, Maarten van Bommel, Jessica Hallett, Ineke Joosten, and Klaas J. van den Berg, "Investigation of Crimson-Dyed Fibres for a New Approach on the Characterization of Cochineal and Kermes Dyes in Historical Textiles," *Analytica Chimica Acta* 897 (October 15, 2015): 117.
65. William Crookes, *A Practical Handbook of Dyeing and Calico-Printing* (London: Longmans, Green, and Co., 1874), 353.
66. Ibid.
67. Ibid.
68. Ibid.
69. Ibid.
70. "Lac Dye," *Natural Pigments*, accessed November 3, 2019, www.naturalpigments.com/lac-dye.html.
71. "Lac Dye," Conservation and Art Materials Encyclopedia Online, accessed November 3, 2019, http://cameo.mfa.org/wiki/Lac_dye.
72. Judy Newland, "Natural Dyes: Lac," *Cloth Roads*, July 9, 2015, www.clothroads.com/natural-dyes-lac/.
73. "Lac Extract," *Botanical Colors*, accessed November 6, 2019, https://botanicalcolors.com/shop/natural-dye-extracts/lac-extract/.
74. Newland, "Natural Dyes: Lac."
75. Ibid.
76. Karen Tranberg Hansen, "The World in Dress: Anthropological Perspectives on Clothing, Fashion, and Culture," *Annual Review of Anthropology* 33, no. 1 (2004): 369.

Bibliography

Adato, Allison. "Heel de France: For the Red Carpet or the Wedding Aisle, Stars Are High on Christian Louboutin's Sexy Stilettos." *People Weekly*, February 10, 2003, 88.

"Armenian Cochineal." *WikiVisually*. Accessed October 10, 2019. https://wikivisually.com/wiki/Armenian_cochineal.

Carvalho, David N. *Forty Centuries of Ink*. New York: Burt Franklin, 1971.

"Channel 4 to Meet Christian Louboutin in New Documentary." *Channel 4*, July 27, 2015. www.channel4.com/press/news/channel-4-meet-christian-louboutin-new-documentary.

"Christian Louboutin." *Business of Fashion*. Accessed October 4, 2019. www.businessoffashion.com/community/people/christian-louboutin.

"Christian Louboutin Biography." *Biography.com*, April 2, 2014; last modified July 23, 2019. www.biography.com/fashion-designer/christian-louboutin.

"Christian Louboutin: First Guest Creator of Crazy Horse Paris." *Crazy Horse Paris*. Accessed September 15, 2019. www.lecrazyhorseparis.com/en/createur/christian-louboutin-en/.

Cosgrave, Bronwyn. *The Complete History of Costume and Fashion: From Ancient Egypt to the Present Day*. New York: Checkmark Books, 2000.

Crookes, William. *A Practical Handbook of Dyeing and Calico-printing*. London: Longmans, Green, and Co., 1874.

DeJean, Joan. *The Queen's Embroiderer: A True Story of Paris, Lovers, Swindlers and the First Stock Market Crisis*. London: Bloomsbury Publishing, 2018.

Di Donato, Jill. "The Inspiration behind Christian Louboutin's Red-Bottomed Soles." *Medium*, August 18, 2017. https://medium.com/the-omnivore/the-inspiration-behind-christian-louboutins-red-bottomed-soles-99985dcdaa3e.

"Feu, The Movie." *Crazy Horse Paris*. Accessed September 15, 2019. www.lecrazyhorseparis.com/en/collaboration/feu-the-movie-by-christian-louboutin/.

Foroudi, Pantea, T.C. Melewar, and Suraksha Gupta. "Corporate Logo: History, Definition, and Components." *International Studies of Management & Organization* 47 no. 2 (Summer 2017): 176–196.

"French National Symbols: The Liberty Cap or Phrygian Cap." *Languedoc*. Accessed September 27, 2019. www.languedoc-france.info/06141204_libertycap.htm.

"From Louis XIV to Christian Louboutin: A History of Red-Soled Shoes." *Forbes*. Accessed December 20, 2016. www.forbes.com/pictures/emjl45ghf/louis-xiv-of-france-posing-in-red-heeled-shoes/#203503751893.

Gibson, Eleanor. "Tree Bark Covers Christian Louboutin Boutique in Miami Design District." *Dezeen*, December 21, 2018. www.dezeen.com/2018/12/21/christian-louboutin-flagship-miami-design-district/.

Greenfield, Amy Butler. *A Perfect Red: Empire, Espionage, and the Quest for the Color of Desire*. New York: HarperCollins Publishers, 2005.

Hansen, Karen Tranberg. "The World in Dress: Anthropological Perspectives on Clothing, Fashion, and Culture." *Annual Review of Anthropology* 33, no. 1 (2004): 369–392.

Jones, Whitney A. and Julie Ann Orsini. *Sole Desire: The Shoes of Christian Louboutin*, exhibition catalogue. New York: Fashion Institute of Technology, 2008.

Kawamura, Yuniya. *Sneakers: Fashion, Gender, and Subculture*. New York: Bloomsbury Academic, 2016.

Knighton, Andrew. "11 Military Uniforms That Got Soldiers Killed." *War History Online*, August 7, 2016. www.warhistoryonline.com/history/11-military-uniforms-got-soldiers_killed.html.

"Lac Dye." *Conservation and Art Materials Encyclopedia Online*. Accessed November 3, 2019. http://cameo.mfa.org/wiki/Lac_dye.

"Lac Dye." *Natural Pigments*. Accessed November 3, 2019. www.naturalpigments.com/lac-dye.html.

"Lac Extract." *Botanical Colors*. Accessed November 6, 2019. https://botanicalcolors.com/shop/natural-dye-extracts/lac-extract/.

Newland, Judy. "Natural Dyes: Lac." *Cloth Roads*, July 9, 2015. www.clothroads.com/natural-dyes-lac/.

O'Donnell, Tanya. "Christian Louboutin Logo Design History and Evolution." *Logo Realm*. Accessed September 21, 2019. https://logorealm.com/christian-louboutin-logo/.

Patton, Temple C. *Pigment Handbook, Volume I Properties and Economics*. New York: John Wiley & Sons, 1973.

Phipps, Elena. *Cochineal Red: The Art History of a Color*. New York: Metropolitan Museum of Art, 2010.

Polhemus, Ted. *Fashion and Anti-Fashion: Anthropology of Clothing and Adornment*. London: Thames & Hudson, 1978.

"Polish Cochineal." *The Craft Atlas*. Accessed October 10, 2019. https://craftatlas.co/natural-dyes/polish-cochineal.

Riello, Giorgio and Peter McNeil. *Shoes: A History from Sandals to Sneakers*. New York: Bloomsbury Academic, 2006.

Sandberg, Gösta. *The Red Dyes: Cochineal, Madder, and Murex Purple: A World Tour of Textile Techniques*. Asheville: Lark Books, 1997.

Serrano, Ana, Andrew van den Doel, Maarten van Bommel, Jessica Hallett, Ineke Joosten, and Klaas J. van den Berg. "Investigation of Crimson-Dyed Fibres for a New Approach on the Characterization of Cochineal and Kermes Dyes in Historical Textiles." *Analytica Chimica Acta* 897 (October 15, 2015): 116–127.

Shadbolt, Peter. "How Important Is It for a Company to Have a Great Logo?" *BBC*, May 7, 2015. www.bbc.com/news/business-32495854.

Smith, Lorenza. "The Red Craze." *Fashion History Timeline of the Fashion Institute of Technology*. Accessed September 19, 2019. https://fashionhistory.fitnyc.edu/the-red-craze/.

Stamberg, Susan. "The Color Red: A History in Textiles." *NPR*, February 13, 2007. www.npr.org/2007/02/13/7366503/the-color-red-a-history-in-textiles.

Tuchman, Barbara W. *The Guns of August*. New York: Ballantine Books, 1962.

Vardinoyanni, Alexia Antsakli. "Wildflowers: Interview with Christian Louboutin." *ArtFlyer*, September 25, 2015. https://artflyer.net/christian-louboutin-exclusive-interview-factory-nerviano-italy/.

"Why Is the French Flag Blue, White, Red?" *Institut Linguistique Adenet*, July 14, 2015. www.ila-france.com/blog/why-is-the-french-flag-blue-white-red.
Wilde, Robert. "Phrygian Cap/Bonnet Rouge." *Thought Co.*, April 2, 2018. www.thoughtco.com/phrygian-cap-bonnet-rouge-1221893.
Yannetta, Tiffany. "Christian Louboutin's New Men's Store Includes a Tattoo Parlor." *Racked*, August 30, 2012. https://ny.racked.com/2012/8/30/7712557/christian-louboutin-new-mens-store-does-include-a-tattoo-parlor.

8 Japan's Fashion Subculture

Lolita, From Cuteness to Feminist Revolution and Escapism

Crînguța-Irina Pelea

Historical Perspective, Characteristics, and Aesthetics

As an independent contemporary street fashion and small-scale subculture, Lolita emerged during the '80s in a Japan, embracing an extraordinary nostalgia of the past (Suzuki 2007). As an attempt to generalize and encompass the quintessence of this subculture, Lolitas are usually teenagers and young adult women who adopt a dress code specific to the Victorian era (1837–1901) and the Edwardian era (1901–1910), or Belle Epoque, with influences that stretch as far back as the Rococo art movement. Thus, the wearers' style is a reflection of a childish and fairy-like image, ornamented with elaborate feminine elements such as frills, ribbons, lace, bonnets, and bell-shaped petticoats, while they intend to mimic Western European porcelain dolls or fairy-tale princess.[1]

With time, the fashion subculture has fragmented into several significant subgenres, which are considered the following: Sweet Lolita, known as AmaRori; Classic Lolita, KuraRori; and Gothic Lolita, as in GosuRori. If the style of Sweet Lolita incorporates calm and warm chromatics of pink, white, and light blue, combined with cute and childish patterns of teddy bears, teacups, and cookies, the style of Gothic Lolita stands out through its longer skirts, dark colors, pessimistic and gloomy impressions, and Christian motifs such as crosses and gothic symbols, inspired by Victorian mourning attire.[2] Classic Lolita is a mature style and features neutral colors and dusty pastels and catches one's attention through the elegance of moderate frills and laces.

Given its visually spectacular and eye-catching nature, this particular fashion subculture has enticed many individuals all over the world. It has developed into a fully global phenomenon that presents unique characteristics in different national cultural contexts: the United States, Sweden, Romania, France, Italy, Great Britain, Australia, Hong Kong, South Korea, and many more. Nevertheless, Lolita brands have been intrinsically and exclusively connected with the original performative space of Japan; thus, these brands are not designed for export, given that they become symbolic and metaphoric carriers for the dreams, anxieties, hopes, and frustrations of young Japanese women.[3]

The subculture leads its followers to a path of creative escapism toward the aesthetics of cuteness, and it manifests itself as a complex matrix of visual and behavioral resistance against the conventional, traditional, and contemporary Japanese culture. Ever since its emergence in the '80s, Lolitas have been perceived continuously as ephemeral and extraordinary beings, given their surreal appearance, which is strikingly different when compared to the modern-day placid environment.

On a side note, although the Lolita subculture bears a resemblance in name to the promiscuous young girl protagonist of the novel written by Vladimir Nabokov, "it . . . has nothing to do with such references. Many Lolita members know nothing about the Nabokov novel."[4]

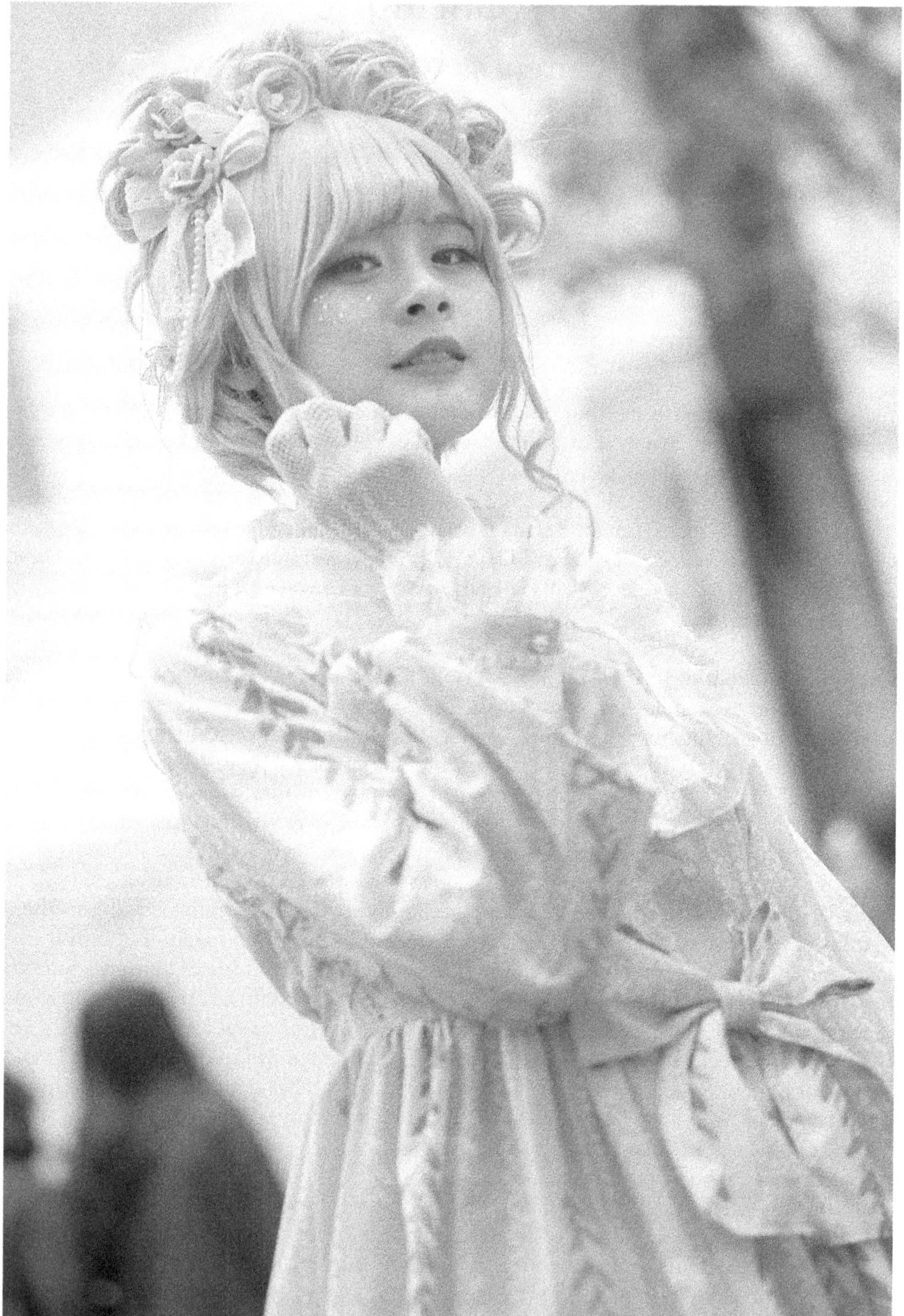

Figure 8.1 Sweet Lolita and "kawaii" style: lace and pastel colors, Pexels.com.

Despite it being a situation perpetrated for many decades, there has been widespread misunderstanding connecting the fashion subculture to the sexual, provocative content of Nabokov's novel; the intended image is one abounding in sweetness and childish innocence, but it often ends up being interpreted by non-followers as an exotic fetish and thus sexualized accordingly.

The aggressive sexualization is due to the Nabokovian association but also to the imagery originating from Japanese popular culture, which tends to objectify and eroticize the adolescent girl. For instance, Lolicon or Roricon as a reference point stands out, a term derived from the words "Loli" and "complex," frequently used to describe erotic and pornographic manga and hentai anime which depict very young and prepubescent girls involved sexually with older boys or adult men. Consequently, the cult of the sexually active female child was transferred to the Lolita subculture solely on the name resemblance.

However, an appropriate symbolic and fictional character for this subculture is considered Alice from Lewis Carroll's *Alice's Adventures in Wonderland*, as she encompasses the archetypical image of the "shōjo girl," even though her purity is exhibited, in sexual and erotic depictions, at the border of childhood and adulthood. As Masafumi Monden points out, the strong appeal of Alice for Japan is related mainly to her strong resemblance to the social construct of the ideal shōjo: "if we consider the typical concept of shōjo as sweet and innocent on the outside, and considerably autonomous on the inside, the imagery of Alice displays similar characteristics."[5]

Consequently, just like shōjo and the fictional character of Alice, Lolitas aim to become "kawaii" (可愛い); this is a general concept within Japanese popular culture, applicable to both a person or a commodity, and it can be defined as "an aesthetic that celebrates sweet, adorable, simple, infantile, delicate and pretty visual, physical or behavioral qualities."[6] Therefore, the cuteness of Lolita has the therapeutic effect of counterbalancing the brutal rigidity of Japanese society.

Hence, the image of Nabokov's highly eroticized preadolescent character, which has stirred undying controversies in many Western societies, highly conflicts with Lolita aesthetics as it exists in Japan, placed at the interweaving of a dull and anxiety-inducing reality and a romantically wild and fantastic world. Nonetheless, one should also consider that Lolita has faced its fair share of criticism in Japan as well, because wearers are perceived as immature and continuously rejecting maturity and the necessity to conform to the Japanese standard criteria of femininity socially. Hence, while in Western societies, the main criticism derives from the abounding and overflowing sexuality, Japan penalizes Lolitas for their vocal and publicly visual divergence from the society's mainstream, which remains a genuine reflection of the cultural uniformity and long-lasting social conformity.

From an aesthetic perspective, it is particularly noteworthy that the childish cuteness represents one dominant subcultural sensibility, because Lolita favors the idealized image of the Victorian female child.

As Kehily and De Lappe have noted, the clothes of the wearers "are designed to de-emphasize the features of an adult female body; they used flattened bodices, high waists, and full skirts with voluminous underskirts to conceal their bust and hips."[7] To add to the dressing style, "the striking pose is intended to evoke the illusion of a very young girl or a porcelain doll" or

> when posing for photographs, Lolis often stand with their knees together and toes pointed inward and their head inclined to one side; a stylization that embodies a regressed state of childhood that is both innocent and knowing at the same time.[8]

For the followers, "being a Lolita becomes more than just a choice of clothing; it comes to be a style and way of being, which defines their identity and life philosophy."[9] Their body language comes only to reflect the romantic and idealized vision the wearers hold of the aristocratic young women living during the eighteenth- and nineteenth-century Europe.

The original philosophy of Lolita does not override the cultural differences, which arise. Consequently, one can consider that there is a clear tendency of fragmentation and transglobalization, which takes place simultaneously with the cultural flow and transmutation of Lolita from the cultural and symbolic context of Japan toward Western societies.

The subculture's references to other cultural products such as manga, anime, or visual kei represent appropriate examples of cultural recycling at the intersection of the West and Japan. Given this dynamic cultural recycling and interconnectivity with other cultural areas, there is a frequent tendency to misunderstand and confuse Lolita with cosplay. Through cosplay, one can understand "an emerging transglobal trend for young adults to periodically dress up in themed costumes assuming the persona of characters from contemporary Japanese comic books, animated cartoons, video, online games, and popular bands."[10]

Even though there are some resemblances between these two subcultural movements, "for the authentic Lolita followers, it is highly offensive for them to be called cosplayers. Lolita is an important part of their life; sometimes, it consumes their entire life,"[11] because this fashion and visual movement does not presume to adopt the childish image of a burlesque doll and princess-inspired clothing: it also pervades the wearer's life to a large extent.

The dynamism of this dichotomy and fusion of meanings, products, and symbolic colportage is reflected in the dual belonging of Lolita, both to an aristocratic era long gone and to contemporary Japan.

Lolita: Luxury Fashion and British Cultural Heritage

Although Lolita remains a relatively small-scale subculture, it has received until now a significant and increasing amount of attention not only from mass media but also researchers from a variety of scientific fields, such as fashion studies, intercultural communication, and cultural psychology but also from the general public.

One of the reasons it continues to be a niche fashion subculture is the luxury one has to afford as a follower, given the high production costs of the clothes. The most famous Lolita brands are "BABY THE STARS SHINE BRIGHT," "Angelic Pretty," "ALICE and the PIRATES," and "Jane Marple."

For each of these brands, every item is handmade and unique, facts that can only contribute to the high value of the clothes. Otherwise, if one considers the clothing material, which is plain cotton, the synthetic leather of the shoes, and purses or the necklaces made of plastic, the price tag could seem an utterly outrageous sum. Accordingly, the previously mentioned Lolita brands stand out and are easily perceived as luxurious because of the high production cost, long period of manufacturing, and uniqueness and quality of each costume and garment.

These brands tap into the rich cultural heritage of an aristocratic Europe, more specifically Great Britain, and a past that has no direct cultural or social connection with Japan. Nevertheless, there are subgenres such as Wa Lolita or Qi Lolita draw upon shared cultural knowledge and connect to some extent with Japan or, in some cases, China's rich history and traditional fashion.

Overall, the brands' value is built only by connecting continuously to the cultural knowledge of Japan, which helps to engage with the arising cultural tensions instead of ignoring them. However, Lolita brands do not only appropriate the cultural past of Victorian fashion but also generate new cultural meanings and practices that emerge from the hybridization of the Victorian dress code and the principles of Japanese mentality and philosophy of life.

Furthermore, Lolita brands emphasize co-creation: manufacturers and buyers end up working together intentionally or unintentionally, thus creating new meanings and adding value to these brands. Sometimes, wearers convert themselves into manufacturers or the other way around and invest in their clothes meanings and emotions associated with various life events or specific contexts, given that this dressing style also contributes to their life experiences in a significant way. Therefore, by creating an emotional luxury experience, the brands manage to embody at the same time the followers' identity, together with the meticulousness of handmade work and the know-how of the art of production.

While the British aristocratic dress code of the Victorian era comes to represent a cultural resource that transcends local and regional borders, the brands also introduce isolated Japanese style elements that correspond to the "kawaii" ideal mentioned previously or other strategically located iconic patterns. Therefore, one can conclude that the basic fashion strategy is to engage the cultural interest of the wearer by confiscating a past foreign to one's reality and intertwining it with Japanese beauty and feminine ideals up to a certain point.

As an effect, this intertwinement places the Lolita follower at the borders of two worlds set in two different spatial and temporal dimensions and challenges the rigidity and the homogeneity of contemporary Japan, as well as obedience as a quality of the feminine ideal.

The brands adopt a similar strategy, which is to position themselves as more than single functions and passing trifles but as lifestyle options. Being a Lolita imprints one's way of life, leading to a special status or ensuring harmonious communication relationships and exchanges with others as well. Hence, as a promotion strategy, brands grow to be more than fashion luxury brands targeted toward a niche segment of the public but more likely a luxury lifestyle brand, blending the heritage of the Victorian dress code with Japanese design, craftsmanship, and national cultural practice.

For instance, the patterns sewn on the dresses represent an accurate reflection of the delicacy, sweetness, and fragility incorporated by the "kawaii" concept. As for historical accuracy, they are nowhere to be associated with authentic Victorian dresses. Besides bunnies, teddy bears, chocolates, cookies, and pink and shiny flowers, tea party patterns are among the most frequently used. The tea culture continues to permeate many aspects of life in contemporary Japan on a multilayered level, not just its past, since it is associated with a unique discourse of aesthetics.

Nonetheless, very little is known about how this fashion subculture draws its stories in the digital era, and limited research has been conducted on Japanese-language social media platforms as a creative space for the subculture's digital storytelling.

One of the reasons behind this academic limitation is that though there are significant differences between Lolita's country of origin and its reception in social media versus other countries where the subculture has gained popularity, most researchers are forced to employ English as an intermediate pivot language when an overwhelming percent of Japanese followers blog in the Japanese language.

Methodology

The empirical section of the present chapter aims to explore the underlying patterns of digital narratives employed by the followers of the Lolita subculture in the Japanese-language blogosphere. Moreover, several questions underpin the research: How do Japanese Lolitas use the blog as an instrument of narrative transportation? Can one identify the essential elements and patterns of their blogging narratives? Are the followers' blogs defined by a multilayered structure, engaging memory, space, and place?

One of the reasons for selecting the blog as a carrier of digital narratives is because of its renowned quality of being almost unlimited for self-expression and for offering the blogger the chance to access an independent and sometimes even unlimited space for storytelling and for creating a proper virtual identity, as one desires. Moreover, by sampling Lolita blogs exclusively in the Japanese language, the present research aims to distance itself from the extremely rich database of academic publications focusing on English-language information on this subject.

Another reason for preferring the blog as the main object of analysis is connected with noticing a collective migrating tendency of Japanese Lolita followers from public, offline, and collective space such as Harajuku or Shinjuku to the virtual one, obviously more individually oriented, like the blogging platform Ameba. Moreover, through their long-time activity, these blogs, written in the Japanese language, become valuable first-hand instruments for transferring subcultural knowledge and commodities, digital handbooks of "how-to," while still being embedded with the enthusiasm, mystery, and personality of a journal.

The existence of virtual space, together with the translocation and emergence of this subculture within it, become necessary conditions for discussing the cyber dimension of Lolita and to what extent these dynamic exchanges have an impact on the quality and quantity of storytelling.

The methodology adopted for the present chapter consists of netnography and content analysis on a sample of sixty blogs of Japanese Lolitas, in the Japanese language, selected from the most popular blogging platforms, until saturation was reached. The research took place between March and November 2019. Visual and textual elements such as banners, blocks, and advertising links have been excluded beforehand, considering that they do not belong to the blog's editorial line and they do not reflect the blogger's will by any means.

Netnography represents "the ethnography of internet or technological network, and is the ethnography that is adapted to our technological modern and social world's complication."[12] The content analysis covers in-depth the field of semiotics and has the capacity to accurately describe and interpret behavior.[13] Therefore, considering the nature of the topic, the linguistic and cultural context, and the selected database, these two techniques have been chosen to strengthen the findings and to help in gathering deeper insights, while placing considerable emphasis on qualitative data.

The sampling took place according to previously established eligibility criteria, such as popularity, recent update, longevity, and diversity (to correspond to as many Lolita trends as possible), and it was conducted using google.jp, with the following keywords: 「ロリータ」 and 「ブログ」 ("Lolita" and "blog"). Additional blogs were selected through blogrolls until the desired sample size was reached.

Findings and Interpretation

For coding and analyzing the digital narratives, the most common blog themes have been organized into several distinct categories, which are identified as follows: "Relationships and Family," "Parenting," "Work," "Food," and "Lolita Universe."

The content of the blogs tends to include specific topics very well organized under tags such as Everyday Life, Selling and Buying, History, News, Lolita Brands, Fashion, or Writer's Spot. Still, it also touches matters of relevance for the entire Lolita community from Japan and, to some extent, worldwide.

Each blog included as a sample in the database is controlled and updated by a single person. It embraces the format of a lifelog, focusing not only on the blogger's activity as a Lolita follower but also on one's everyday life, continually reflecting her mental and physical interaction with the Lolita subculture's philosophy. Even though, at first glance, the blogs might seem individually oriented, they are also characterized by a high degree of interactivity: in most cases, elements of the personal homepage are combined with marketing attempts and promotional messages, and the blogger frequently launches invitations to various fashion events.

Furthermore, besides comments, blogroll hyperlinks, or embedded codes, many different sharing platforms such as Facebook, Line, Instagram, or Twitter are available for spreading content and adding value to the blog by increasing its visibility.

After identifying the categories as mentioned previously, the present chapter focuses on exploring the digital narratives assigned to the "Lolita Universe" category, which, in most cases, is overwhelmingly represented by a high number of blog posts.

Some bloggers reposted articles or prints of Lolita magazines. Thus, a notable goal of this predominant youth subculture is providing an alternative mass media space within the subculture, designed as a critical and constructive space where the members have the chance to counteract the ideological misconceptions and hostility or to manifest themselves. The existence of an alternative Lolita press, through magazines such as *Tulle*, *Kera*, *Miel*, *Doll Siesta*, *Le Panier*, *Gothic & Lolita Bible*, and so on, proves that describing oneself as a Lolita represents more than adopting a particular eccentric fashion style.

Moreover, internal subcultural hostilities tend to arise continuously, as a consequence of the subgenres' diversity, style variety, and ideological differences concerning aesthetic values. For instance, a Gothic Lolita might have a stronger personality, emphasized by piercings; a preference for black in clothing and dark make-up; and interest in fantasy, magic, and mysticism; however, a Sweet Lolita will stand out as being romantic, with a flowing, colorful, pastel wardrobe, which represents the creative personality of a dreamer, an artist, or an innocent fairy.

Many Japanese Lolita bloggers make use of a Lolita name, different from their legal surname, a fact which confirms that for them blogging and flowing into the Lolita universe represent a way of exploring, negotiating, or projecting their identity through online social media platforms. For instance, one blogger edited her "Personal Introduction" as it follows:

> 【自己紹介：普段は「さとみ」、　ロリィタ時は「たまき」と名乗っております。 お好きな方でお呼び下さいませ♪．．．】
>
> Personal Introduction: Usually, I go by Satomi, but when I dress/act/am a Lolita, my name is Tamaki. Please call me as you wish.[14]

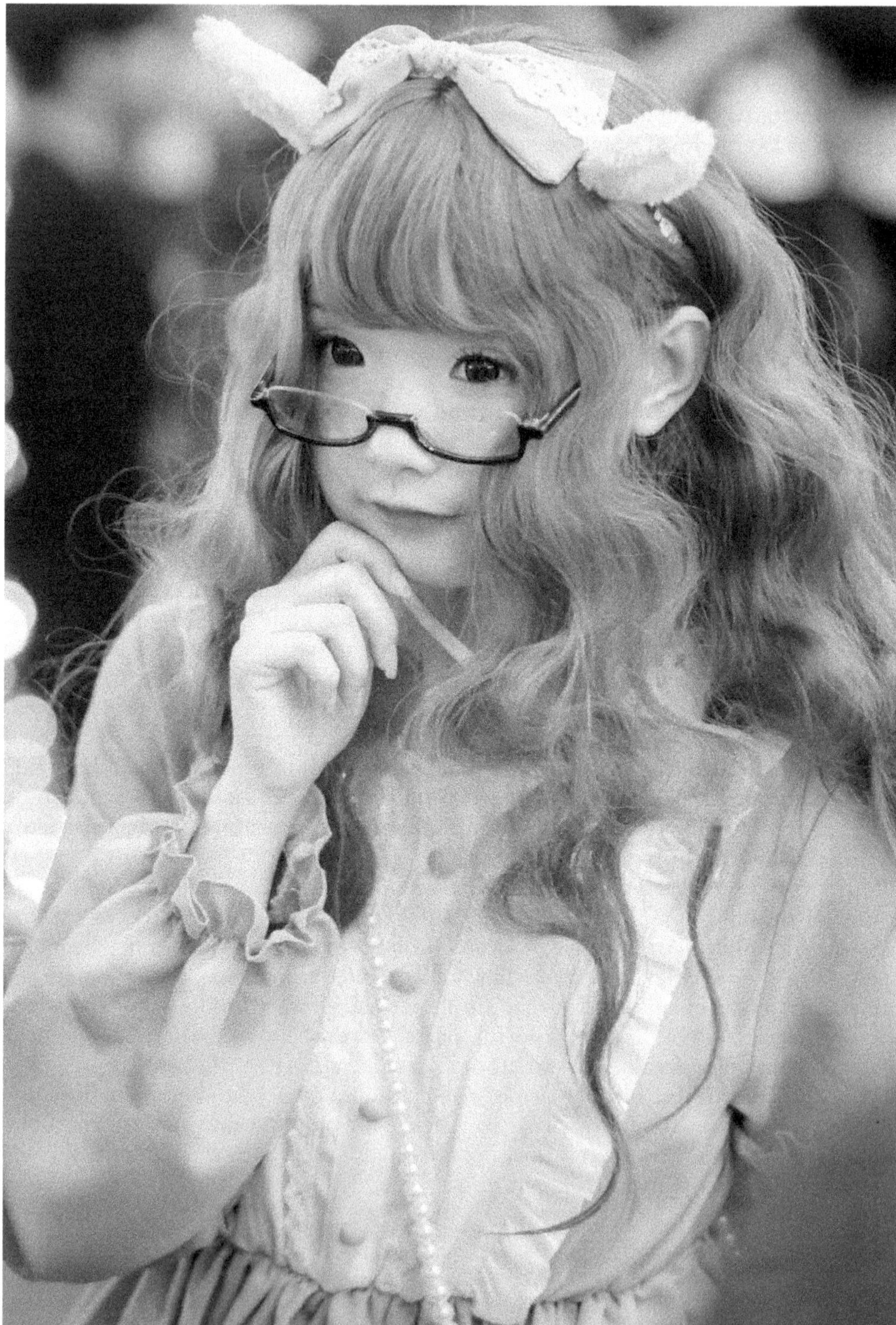

Figure 8.2 Recreating one's identity through fashion, Pexels.com.

The following exciting and unique aspect worth mentioning concerning the patterns of digital storytelling is the existence of several significant and almost untranslatable Lolita linguistic markers, up until the point the subcultural style is defined by Japanese slang expressions and a unique speaking style. The members of the subculture engage an alternative distinct linguistic practice, similar to "a lady's language," overusing honorifics, speaking very slowly, or reinforcing the feminization of certain words. Moreover, new words emerge by clipping, for instance, 「毎日ロリ」, 「土日ロリ」, and 「ロリカワ」, a fact that adds to the linguistic richness of the Japanese language but also emphasizes the difficulty of translating these culturally imprinted linguistic nuances into Western cultural contexts.

Lolita events or group gatherings represent another prevailing narrative direction identified in the blogs; as symbolic forms of the subculture, they crystallize, objectify, and communicate the subculture's values while increasing social cohesion and encouraging both virtual and non-virtual interconnection and friendship between its members.

Regarding the category of Lolita Universe, two key themes have been identified as significant: feminism and escapism.

Enfolding the Story: The Silent Feminist Revolution of Lolita

Given the longstanding and complex historical background, alongside the multilayered globalizing present, the Lolita subculture stands apart by revealing the rebellious nature of cuteness. The members' behavior can be easily interpreted as a form of ideological resistance against the conservative and rigid customs of Japanese culture, and this becomes one of the subculture's digital stories as narrated in the blog posts.

At first glance, the weakness, the frailty, and the pretended innocence, all together with portraying the silly yet pretty girl image might seem antagonist to feminist values; however, the spectacular character of this subculture lies in expressing a forbidden narration and transgressing the classical, most expected and well-known behavioral code for Japanese woman. The followers' stance and attitude are most likely perceived as unnatural, especially outside Harajuku, the temple of the extravaganza, where no rules are to be followed in matters of aesthetics. Thus, the subculture allegorically challenges the existing symbolic order, status, and position of the Japanese woman and converts itself into an ideological force with high potential for a woman. By adopting and otherwise adapting a fashion code with literally no connection to Japan's history and culture, the Lolitas deliberately obscure their origins, refusing and denying the values of their parent culture.

Though the followers are fashioning themselves into innocent and helpless children, there is little to no erotic intention, given that most Lolitas complain of having problems connecting with the opposite sex and state Lolitas' popularity with men is relatively low.

> 「男ウケのためにロリータやめるなんて無理！自分をつらぬく！結婚して子供を産むことも、好きな事を仕事にしてそれを貫くことも同様に尊い！」
>
> It is out of the question to give up Lolita only to be popular with men! I'll stick to it! It's something I devoted myself to, just as precious as doing the job one likes, getting married and having kids![15]

Misako Aoki, known for being the president of the Japan Lolita Association for Lolita fashion, also underlined in one interview for *Huffington Post*, available on her blog, the same facts regarding Lolitas' popularity with Japanese men.

> 「一方で、ロリータ服は「男性ウケが最強に悪いファッション」（青木さん）とされる。青木さん自身、出会い系アプリで知り合った男性からことごとく「ドン引き」されたという。」
> On the one hand, Lolita clothes are known to be the fashion with the worst appeal in men, says Ms. Aoki. Ms. Aoki herself has been rejected by men she has met through online dating applications.[16]

Thus, Lolitas are often perceived in Japan as women who encounter problems in their love life, getting married, or having children. In this context, embracing the fashion subculture can be associated with entitling a feminist declaration by placing oneself outside the normality and the routine.

Besides accepting that one's love life is prone to fail, a Japanese Lolita will also face bullying and cyberbullying. Yet one continues and perseveres in her lifestyle, values, and beliefs.

> 「ロリータ服って、街を歩くだけで指をさされたり勝手にカメラむけられたり笑われたりするし、男ウケなんか興味ないのに「男ウケ悪いよ」なんて謎に上から目線なアドバイス受けたりするし、「ゴスロリ」とか「コスプレ」という正しくない括られ方をしたり、青木さんも嫌な思いをたくさんしてきてると思う。」
> Wearing Lolita clothes, just by walking the streets, you will be laughed at, you will be photographed against your will or pointed at. Even though you have no interest in being popular with men, you will be advised with an arrogant attitude about it. There will be people who can't make the difference between GosuRori and Cosplay.[17]

Hence, most Lolitas choose to ignore the bullying and to stick to their life and style choice as a form of denying and proclaiming their power confiscated by a patriarchal and hegemonic discourse widely representative for Japan nowadays. Their voice, though it remains silent, speaks through fashion, defies the standards and the norms of a male-dominated society, and marks the transgression of the paradigm of the pretty and daring Japanese woman. Their cuteness surpasses challenges and rivals the status and boundaries of traditional cuteness.

Many blog posts tackle another sensitive subtheme of feminism, the relationship between a woman's age, beauty, social worth, and the fashion norms one should follow according to her age.

Similarly, being a Lolita in one's 30s (an age group named "Arasa" in Japan: 「アラサー」) might become problematic for the follower and even contribute to increasing the bullying one has to face sooner or later. The older a follower gets, the harder it becomes to represent and incorporate the Lolita aesthetic successfully. One member admits she grew out of this subculture because she thought it wasn't appropriate anymore for her age and that it was devastating to accept this reality.

> 「突然ですが、わたしは26歳でロリィタファッションを卒業しました。」
> It was sudden, but I grew out of Lolita fashion when I was 26 years old.

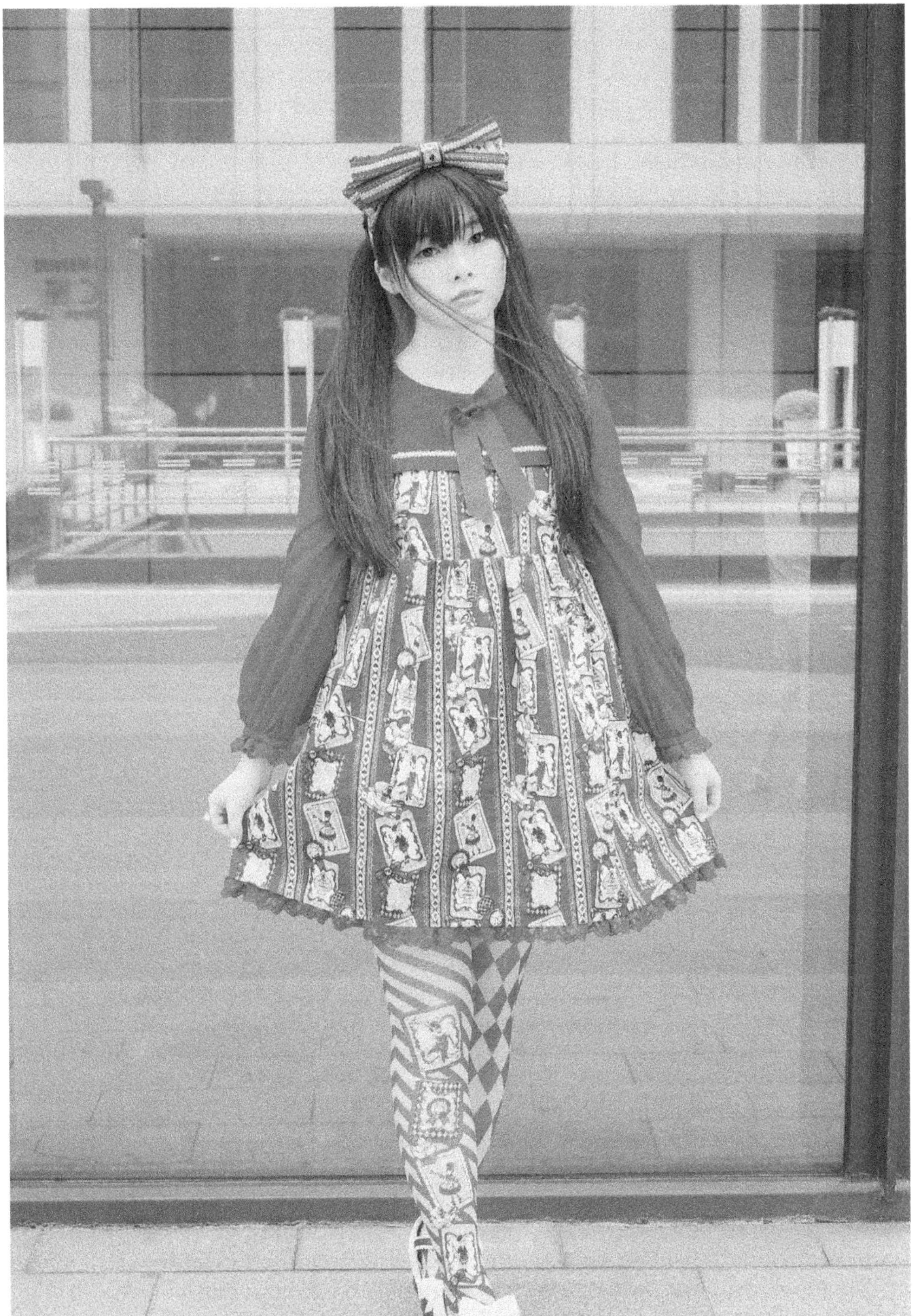

Figure 8.3 Street style: Lolita is taking on the world.

> 「大切なもの失った虚無感に駆られる。これが一番辛い段階です。今まで大切にしてきた価値観や思想を手放す瞬間ってものすごく怖いんです。」
> I was driven by a sense of emptiness and meaningless of having lost something precious. This was the most painful part. It is so terrifying to let go in one moment of values and a way of thinking I have come to cherish until now.[18]

As an attempt to reinforce the empowerment of members in their 30s, the Lolita fashion magazine *Eternita*, dedicated mostly to adult women, appeals to potential readers through a catchy phrase: "What would Alice as an adult wear?" (「大人になったアリスは何を着る？」) thus implying that Alice, as an adult, would persevere in her fashion style, only slightly adapted to the age requirement.

However, other members frequently state on their blogs that Lolita fashion is to stay in their lives forever and reaffirm their unbreakable attachment toward the subculture.

> 「１日でも長くロリィタ着てたい」有坂愛海が語るロリィタ服への情熱」
> Even for one more day, I want to wear Lolita, stated Emi Arisaka, confessing her enthusiasm towards Lolita.[19]

Arisaka is also well known for being a representative personality among the members of the subculture, with longstanding activity as a model, songwriter, fashion editor, and designer. One of the songs she composed, "A 30-Year-Old Lolita in Harajuku" (「アラサーロリータ、原宿に立つ」), is a genuine reflection of the struggles a Lolita around this age must confront:

> 「もう私もアラサーよね
> facebookは憂鬱だなぁ
> 中学のクラスメイトはみんな結婚して子持ち
> 大学の友達はいいお給料でモルディブ旅行
> それなのにあたしは親戚に合わせる顔がない
> 今日も私は一人原宿に立つ
> 三万のスカートゲット！
> 明日からモヤシで暮らす」
> I am already in my 30s,/Surfing on Facebook is depressive/ My junior high school classmates are all married with kids/My university friends have good salaries and take trips to Maldives/Despite this, I am too ashamed to meet my relatives/Today as well I am staying alone in Harajuku,/With a 30,000 yen dress, / Starting tomorrow, I am living off red beans.[20]

These lyrics sit at the heart of some longstanding, deep social tensions that underpin the realistic portrayal of Japanese Lolitas in their 30s and reflect how this clothing style represents a flexible metaphor for concealing the followers' emotional issues and the social problems one encounters over time.

Thus, Lolita fashion becomes the language of a symbolic universe that undoubtedly would face difficulties in crossing the spatial and temporal boundaries of contemporary Japan, while it intertwines specific, culturally, and geographically restricted signs of social and cultural oppression and the arduous struggle for liberation.

Fashioning one's body and spirit according to the subculture's norms, values, and ideas reveals a strong tendency toward escapism as another side of this culturally reconstructed identity that challenges the dominant patriarchal authority. As part of the subculture's digital story, together with feminism, escapism becomes an expression of identity surpassing the aesthetic form.

Escapism: Running Back to Where One Has Not Been Before

Cultivating one's looks according to the aesthetic criteria of the subculture has more than a liberating character. It turns into a manifestation of emancipation, because embracing this subculture diverts considerable attention away from other forms of social action and interaction with non-followers. Lolitas are childish, and this is a common characteristic reflected in both language and behavior. These women not only adopt the dress code of children but also behave like children, despite reaching the age of adulthood: they play with dolls and stuffed animals and eat sweets, mimicking children.

As such, they create for themselves an imaginary self, helping them to cope with their frustrations, anxieties, and depression, while liberating them, even for a short time, from all the pressures imposed by Japanese society on adults. This intended childish and immature self represents one's declaration of refusing or at least temporarily denying adulthood. In consequence, it reflects an escapist attitude when confronted with Japan's rigorous social etiquette.

Worth mentioning as related to this aspect is a minor substyle of the subculture known as Grotesque Lolita, "GuroLoli," that makes use of the grotesque and erotic imagery of a broken doll; the followers use spatters of fake blood atop second-hand white fabrics, ripped bandages, or eye-patches, accessorized with dolls in a similar style.

Although this alternative and rare subgenre comes to counterbalance the pristine sweetness and the excessive feminine cuteness displayed by most Lolitas, it is not easily formatted for daily wear, unlike other styles. Thus, the clothing is worn on rare and special occasions. Their blood-soaked bandages could metaphorically represent emotional and spiritual wounds, a cry for help, or, in other words, through its aggressive visual imagery, it vocalizes more loudly than others do their allegoric complaints to the ones bearing responsibility.

As mentioned before, fashioning one's appearance can also have a therapeutic effect and becomes a way of managing personal dissatisfaction or failure in private life.

> 「私がそこまでロリィタにこだわる理由は多分冴えない現実を忘れられる手段だからだと思う。仕事もずっと非正規で正社員求人にも何度も応募したけどいつも不採用。恋人も生まれてこの方出来たこともないいわゆる喪女である。友達も高校卒業してからおらず、ツイッターでもフォロワーはほとんどなし。そんな誰にも必要とされていない私の現実逃避の手段がロリィタファッションなのだ。」
>
> The reason why I am so obsessed with Lolita is that it is a way to make me forget the dark and dull reality. I have been for a long time, a non-regular worker, and although I have applied countless times to become a regular employee, I have always been turned down. I am an unpopular woman who was never capable of getting a boyfriend. I have no friends since I graduated high school, and I have almost no followers on Twitter. Lolita fashion is a way of escaping reality for me. I am of no use to anyone.[21]

The subculture allows free movement for playing with gender borders without much judgment, a fact that explains the existence of "Ouji" or "Aristocrat" Lolita, a unisex style, embraced both by girls who are fond of a manlier style and boys wishing to approach the clothing as well. Therefore, escaping outside one's gender identity goes both ways, for female and male followers, until the point it frequently intersects with the LGBT subculture and community located in Japan.

The presence of Lolita in Harajuku becomes a ritual that enables the follower's temporary abandonment of his/her usual identity and marks the withdrawal starting point from community participation and interaction. Furthermore, confiscating and contextualizing the Victorian dress code in a postmodern space represents a metaphor for "time traveling," which remains to this day one of the most popular tropes in Japanese popular culture. However, this is nothing more than a failed attempt to recreate and live once again the eternal childhood or, at most, to appropriate the desired identity, as each follower knows that this complete isolation through dress code and behavior that have no historical and cultural connection to Japan is only temporary.

Conclusions

In conclusion, the present chapter aimed to provide a framework for researchers and the public by highlighting recognizable storytelling patterns engaged in by Japanese Lolita followers on their blogs. While exploring the Lolita Universe, two main themes have been identified and analyzed by employing the Japanese language as a pivot of the research: feminism and empowerment, respectively, escapism of one's identity, gender, and spatial and temporal settings.

Even though the Lolita subculture refers to Victorian fashion as a leading cultural source and incorporates many elements of Victorian dress, it lacks historical accuracy to a great degree, which is by no means a priority for its followers.

From the Western point of view, Lolitas are prone to be easily associated with fetishistic imagery and supporting the aggressive sexualization of very young girls by exhibiting their pretended childish innocence as an aphrodisiac. However, if analyzed within the context of contemporary Japanese society and through the lens of the Japanese language, most Lolitas state that being a follower will brand them as unsuccessful in men and probably have severe repercussions on one's love life.

Nevertheless, by choosing to adopt this luxurious yet liberatory fashion style, the wearers challenge the beauty and social ideals promoted by Japanese popular culture, tracing back to the rigid definition of Japanese femininity.

Stating one's individuality in a highly homogenous and collective society, even with the high risk of being marginalized, stigmatized, and bullied, represents a significant narrative line of their digital stories and simultaneously a declaration of empowerment and feminism. Henceforth, the Lolita subculture should be interpreted as reflecting the personality of the wearer rather than merely pointing out a disconnecting and extravagant clothing style. As frequently highlighted in various blog posts, becoming a member represents an act of self-expression, in which one finally has the chance to construct for oneself a new identity, thus reasserting legitimacy, the feminine power of the individual, and control over one's body.

As noticed from the digital stories narrated by the followers on their blogs, the aesthetic cult of the Lolita subculture has a fundamentally contradictory nature. Although it displays unwitting complicity with aesthetic values of Japanese popular culture, by perpetuating to no small extent the stereotypical association of the feminine with childish cuteness, it also defeminizes the body of the wearer by intentionally hiding the mature and womanly silhouette under bell-shaped skirts and blouses with puffy sleeves. Nevertheless, this is a story of a different "kind" of cuteness, which becomes visually aggressive in the realms of a society pleading for homogeneity.

On a side note, a well-known Japanese proverb that accurately reflects this socially and culturally constructed imperative for homogeneity is 「出る杭は打たれる」, meaning, "the nail that sticks out gets hammered down." At first glance, one could think that a Lolita is like this nail and is prone to be oppressed and reduced to silence. However, the other side of the same proverb mentions that 「出過ぎない杭は打たれない」, as in "the nail sticking way too out does not get hammered down." As history has shown to now, the Japanese Lolita metaphorically represents that one nail sticking out too much and thus has many more new stories to share.

Notes

1. Isaac Gagné, "'Hyperfeminine' Subcultures: Rethinking Gender Subjectivity and the Discourse of Sexuality among Adolescent Girls in Contemporary Japan" in *Girls' Sexualities and the Media*, ed. Kate Harper, Yasmina Katsulis, Vera Lopez, and Georganne Scheiner Gillis, 158.
2. Valerie Steele and Jennifer Park, *Gothic: Dark Glamour*. 3rd ed. (New Haven: Yale University Press, 2008), 105.
3. Vera C. Mackie, "Transnational Bricolage: Gothic Lolita and the Political Economy of Fashion," *Intersections: Gender and Sexuality in Asia and the Pacific* 20 (2009), http://intersections.anu.edu.au/issue20/mackie.html.
4. Yuniya Kawamura, *Fashioning Japanese Subcultures* (London: Berg Publishers, 2012), 66.
5. Masafumi Monden, "Being Alice in Japan: Performing a Cute, 'Girlish' Revolt," *Japan Forum* 26 (2), (2015): 266, doi:10.1080/09555803.2014.900511.
6. Ibid, 268.
7. Mary Jane Kehily and Joseph De Lappe, "Lolita: Case Study of a Contemporary Youth Subculture," in *Children, Sexuality and Sexualization* (Bristol: Palgrave Macmillan, 2016), 62.
8. Ibid, 63.
9. Tiffany Godoy and Ivan Vartanian. *Tokyo Street Style* (London: Thames & Hudson, 2008), 144.
10. Anne Peirson-Smith, "O Brave New World That Hath Such Costumes in It: An Examination of Cosplay and the Fantastical Presentation of Self," in *Transglobal Fashion Narratives: Clothing Communication, Style Statements and Brand Storytelling* (Bristol: Intellect Books, 2018), 255.
11. Yuniya Kawamura, *Fashioning Japanese Subcultures* (London: Berg Publishers, 2012), 73.
12. Robert V. Kozinets, "The Field behind the Screen: Using Netnography for Marketing Research" in Online Communities," *Journal of Marketing Research* 39 (1), (2002): 68, doi:10.1509/jmkr.39.1.61.18935.
13. Satu Elo and Helvi Kyngäs. "The Qualitative Content Analysis Process," *Journal of Advanced Nursing* 62 (1), (2008): 108, https://student.cc.uoc.gr/uploadFiles/192-%CE%A3%CE%A0%CE%95%CE%9D407/CONTENT%20ANALYSIS.pdf.
14. Satomi Sakuragawa,„ 自己紹介", さとみたまきの、あれがそれなブログ。 (blog). *Personal Introduction: The Blog of Satomi Tamaki*. Accessed November 2019. https://ameblo.jp/sa-tamaki0515/theme-10075085099.html.
15. Momo, „ロリータ服って可愛いよね", 汚れてもいいの (blog). September 6, 2018. Accessed November 2019. http://yogoretemoiino.hatenablog.com/entry/2018/09/06/172441.
16. Misako Aoki, „ロリータ趣味の女性は「生産性」が低いのか。モデルの青木美沙子さんが出会い系アプリを使って考えたこと", interview by Kazuhiro Sekine, *HuffPost* (newspaper). December 12, 2018. Accessed November 2019. www.huffingtonpost.jp/entry/misako-aoki_jp_5c5d8baee4b0974f75b3bdae.

17. Momo, „ロリータ服って可愛いよね“, 汚れてもいいの (blog). September 6, 2018.
18. White Lily, „元ロリィタが語る、ロリィタを卒業したあとのお話。～大好きだったお洋服とのお別れ～”, interview, *Twinkle* (blog). February 8, 2019. Accessed November 2019. https://twinkletwinkle.love/graduate-lolita/#toc4.
19. Emi Arisaka, „アラサーロリータ、原宿に立つ”, *Emi Arisaka Official Blog* (blog). June 16, 2015. Accessed November 2019. https://ameblo.jp/arisakaemi/entry-12039780881.html.
20. Ibid.
21. Anonymous Author, „私がロリィタにこだわる理由”, *HatelaBo Anonymous Diary*, (blog). February 4, 2015. Accessed December 2019. https://anond.hatelabo.jp/20170204213544.

Bibliography

Anonymous Author, „私がロリィタにこだわる理由," *HatelaBo Anonymous Diary*, (blog) February 4, 2015. Accessed December 2019. https://anond.hatelabo.jp/20170204213544.

Elo, Satu, and Helvi Kyngäs. 2008. "The Qualitative Content Analysis Process." *Journal of Advanced Nursing* 62 (1): 107–115. doi:10.1111/j.1365-2648.2007.04569.x. Available at {https://student.cc.uoc.gr/uploadFiles/192-%CE%A3%CE%A0%CE%95%CE%9D407/CONTENT%20ANALYSIS.pdf}

Gagné, Isaac. 2008. "Urban Princesses: Performance and 'Women's Language' in Japan's Gothic/Lolita Subculture." *Journal of Linguistic Anthropology* 18 (1): 130–150.

Gagné, Isaac. 2013a. Bracketed Adolescence: Unpacking Gender and Youth Subjectivity through Subcultural Fashion in Late-Capitalist Japan. *Intersections: Gender and Sexuality in Asia and the Pacific* 32.

Gagné, Isaac. 2013b. " 'Hyperfeminine' Subcultures: Rethinking Gender Subjectivity and the Discourse of Sexuality among Adolescent Girls in Contemporary Japan." Pp. 157–171 in *Girls' Sexualities and the Media*, ed. Kate Harper, Yasmina Katsulis, Vera Lopez, and Georganne Scheiner Gillis. New York: Peter Lang Pub Inc.

Godoy, Tiffany, and Ivan Vartanian. 2008. *Tokyo Street Style*. London: Thames & Hudson.

Hardy Bernal, Kathryn A. 2011. "The Lolita Complex: A Japanese Fashion Subculture & Its Paradoxes." Master of Philosophy, School of Art and Design, Auckland.

Kawamura, Yuniya. 2012. *Fashioning Japanese Subcultures*. London: Berg Publishers.

Kehily, Mary Jane, and Joseph De Lappe. 2016. "Lolita: Case Study of a Contemporary Youth Subculture." In *Children, Sexuality and Sexualization*. Bristol: Palgrave Macmillan.

Kozinets, Robert V. 2002. "The Field behind the Screen: Using Netnography for Marketing Research in Online Communities." *Journal of Marketing Research* 39 (1): 61–72. doi:10.1509/jmkr.39.1.61.18935.

Mackie, Vera. C. 2009. "Transnational Bricolage: Gothic Lolita and the Political Economy of Fashion." *Intersections: Gender and Sexuality in Asia and the Pacific* 20. Available at http://intersections.anu.edu.au/issue20/mackie.html.

Monden, Masafumi. 2008. "Transcultural Flow of Demure Aesthetics: Examining Cultural Globalisation through Gothic & Lolita Fashion." *New Voices* 2: 21–40. doi:10.21159/nv.02.02.

Monden, Masafumi. 2014. "Being Alice in Japan: Performing a Cute, 'Girlish' Revolt." *Japan Forum* 26 (2): 265–285. doi:10.1080/09555803.2014.900511.

Monden, Masafumi. 2015. *Japanese Fashion Cultures: Dress and Gender in Contemporary Japan*. London: Bloomsbury Publishing.

Peirson-Smith, Anne. 2018. "O Brave New World That Hath Such Costumes in It: An Examination of Cosplay and the Fantastical Presentation of Self." Pp. 253–275 in *Transglobal Fashion Narratives: Clothing Communication, Style Statements and Brand Storytelling*. Bristol: Intellect Books.

Steele, Valerie. 2010. *Japan Fashion Now*. New Haven: Yale University Press.

Steele, Valerie, and Jennifer Park. 2008. *Gothic: Dark Glamour*. 3rd ed. New Haven: Yale University Press.

Suzuki, Mariko. 2007. "Gothic, Lolita, Visual-Kei: First Kansai then the World (via Harajuku)." Pp. 134–165 in *Style Deficit Disorder: Harajuku Street Fashion*, ed. Tiffany Godoy. San Francisco: Chronicle Books.

Online Resources

Aoki, Misako, „ロリータ趣味の女性は「生産性」が低いのか。モデルの青木美沙子さんが出会い系アプリを使って考えたこと", interview by Kazuhiro Sekine, *HuffPost* (newspaper). December 12, 2018. Accessed November 2019. www.huffingtonpost.jp/entry/misako-aoki_jp_5c5d8baee4b0974f75b3bdae

Arisaka, Emi, „アラサーロリータ、原宿に立つ", *Emi Arisaka Official Blog* (blog). June 16, 2015. Accessed November 2019. https://ameblo.jp/arisakaemi/entry-12039780881.html

Momo, „ロリータ服って可愛いよね", 汚れてもいいの (blog). September 6, 2018. Accessed November 2019. http://yogoretemoiino.hatenablog.com/entry/2018/09/06/172441.

Sakuragawa, Satomi, „Jikoshoukai", „さとみたまきの、あれがそれなブログ。" (blog). Accessed November 2019. https://ameblo.jp/sa-tamaki0515/theme-10075085099.html.

White Lily, „元ロリィタが語る、ロリィタを卒業したあとのお話。～大好きだったお洋服とのお別れ～", *Twinkle* (blog). February 8, 2019. Accessed November 2019. https://twinkletwinkle.love/graduate-lolita/#toc4.

Part III

Spaces and Technologies

9 Constructing an Affective Retail Space

Bodily Engagement With a Luxury Fashion Brand Through Spatial and Heritage Storytelling

Peng Liu and Lan Lan

This chapter explores the cultural encounter of consumers with a luxury fashion brand as a way of promoting its business, where the engagement is reflected through the bodily movement within a designed affective retail space. The investigation focuses on the Chinese brand Wuyong, founded in 2006 by the Chinese fashion designer Ma Ke. Wuyong products are only sold through Useless Space. Established in 2014, the store is housed in an old factory building located in the central district of Beijing, which has been redesigned into a culture-centered retail precinct. This area, comprising a group of four brick buildings, was a printing factory established in 1954 and had been operating until 2011. The factory was relocated in 2012 due to the decline in its business, as well as the excessive noise and odor being emitted. The local government in collaboration with a private company subsequently reopened the area in 2014 as a cultural precinct called 77 Culture Garden, which features the four buildings and the courtyard formed in the center with the main gate facing east. Within this precinct, there are shops, as well as a gallery, theater, and museum. Useless Space occupies a single building on the left of the courtyard next to the main gate (Figure 9.1).

The Wuyong brand's retail space is dedicated to providing consumers with experience of handmade products through multiple means of cultural exhibition, spatial interaction, and shopping in one place, where the main message of the space speaks to all the craftspeople in China,[1] with all the products advocating handmade techniques of spinning and weaving, hand-stitching, plant dyeing, printing, and so forth. In addition to a custom production service where the ordered garments such as oversized apparel take extra time to complete, the handmade products sold at Useless Space, mainly garments for women, along with a selection of unisex and children's apparel, bed linen, and daily artifacts, are all ready to wear/use. Furniture items need to be ordered and measured first and picked up at a later date. The space occupies the whole ground floor of the building with a total of 12,000 square meters. Of particular note, the space is divided into two sections—digital tools are used in the outer section to facilitate heritage storytelling, while the inner section has been set up to generate a spatial narration; both sections engage the body with/in the space to create affective bodily experience in communicating the message of the brand. Accordingly, our investigation examines bodily experience in the retail space in terms of heritage storytelling drawing on museological and curatorial studies, as well as spatial storytelling with reference to affective heritage architecture studies.

Our analysis of Useless Space finds that the space offers customers a culturally contextualized retail experience and focuses on how the ensuing bodily experience reflects the Chinese cultural heritage being communicated in the space through not

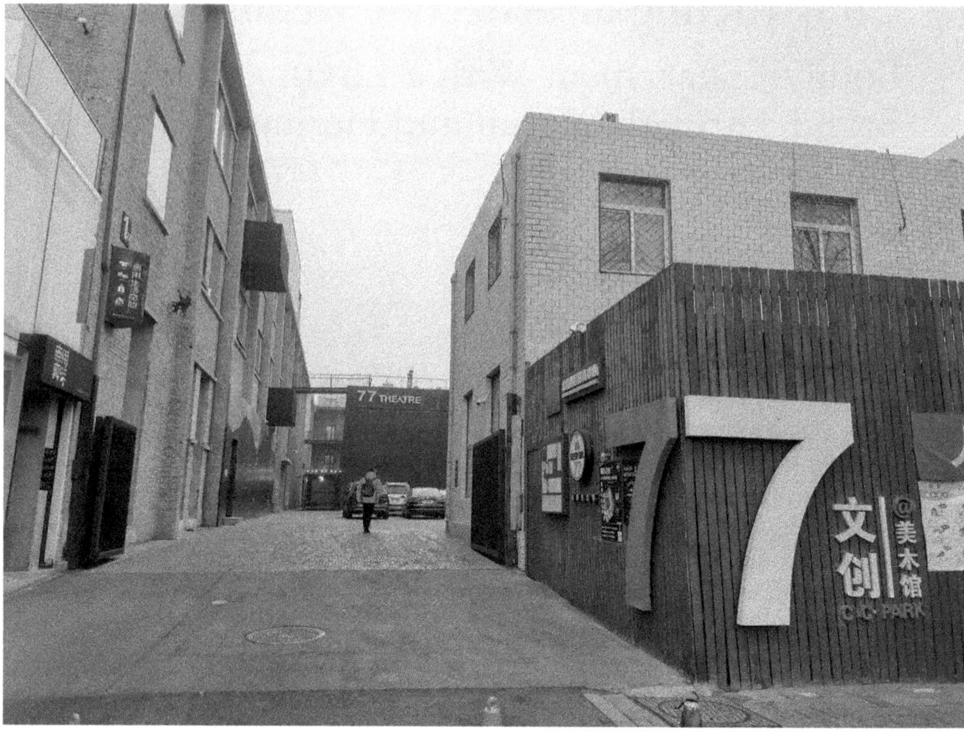

Figure 9.1 View from the entry point of 77 Culture Garden directly facing the 77 Theatre located at the far end. Useless Space is the brick building on the left, with the entrance facing the center courtyard.

Source: Photo: Peng Liu, December 2019.

only engagement with the physical cultural artifacts situated in the narrative space but also their virtual presentation via digital tools, which is further reflected in the bodily movement through this space. Our field visits to Useless Space were conducted in April 2017 and March, July, and December 2019. The primary field study for the in-store walkthrough was conducted in March 2019 by Peng Liu, who was born and raised in Beijing with western education, and whose research is primarily interested in bodily engagement with spatial constructs.[2] The account of the bodily engagement with/in Useless Space has been written from his firsthand perspective. By examining affective experience as our fieldwork methodology in this way, we acknowledge that bodily engagement is both personalized and subjective.

This chapter aims to articulate how the heritage and spatial narrations have been constructed, as well as how the storytelling is being enabled and supported through the use of visual culture and digital technology. Therefore, the body is brought into the retail space to experience heritage storytelling through the display artifacts and their enhancement by the digital tools in the outer space and spatial storytelling through walking in the inner space. The two narratives and the intersection between them not only tell affective stories that provoke the Chinese traditional sense in the space but create embodied responses toward the fashion brand. The cultural encounter of the walkthrough concludes with a reminder that the space is in the end a retail space offering a culturally contextualized retail experience. The retail display reflects how the space has been set up for purchases to be made and how it functions to shape consumer experience through the designated walking route. The staging of the showrooms as domestic environments toward the end of the walking experience is a constitutive part of this spatial logic and cultural narration.

Heritage Storytelling, Spatial Storytelling, and Using Visual Culture and Digital Technology to Construct Affective Storytelling

Storytelling, or narrative in academic terms, has been widely discussed and used as a research methodology across various disciplines in the humanities in recent decades, such as cultural studies, geography, history, psychotherapy, museology, and education. As "[h]uman beings are natural storytellers,"[3] storytelling allows the expression of personal interpretation and the interpretation of various perspectives. The method of theorizing from personal experience is a common practice in qualitative research in apprehending the world, in which narrative is an important means to reflect individual experience in order to form the line of the argument. As psychologist Jerome Bruner notes with regard to how storytelling organizes social and cultural experience, "[t]he organizing principle is narrative rather than conceptual"—"people organize their experience in, knowledge about, and transactions with the social world" through storytelling.[4] There is always a concrete point of view in stories. While allowing for the readers'/listeners' own personal experiences to be connected to the stories, storytelling "make[s] the concrete details of the story represent something much larger"[5] and complex in order to understand the world. As Leslie Bedford points out, storytelling "open[s] up a space into which the listener's own thoughts, feelings, and memories can flow and expand . . . [inspiring] an internal dialogue and thus ensur[ing] a real connection"[6] to the world. That is the power of storytelling, which becomes an essential approach to making sense of humans in relation to the world, as well as a way to realize ourselves.

Heritage Storytelling

This chapter investigates the application of heritage storytelling at Useless Space, particularly in relation to the outer section that has an exhibition area. This section comprises an exhibition space, a designated area with traditionally handmade products available for sale next to the entry, and a desk counter at the far end. The exhibitions are curated by Ma Ke. Each exhibition is normally held for six months, but *Yong Geng Hao Geng Shao De Dong Xi, Guo Geng You Yi Yi De Sheng Huo* (To Have Greater Meaningful Life by Having Better and Fewer Things), as shown in Figure 9.2, specialized in the display of handmade crafts and ran for twelve months, from April 2019 to March 2020. In general, the exhibition themes focus on traditional handcrafts and sustainable materials favored by the brand, with display objects ranging from heritage antiques to recently collected daily artifacts by the designer.

Despite the connotation of the name of the space, which is interpretive and metaphorical in a Chinese cultural context,[7] the retail space at Useless Space is, by contextualizing Chinese culture, capitalizing on topical discourses in the global fashion industry, particularly with regard to advocating traditional handmade techniques and artifacts. The outer section of the retail space facilitates and capitalizes on this

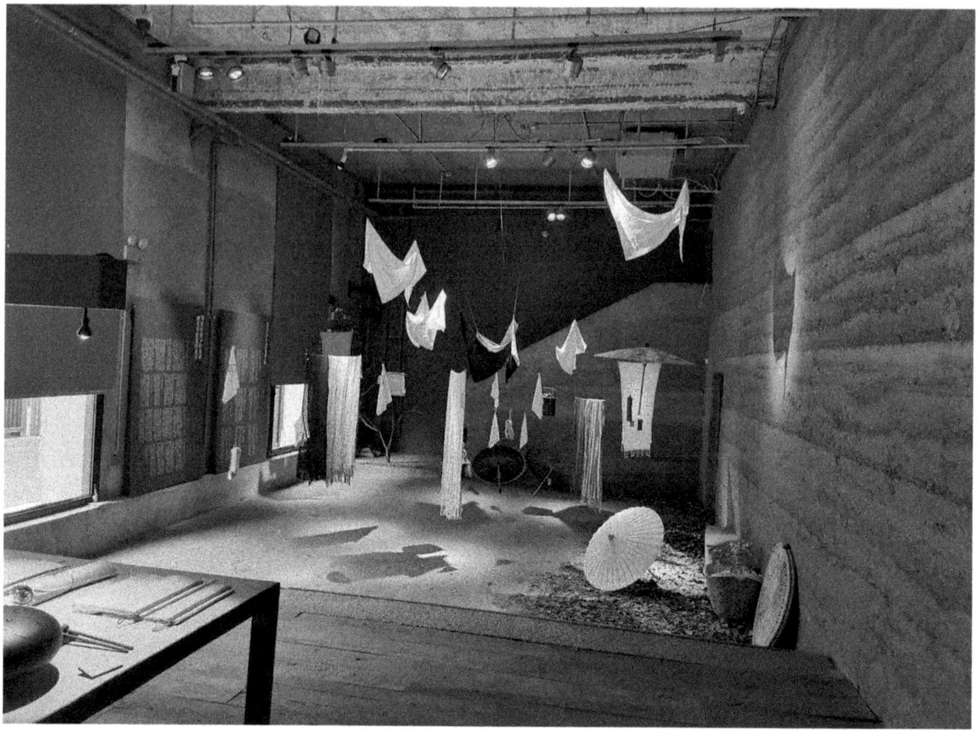

Figure 9.2 Handmade artifacts are on display in a museum-like setting. Each object is attached with a label providing essential information, such as the materials, techniques, cultural background, and so on. Posters of the exhibition are stuck to the wall on the left, with a doorway and stairs on the right which provide access to the inner space. Track lighting is also visible overhead. There is a digital projector and screen mounted on the far corner opposite the stairs. The wall on the right divides the space into two.

Source: Photo: Peng Liu, December 2019.

message through heritage storytelling supported by digital tools in the exhibition area. As Kimberley Wilson and Cheryl Desha note, "heritage storytelling can contribute to long-term cultural, environmental and economic outcomes through facilitating cultural connectedness, participatory engagement, behaviour change."[8] Cultural interpretations are offered to the heritage and cultural artifacts displayed in the exhibition and the handmade items in the sale section via posters with extended explanations, with labels on each display item (Figure 9.3), and as explained by the staff; those objects are understood and capitalized through heritage storytelling. This storytelling always offers concrete details of the story that situates the object in a concrete scenario involving place. Therefore, the heritage storytelling functions to contextualize the objects with reference to the historic place they were originally situated in. In other words, the place is reattached to and realized together with the cultural artifact through heritage storytelling, and it is precisely "through such interpretation that tangible [cultural artifacts and] historic places begin to have meaning"[9]—or, in Dawson Munjeri's words, "the tangible can only be understood and interpreted through the intangible."[10]

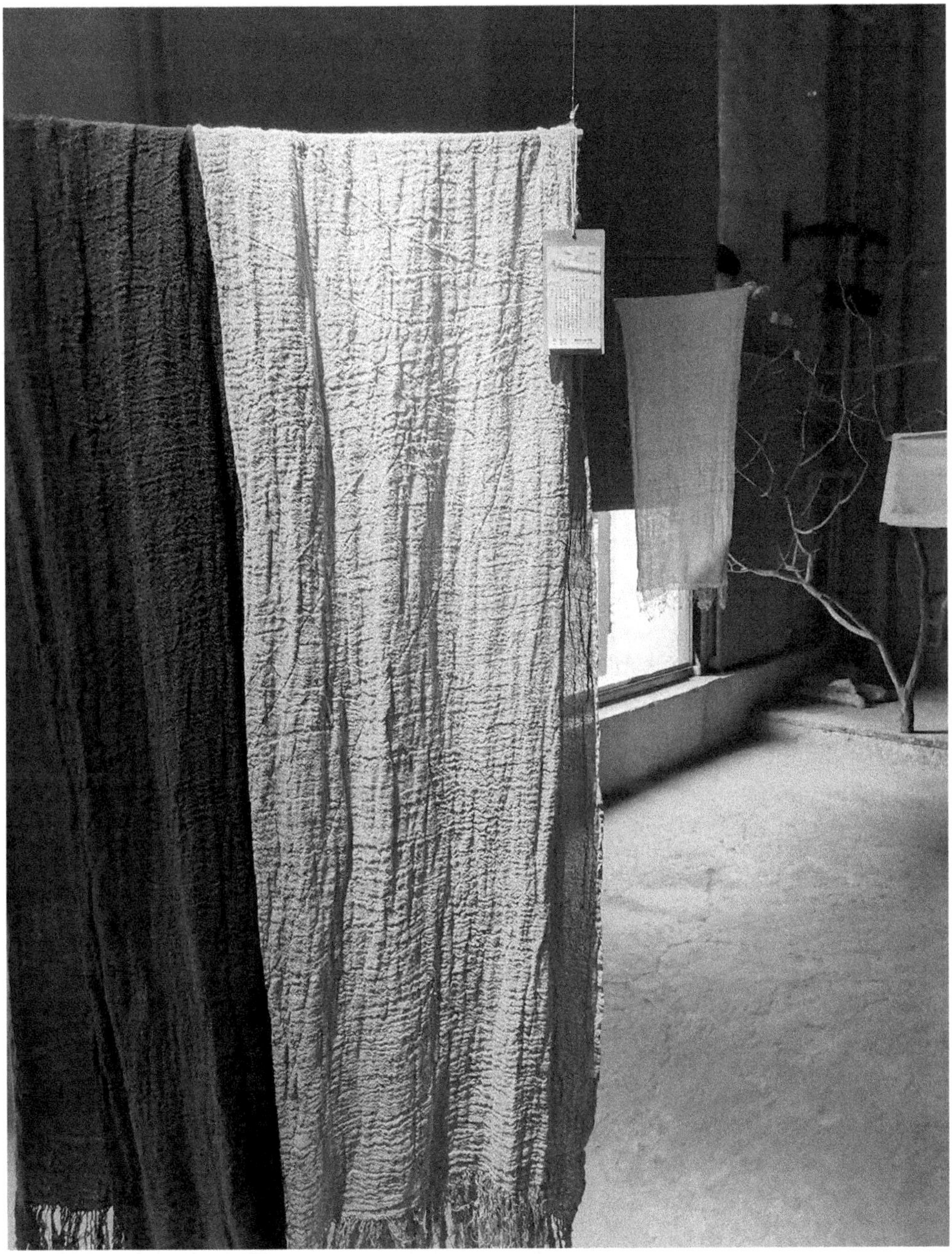

Figure 9.3 An explanatory label is attached to every displayed item.

Source: Photo: Peng Liu, December 2019.

In the case of Useless Space, these objects are specially sourced for each exhibition that presents both the handmade tangible materials and the intangible stories behind them, which in turn reflect the latest fashion collection being sold in the space featuring those particular traditional techniques and sustainable materials. For example, the exhibition we previously visited in April 2017 called *Xun Yi Wen Dao* (Seeking Clothing as Pursuing Truth) featured more than fifty handmade garments selected from a nationwide call for entries. Each garment is presented along with audio equipment with which visitors can hear the story of the garment via earphones while visually perceiving the materials and the patterns. The audio story is read out by a third-person narrator, and the content mainly focuses on the experience of wearing the garment, reflecting the emotional connection with it, as well as the materials and techniques used, such as a garment made with an expensive material embroidered with traditional patterns for a great-grandma's wedding. Moreover, a special event was held on October 29, 2016, during the exhibition opening at Useless Space, with a total of six invited makers from the exhibition selection who shared not only the technical aspects of making their garments but also stories about how those garments have lasted through wars and other difficult times or how the exhibited garments have been passed down through three or four generations in their family history.

Spatial Storytelling

While heritage storytelling at Useless Space offers interpretations of the display objects and provides their social and cultural context, another approach is employed in the form of spatial storytelling, which is used to allow the body to be affected in the cultural space. This chapter investigates spatial storytelling and the associated bodily experience in the inner section of Useless Space. The spatial storytelling engages the body in the mediated environment where the historic and curated space is the essential communication medium, in which the discovery of the bodily experience in the spatial storytelling plays out as a non-linear narrative.[11] By doing so, the inner space facilitates the message of the brand through shaping bodily experience in the designated spatial narrative space. The design uses spatial narration to "uncover, collate and communicate the historic [and cultural] details of buildings and the surrounding place . . . [and] evolve the existing story,"[12] which is perceived by my body while walking through the inner section. Useless Space is created from a former printing factory that was originally designed for and reproduced by the interaction between building materials, operating machines, and workers over decades; the remnants of the factory, such as steel tubes, columns, and walls, already have stories—the space is historically inherited and culturally embodied. The preserved visual elements in the mediated environment is inherited by the designer and turned into part of the cultural space with the presence of handmade artifacts as domestic settings that create impact upon my body, which will be elaborated on later in the chapter. The domestic recreation comes across as an artifice that seems to jar with the industrial remnants; however, my body does not experience the space as seemingly divergent histories/stories. Rather, the preserved visual elements prompt my body to wonder and imagine the former life of the space, which involuntarily applies to the heritage/cultural objects in the present space, too. For example, my body not only interacts with *a* wooden dining table displayed in the space but appreciates *the* wooden top of the table that has been repurposed from an old door panel collected during the designer's field trip. Such experience with heritage/cultural objects in terms of both their current form and previous life is the cultural quality that has been created spatially at Useless Space, an experience that is coherent with the industrial remnants in terms of bodily experience as a non-linear narrative. The seemingly divergent histories/stories between industrial remnants and collected cultural artifacts, therefore, are captured, mixed, and processed within my body and released back to the space through bodily movement, to affect the space and be affected by the space. The interaction between my body and the space makes the space dynamic so that the cultural encounter can take place to produce affect. The interaction, seen as bodily movement in response to the narrative space, is accordingly an affective encounter that occurs via bodily engagement with/in the cultural/heritage space.

Using Visual Culture and Digital Technology to Construct Affective Storytelling

Visual culture and digital technology are used to construct affective storytelling at Useless Space. In the context of this chapter, visual culture can be regarded as all manifestations of the visual environment and experience in the affective cultural space. According to Nicholas Mirzoeff, "[t]he constituent element of visual culture's practice is the visual event,"[13] in which audiences seek information, meaning, or pleasure at the interface with visualized media. More importantly, "the event is the effect of a [cultural and social] network in which subjects operate and which in turn conditions their freedom of action."[14] In other words, while the study on the structure of an image, for example, remains a focal point in visual culture studies, it is the relationship between images/visual environment and audiences within the cultural and social network that is to be evaluated for the cultural significance. That is to say, in the case of Useless Space, rather than decoding a particularly Chinese traditional pattern on the cultural artifacts in the space or identifying the definitive meaning of the pattern in a particular cultural context, visual culture has been used to demonstrate how the visually perceived cultural environment functions in the web of connotations and cultural significance that make the retail space affective and create impact upon the body. The affective encounter between the body and the cultural space through storytelling produces affect that is reflected in the ensuing bodily movement in the retail space. The cultural space is also made affective with the mediation and extension of visual experience through technology.

Many museums today are increasingly focusing on the communication of heritage via digital storytelling to engage their audiences and create or curate affective spaces for encountering stories.[15] Digital technology provides new ways for concepts to be communicated. Carl Hogsden and Emma Poulter consider digital experience "an alternative reciprocal model,"[16] while Laura King, James F. Stark, and Paul Cooke regard the digital encounter as a "different category from physical encounters."[17] For Michael Heim, "virtual worlds . . . do not simply reproduce the existential features of reality but transform them beyond immediate recognition."[18] In short, the use of digital technology offers a type of new bodily experience.

Of particular relevance to this chapter is bodily experience in relation to digital enhancement in the space, where "authenticity, authority, interpretation, representation, knowledge, and affect"[19] are co-produced during the affective encounter with the material objects in the space. In the case of Useless Space, the use of digital technology acts as an enhancement of the material objects in co-producing the affective outcome. The visual environment is culturally contextualized in relation to our bodies as culturally embodied beings through visual culture, while the use of digital tools extends this relationship through technological mediations which enhance our experience beyond the physical space.

Chinese Luxury Fashion Brands

Recent discussions on Asian fashion designers and brands have been analyzed from various perspectives, including education,[20] social changes,[21] immigration,[22] and, most commonly, the economy.[23] This chapter leans more toward the cultural and aesthetic approach to Chinese fashion, such as the ethnicity of Chinese native designers in relation to a larger global fashion world[24] and "national fashion in a global age."[25] Published literature on the study of Chinese fashion history shows a binary point of view in understanding Chinese fashion. For example, Simona Segre Reinach notes that designers born in China before the 1980s have a more " 'serious' and scrupulous approach in presenting China and 'Chineseness,' [while] the younger ones . . . are full of deconstructive self-irony."[26] Hazel Clark notes the two design stereotypes associated with Asian fashion designers are those who use "traditional Orientalist and Chinoiserie motifs, such as dragons or exotic birds" as cultural representation and those who use "the loose body-modifying shapes introduced by the Japanese avant-garde designers in the 1980s"[27] in their designs. This chapter, however, investigates the case of Useless Space as a Chinese contemporary fashion practice engaging with consumers through bodily experience in the affective space via storytelling.

Chinese luxury brands created by mainland Chinese designers have been developing rapidly in recent years, such as Ji Cheng's La Vie, Liangzi's Shuliang, Wang Yiyang's Chagang, and Ma Ke's Exception and Wuyong. These brands have been further grouped into two styles in traditional study: one is fascinated with reflecting ancient philosophical ideology in their design, while the other aims to be more modern by using everyday objects.[28] Both styles, which move away from the visual representation of traditional Chinese symbols and instead focus on the ideas of the Chinese spirit in their designs, are considered progressive by Christine Tsui. For example, Tsui suggests that Uma Wang and Wang Yiyang can be interpreted as Zen designers, as seen in the former's use of fabric textures and in her knitwear line and the latter's Chagang collection, which offers feelings of "peace, simplicity, and calm."[29] Their designs are "in the form of pale and/or neutral colors, natural fabrics, and simply cut shapes that flow with the body,"[30] which imply ancient Chinese ideology. Although further investigation is needed to consolidate the relationship between the particular spiritual ideology and the manifest design practice, Tsui's approach in understanding the development of Chinese brands in past decades proposes a changing view over the persistent sense of "Chineseness"[31] reflected in the apparel and embedded in Chinese designs and brands.[32] In other words, there has been a change from an old style of cultural representation of "an *explicit, direct*, and *exterior* form" to a new style of "a *subtle, indirect*, and *hidden* form" of spiritual expression.[33] Or, as noted by Segre Reinach, Chinese designers have made the "move towards a common aesthetics which is China-based while speaking an international language . . . as a new configuration for contemporary fashion in China,"[34] and such form switching can be understood as Chinese native designers' response to the changing paradigm in terms of comprehending the world through bodily engagement and lived encounter. This chapter focuses on Chinese fashion designers who voluntarily/involuntarily respond to the changing paradigm in their practice by emphasizing affective bodily experience in the lived encounter between the design/brand, the retail space, and the consumers through the use of storytelling facilitated by visual culture and digital technology.

Ma Ke's design practice and philosophy for Wuyong and Useless Space reflect her ethical commitment to natural and sustainable living, as well as the history and culture of China. Of particular note, her designs are all characterized as handmade, and the products sold in the retail space are made from sustainable and recyclable natural materials, such as cotton, linen, and silk. At the same time, focusing on the handmade contextualizes the brand in relation to Chinese traditional culture in that all the products are made using traditional techniques, such as hand embroidery and natural dying. Moreover, according to the staff at Useless Space, the net income of everything sold at the store after deducting the cost of management is used to support traditional craftspeople. For instance, new designs are sent to the craftspeople who are commissioned to produce the artifacts or hired to work at the studio in Zhu Hai. According to the staff, the space has been designed by Ma Ke to showcase the handmade artifacts and, in turn, Wuyong's brand values by association. The concept of the traditional handmade item as a reflection of Chinese ancient philosophical ideals is essential to the branding for Wuyong and applied to every object displayed in Useless Space in order to create a cultural space, one that is in the end offered as a culturally contextualized retail experience to customers. The implication of positing handmade artifacts as a brand value is to see them as heritage items or practices, thereby promoting the handmade as a signifier of traditional craft/culture that needs to be maintained today. In doing so, the store's space and in-store storytelling are mobilized in Useless Space.

Such in-store storytelling is commonly used and represents an important aspect in fashion and fashion branding. Many established international luxury brands, such as Hermès, Chanel, and Burberry, either use their own history or attach themselves to a historic period where stories can be told in their stores to provoke visitors' memories and feelings. This particular approach allows a multisensorial experience to take place whereby the brand is received through multiple means; hence a physical, social/cultural, and sentimental connection can be made between customers and the brand through spatial experience. Consequently, the drive of store design toward the focus on branding pays more attention to offering cultural experience within stores, so much so that, for example, the boundaries between design and art, retail space and gallery space,[35] virtual and actual, and so on are increasingly becoming indistinct in fashion retail. Many other international fashion brands have used and harnessed these indistinct boundaries to varying degrees as a fashion retail and branding strategy, such as the Fondation Louis Vuitton;[36] Fondazione Prada Milano;[37] Dior's exhibition at the Victoria and Albert Museum, London;[38] and Cartier's exhibition at The Palace Museum,[39] located in the Forbidden City, Beijing. The indistinct boundaries that affect bodily experience within Useless Space will be examined in the next section.

Bodily Experience in Useless Space

The store is a rectangle-shaped retail space occupying an entire ground floor of the building. The space is divided into two sections by an additional internal brick wall. When my body enters the building, I encounter the outer section of Useless Space, which is open to the public during opening hours. In this outer section, facing the inner wall, there is an exhibition area on my left, with a sales section on my right, as well as stairs leading to a counter area upstairs. The inner section is located on the other side of the brick wall and cannot be seen directly; an appointment must be made in advance to visit it. Internally, Useless Space has an approximately six-meter-high ceiling that allows a mezzanine floor to be added, which further subdivides the space into smaller sections, with a flight of stairs to access them. Notably, elements such as fire hydrants are present in certain spots, because of the building safety regulations, and some details of the old factory, such as various factory steel tubes running overhead, have been intentionally retained and redesigned in coherence with the overall space making.

I am assigned a staff member at the reception area upon my arrival, and I later observed four other visitors in two groups during my two-hour stay. According to the staff, the number of appointments varies from day to day. As explained, the aim of requiring appointments to visit the inner section of Useless Space is for crowd control purposes and to ensure a relatively discreet visit without interruption from other visitors. This amplifies the anticipated bodily experience in the space, as the walking route is predetermined and the walking pace is moderated by the staff; so, too, the bodily movement is guided. The guided tour is offered to both first-time visitors and regular or returning customers, who are mainly Chinese. The personalized appointment is also offered to international visitors, with English-speaking staff available. The space is primarily for display and sales purposes, with the studio, where the handmade garments and daily artifact products are made, located elsewhere. There are no traditional sales assistants in the space; instead, every visitor is assigned a Useless life consultant, who accompanies the in-store guided walking journey while telling stories about the design of the space, the concept of the brand, and the products for sale, which are all closely associated with Chinese traditional culture.

Outer Section

While waiting for my assigned consultant to arrive, I begin exploring the exhibition area, which is approximately 400 square meters, located in the outer section. The exhibition was called *Sheng Huo Zai He Chu? Yang, Luo Tuo, Mao Niu He Mu Ren Yuan Qu De Bei Ying* (Where to live? The back of sheep, camel, yak and shepherd) and themed on an ethnic group. The space is filled with objects displayed in a museum-like setting, featuring cultural and heritage artifacts made using handmade techniques.[40] These artifacts are culturally contextualized and connected using digital technology.[41] Video documentations play in a loop using a digital projector, with a screen and speakers installed in one corner of the rectangular space. The videos have been shot and edited by the Wuyong team, recording various scenes such as the designer visiting craftspeople in various Chinese villages. Apart from the footage showing the natural environments of the field visits, which take us temporarily out of the museum-like setting, the projected video visualizes scenarios featuring the daily process of making handmade products using traditional techniques, such as natural dying, and, more importantly, the way the artifacts are used by people in their authentic home environments. The video also includes conversations between the designer and the craftspeople, who tell stories associated with the making process and the cultural significance of the objects. The use of the digital projector presents the interaction of the artifacts with the human body, which allows the objects to be variously shown in context: on the move, covered in dust, placed in relation to other objects, and even presented as partially broken, as part of the changing world.[42] The digital restoration of the relation of the artifacts to the human body situated in a narrative environment can be an important perspective for understanding the cultural object, one that allows us to perceive the artifacts as moving objects in interaction with bodily actions rather than as fixed, isolated, cleaned, and protected objects in a museum environment. The heritage artifacts in the display, therefore, are contextualized in the narration, and the narration is visualized through the use of the digital projector.

In this respect, the cultural artifacts and heritage stories are perceived via digital enhancement alongside the material objects themselves and create new experience upon my body. It is equally important, too, to acknowledge that engaging with digital tools does not mean that the material objects are left behind. Rather, such engagement contributes to a reading of Useless Space as a digitally enhanced heritage narrative, one that provokes the new bodily experience aimed at by the brand. As noted by King, Stark, and Cooke, the digitally enhanced heritage narrative is

> a qualitatively different *kind* of experience, generating a set of values that are dependent on both the original material, place or object, as well as the medium through which it is presented . . . [and] offer[s] . . . [a] new form of engagement. . . . [A]s a consequence, the real value of digital engagement with digital heritage lies in a different *type* of encounter, which seeks not to replace the tangible aspects of material culture, but rather to add additional explanatory layers to visitor experience.[43]

King, Stark, and Cooke further note that "digital tools should enhance rather than replace the cultural value located within objects, artifacts, and places."[44] The case of Useless Space shows that the virtual experience of Chinese traditional artifacts, made available by the implementation of digital technology, provokes a particular cultural sense in my body, specifically as one who was born after New China had been established. The Chinese central government's advocacy on recalling tradition, such as culture confidence,[45] not only offers a recurrence of traditional culture/ideology in contemporary China to what it was before 1949 but provokes a new bodily experience of reconciliation with tradition reappearing in contemporary society—or, in other words, a response to the new experience of the absence of the culture in the twenty-first century. That is to say, the reappearance of traditional culture/value in the contemporary time, manifested as sustainable materials and handmade techniques in Wuyong products, provokes a sense of the absence of the traditional culture on my body, besides the traditional cultural value itself. The artifacts displayed in Useless Space are a reminder of the traditional culture and techniques that have been absent for decades and how the use of digital tools enhances the way to present and interpret the sense of absence, as the digital itself is perceived to be both virtual and actual. Therefore, the realization of the cultural absence is also a part of the affective encounter while walking in Useless Space, where my bodily experience is enhanced by digital storytelling as a type of new experience. My body, therefore, reacts strongly, in an emotional sense, in the space, not to the cultural heritage being told and visualized in the stories but to the realization that my body can connect to this culture, albeit with the feeling that it is at once familiar, yet strange.

Inner Section

When the assigned consultant arrives, my walking journey through the store begins in a ritualistic way. I am asked by the female consultant to push open the double-panel timber entry door at the brick wall on the ground floor, which marks the starting point of my body entering the inner section of Useless Space. The touching of the wooden surface becomes my very first sensorial experience of exploring the curated narrative of the inner space. Stepping through the doorway and immediately moving into the atrium, which is illuminated by natural light from the windows on the other side of the building, my body is surrounded by a simple and unadorned environment. I experience the sense of an everyday Chinese traditional lifestyle, which is consolidated by the domestic display setting later on, that is quite different from experiencing the space of royal palaces, for example, despite the lack of clarity about the exact period or historical context of the setting I am in. After spending a few quiet minutes allowed by the consultant during which my body can walk around within an approximately fifteen-square-meter area to explore the details of the atrium, including the texture of the ground, walls, plants, reflections on various surface, and so on, my body starts to engage with the quality of the space, recalling associated memories.

Allowing time and space for self-reflection is important in storytelling, as stated previously, and in Useless Space, the spatial narration affects my body through multisensory means whereby my bodily movement is co-producing affect with the spatial narration in the space, accompanied with stories told by the consultant. Under her constant watch, while my body is still in motion, the first story relates to the wooden entry door. The door panels were collected along with many other handmade daily artifacts and transported back to the retail space by the designer while conducting field studies in villages across rural China where ethnic groups still live by their traditions. This story, along with the space filled with cultural artifacts in a domestic setting, reminds me of the documentaries I had watched in the outer section, reiterating the ideas associated with sustainable materials and traditional handmade techniques. Images of the previous field scenes emerge in my mind in concert with the stories I am being told and merge with my multisensory experiences in that space; random memories are recalled and my body gains a better connection with the space.

The brand advocates the concept of handmade and sustainable products, which is expressed via the stories told and discussed with the consultant while walking. She watches my bodily movement and mindfully answers my queries while inserting relevant ideas and concepts when appropriate. There is invariably a connection between the stories and products for sale in the space. For instance, the consultant describes how the crew had to overcome difficulties during field trips to visit the traditional craftspeople in remote villages, such as walking miles without transportation, and then goes on to explain that the cultural objects discovered and collected on these trips have been subsequently redesigned by the designer and that these items are available for sale. These new designs are sent to the craftspeople, who are commissioned to produce them. While talking, the consultant determines when and how much advocacy of the brand is to be disclosed based on her observation of my bodily expressions conveyed through the change of tone, facial expressions, and bodily gestures in response to the stories and concepts while moving through the space. In other words, the walking experience is the combination of visualizing cultural objects, hearing narrative stories, and touching cultural artifacts and redesigned handmade products while moving through Useless Space.

The guided walking experience passes through different sections, which entail changes in the quality of light, the scale of space, the air flow, and so forth. After spending a few moments in the atrium, my body is directed into a dark narrow corridor where I can easily touch the surrounding stones while walking through an approximately ten-meter distance. The darkness of the corridor fades when my body steps out at the other end, with direct sunshine through the building windows illuminating the area which has a high ceiling. Almost immediately, however, my body is asked to enter the adjacent living room that is furnished with traditional everyday artifacts, such as a bed, tables, and chairs collected by the designer and placed in a dark environment. My body is left alone in the room for around five to ten minutes with the door shut and encouraged to walk further down to the end of the room. The rather dark room is approximately twenty square meters illuminated by a little window and two dimmed lamps. My body is immersed in this staged environment. I walk around and touch the relocated traditional furniture;[46] the tactile impression is active, but the dark environment limits my vision. The quiet moment allows more memories to be recalled while the just-told stories are still in the ear.

When time is up, my body is brought out of the dark living room and directed to a kitchen area located in the middle of the inner ground floor. There is reasonable illumination, and I can see every artifact in detail. There is a huge dining table (a repurposed door panel), which is surrounded by chairs, a couch, cabinets, cooking tools, and so on, that are all handmade from sustainable materials. While the kitchen setting is consistent with the presentation of the everyday traditional lifestyle that I have encountered thus far, nonetheless, there are price tags attached to the displays here, which is my first encounter with them since entering the inner section of Useless Space. As soon as the price tags appear, my body realizes the space is starting to shift its emphasis from a curated setting dominated by the designer's ideas and philosophies to a retail space. Even as the visual and spatial narration starts to change, my cultural body is still in the moment of resonating with the stories attached to the displayed cultural materials while already physically stepping into the sales space. The freshly gained affective bodily experience toward the cultural space in understanding the brand inevitably also applies to the handmade products available for sale. The emotional response to these stories ultimately comes to rest upon the retail products in the space.

Conclusions

My walking journey continues through a corridor to reach the other end of the building, where stairs connect to the upper floor and where a few more items appear, such as a traditional loom, which offer more stories to restate the brand's concept. At this end of the space, both on the ground and the mezzanine floor, which is the final section before leaving the inner space, I realize that the space presents a series of domestic settings, such as bedrooms for adults, a bathroom, a living room, and a reading room on the ground floor, as well as a child's room and child's living room of an equivalent size located upstairs, which are fully furnished with handmade products available for sale. Visitors can view and try on the ready-to-wear/use garments, bed sheets, accessories, and so on, for immediate purchase, except for the furniture, which needs to be ordered and picked up at a later date. Useless Space maintains its visual and cultural consistency throughout and concludes in the upper floor with the realization for visitors that this is in the end a retail space. The bodily experience in the affective space, constructed through heritage and spatial storytelling facilitated by visual cultural and digital technology, is in the end a culturally contextualized retail experience. In other words, the brand builds connection with customers through bodily experience in the retail space.

Wuyong and Useless Space are both evidently part of the global trend of the return of customization and the handmade in questioning "*fast fashion* and *fast luxury*."[47] The research in this chapter engages with bodily experience in the retail space to better understand how the brand shapes consumer experience through storytelling as a contemporary approach in fashion. The retail space is seen as an historical and cultural narrative that engages consumers through walking, in which the cultural power of the space moves consumers in a predetermined way. New bodily experience in the retail space is created via multiple means of storytelling, whereby the provocation of the cultural sense prompts an emotional response to the space and so toward the brand. Through the use of storytelling to create a sense of cultural richness that is to be associated with the brand, the space allows visitors to first observe the designer's field trip experience on the digital projector while supplementing the cultural awareness with direct reference to the collected cultural artifacts exhibited in the museological setting. Following this, the inner space invites visitors to interact with the handmade cultural objects, comprising artifacts collected from the field trips and redesigned products in a contemporary setting. The in-store space is staged like the domestic scenes previously seen in the documentaries, which in turn reinforces the cultural connection with the brand. The staging of the upstairs rooms as domestic environments is a constitutive part of the spatial logic and narration. A sense of Chinese culture is being accumulated while visitors experience Useless Space, whereby cultural awareness and bodily understanding toward the brand are built up along the walk, which makes the brand culturally rich and affective. The 'luxury' aspect of the brand is not passively perceived by but completed through the bodily experience in the space. The retail space facilitates the brand's concept as a message to respond to current contestations and conversations in the fashion industry while capitalizing on this concept as a commodity.

Acknowledgments

This work was supported by the Faculty Research Grant of the Macau University of Science and Technology.

Notes

1. Ma Ke, "馬可：一個用衣裳造船的設計師 (Ma Ke: A Designer Creates Ships from Clothing)." Interview by Zhong Weizhi, *Sou Shen Ji*, May 14, 2018. www.huxiu.com/article/244121.html.
2. The author's recent research focuses on the body and examines lived bodily experience and embodied knowledge in affective architectural space. See: Peng Liu, "Walking in the Forbidden City: Embodied Encounters in Narrative Geography," *Visual Studies* 33, no. 2 (2018): 144–160; and Peng Liu, "Body in the Forbidden City: Embodied Sensitivities and Lived Experience in the Affective Architecture," in *Affective Architectures*, ed. Jacquelyn Micieli Voutsinas and Angela Person (New York: Routledge, 2020).
3. Leslie Bedford, "Storytelling: The Real Work of Museums." *Curator: The Museum Journal* 44, no. 1 (2001): 28.
4. Jerome S. Bruner, *Acts of Meaning* (Cambridge: Harvard University Press, 1990), 35.
5. Bedford, "Storytelling," 29.
6. Ibid.
7. 無用 (useless) is a term in "人皆知有用之用，而莫知無用之用也", originally quoted from "Ren Shi Jian," in *Zhuang Zi* (B.C. 369—B.C. 286), which refers to the Chinese ancient philosophical and dialectical approach to understanding the world as a whole and as ever-changing, instead of being seen from a fixed, binary point of view as either useful or useless.

People tend to pay attention to useful things but cannot realize that the so-called 'useless' aspects have a larger meaning. See: https://baike.baidu.com/item/%E4%BA%BA%E9%97%B4%E4%B8%96/2110596?fromtitle=%E5%BA%84%E5%AD%90%C2%B7%E5%86%85%E7%AF%87%C2%B7%E4%BA%BA%E9%97%B4%E4%B8%96&fromid=10162802#2_3.

8. Kimberley Wilson and Cheryl Desha, "Engaging in Design Activism and Communicating Cultural Significance through Contemporary Heritage Storytelling: A Case Study in Brisbane, Australia," *Journal of Cultural Heritage Management and Sustainable Development* 6, no. 3 (2016): 273.
9. Ibid, 272.
10. Dawson Munjeri, "Tangible and Intangible Heritage: From Difference to Convergence," *Museum International* 56, nos. 1–2 (2004): 13.
11. Liu, "Body in the Forbidden City."
12. Wilson and Desha, "Heritage Storytelling," 273.
13. Nicholas Mirzoeff, "The Subject of Visual Culture," in *The Visual Culture Reader*, 2nd edition, ed. Nicholas Mirzoeff (London and New York: Routledge, 2002), 6.
14. Ibid, 6.
15. See: Carl Hogsden and Emma Poulter, "Contact Networks for Digital Reciprocation," *Museum & Society* 10, no. 2 (2012): 81–94; and Laura King, James F. Stark, and Paul Cooke, "Experiencing the Digital World: The Cultural Value of Digital Engagement with Heritage," *Heritage & Society* 9, no. 1 (2016): 76–101.
16. Hogsden and Poulter, "Contact Networks," 82.
17. King, Stark, and Cooke, "Digital World," 86.
18. Michael Heim, *The Metaphysics of Virtual Reality* (London: Oxford University Press, 1993), 32.
19. Fiona Cameron and Sarah Kenderdine, "Introduction," in *Theorizing Digital Cultural Heritage: A Critical Discourse*, ed. Fiona Cameron and Sarah Kenderdine (Cambridge, MA: MIT Press, 2007), 5.
20. Eric Wilson, "Asian-Americans Climb Fashion Industry Ladder," *The New York Times, Fashion & Style* section, September 4, 2010, www.nytimes.com/2010/09/05/fashion/05asians.html.
21. Juanjuan Wu, *Chinese Fashion: From Mao to Now* (Oxford: Berg, 2009).
22. Thuy Linh Nguyen Tu, *The Beautiful Generation: Asian Americans and the Cultural Economy of Fashion* (Durham, NC and London: Duke University Press, 2011).
23. Linda Welters and Arthur C. Mead, "The Future of Chinese Fashion," *Fashion Practice* 4, no. 1 (2012): 13–40.
24. Hazel Clark, "Chinese Fashion Designers: Questions of Ethnicity and Place in the Twenty-First Century," *Fashion Practice* 4, no. 1 (2012): 41–56.
25. Simona Segre Reinach, "The Identity of Fashion in Contemporary China and the New Relationships with the West," *Fashion Practice* 4, no. 1 (2012): 59.
26. Ibid, 61.
27. Clark, "Chinese Fashion Designers," 43.
28. Christine Tsui, "From Symbols to Spirit: Changing Conceptions of National Identity in Chinese Fashion," *Fashion Theory* 17, no. 5 (2013): 579–604.
29. Ibid, 587.
30. Ibid, 588.
31. Ibid, 586.
32. Antonia Finnane, *Changing Clothes in China: Fashion, History, Nation* (New York: Columbia University Press, 2008).
33. Tsui, "Symbols to Spirit," 590–591, original italics.
34. Segre Reinach, "Contemporary China," 63–64.
35. See: Robert V. Kozinets, "Brands in Space: New Inking about Experiential Retail," in *Brick & Mortar Shopping in the 21st Century*, ed. Tina Lowrey (New York: Psychology Press, 2007), 1–13; Charles Mclntyre, "Designing Museum and Gallery Shops As Integral, Co-Creative Retail Spaces within the Overall Visitor Experience," *Museum Management and Curatorship* 25, no. 2 (2010): 181–198; and Jeff Weinstein, "Is Clothing Art?" in

Fashion Statements, ed. Ron Scapp and Brian Seitz (New York: Palgrave Macmillan, 2010), 69–72.
36. Fondation Louis Vuitton, www.louisvuitton.cn/zhs-cn/art/espaces-louis-vuitton#.
37. Fondazione Prada, www.fondazioneprada.org/?lang=en.
38. Victoria and Albert Museum, "Christian Dior: Designer of Dreams," February 2–September 1, 2019, www.vam.ac.uk/exhibitions/dior-designer-of-dreams.
39. The Palace Museum, "Beyond Boundaries: Cartier and the Palace Museum Craftsmanship and Restoration Exhibition," June 1–July 31, 2019, https://en.dpm.org.cn/exhibitions/current/2019-04-17/2933.html.
40. Official images are available at www.wuyong.org/Default.aspx.
41. The digital technology has been used to provide additional cultural context in terms of the cultural objects and act as a connective tool between displays to construct a correlated cultural background for the exhibition.
42. One of the past exhibitions, titled *Bu Wang Lai Shi Lu* (Do Not Forget the Way You Came) and opened in April 2018, exemplified the use of digital projectors to showcase more than 400 pairs of handmade shoes.
43. King, Stark, and Cooke, "Digital World," 85–86, original italics.
44. Ibid, 94.
45. Li Xia, ed, "文化自信—習近平提出的時代課題 (Cultural Confidence–An Era Topic Raised by Xi Jinping)." *Communist Party Member*, December 31, 2019. www.12371.cn/2016/08/05/ARTI1470380463155466.shtml.
46. We acknowledge that Useless Space may be critiqued for the removal of heritage objects from their original context and displaying them in another one. Nevertheless, this chapter leans towards how the space shapes the overall consumer experience of it as a retail space rather then being solely concerned with associated ethical issues about the cultural appropriation and decontextualization of heritage objects displayed in a museum/gallery space, for example.
47. Segre Reinach, "Contemporary China," 60, original italics.

Bibliography

Bedford, Leslie. "Storytelling: The Real Work of Museums." *Curator: The Museum Journal* 44, no. 1 (2001): 27–34.

Bruner, Jerome S. *Acts of Meaning*. Cambridge: Harvard University Press, 1990.

Cameron, Fiona, and Sarah Kenderdine. "Introduction." In *Theorizing Digital Cultural Heritage: A Critical Discourse*, edited by Fiona Cameron and Sarah Kenderdine, 1–18. Cambridge, MA: MIT Press, 2007.

Clark, Hazel. "Chinese Fashion Designers: Questions of Ethnicity and Place in the Twenty-First Century." *Fashion Practice* 4, no. 1 (2012): 41–56.

Finnane, Antonia. *Changing Clothes in China: Fashion, History, Nation*. New York: Columbia University Press, 2008.

Fondation Louis Vuitton. "Louis Vuitton ESPACE Culture and Art Space." www.louisvuitton.cn/zhs-cn/art/espaces-louis-vuitton#.

Fondazione Prada. "The Porcelain Room Chinese Export Porcelain." www.fondazioneprada.org/?lang=en.

Heim, Michael. *The Metaphysics of Virtual Reality*. London: Oxford University Press, 1993.

Hogsden, Carl, and Emma Poulter. "Contact Networks for Digital Reciprocation." *Museum & Society* 10, no. 2 (2012): 81–94.

King, Laura, James F. Stark, and Paul Cooke. "Experiencing the Digital World: The Cultural Value of Digital Engagement with Heritage." *Heritage & Society* 9, no. 1 (2016): 76–101.

Kozinets, Robert V. "Brands in Space: New Thinking about Experiential Retail." In *Brick & Mortar Shopping in the 21st Century*, edited by Tina Lowrey, 1–13. New York: Psychology Press, 2007.

Li Xia, ed. "文化自信—習近平提出的時代課題 (Cultural Confidence–An Era Topic Raised by Xi Jinping)." *Communist Party Member*, December 31, 2019. www.12371.cn/2016/08/05/ARTI1470380463155466.shtml.

Liu, Peng. "Walking in the Forbidden City: Embodied Encounters in Narrative Geography." *Visual Studies* 33, no. 2 (2018): 144–160.

Liu, Peng. "Body in the Forbidden City: Embodied Sensitivities and Lived Experience in the Affective Architecture." In *Affective Architectures*, edited by Jacquelyn Micieli Voutsinas and Angela Person. New York: Routledge, 2020.

Ma Ke. "馬可：一個用衣裳造船的設計師" (Ma Ke: A Designer Creates Ships From Clothing)." Interview by Zhong Weizhi. *Sou Shen Ji*, May 14, 2018. www.huxiu.com/article/244121.html.

Mclntyre, Charles. "Designing Museum and Gallery Shops As Integral, Co-Creative Retail Spaces within the Overall Visitor Experience." *Museum Management and Curatorship* 25, no. 2 (2010): 181–198.

Mirzoeff, Nicholas. "The Subject of Visual Culture." In *The Visual Culture Reader*, 2nd edition, edited by Nicholas Mirzoeff, 3–23. London and New York: Routledge, 2002.

Munjeri, Dawson. "Tangible and Intangible Heritage: From Difference to Convergence." *Museum International* 56, nos. 1–2 (2004): 12–20.

Segre Reinach, Simona. "The Identity of Fashion in Contemporary China and the New Relationships with the West." *Fashion Practice* 4, no. 1 (2012): 57–70.

Taylor, Bradley. "Reconsidering Digital Surrogates: Towards a Viewer-Orientated Model of the Gallery Experience." In *Museum Materialities: Objects, Engagement, Interpretations*, edited by Sandra Dudley, 175–184. London: Routledge, 2010.

The Palace Museum. "Beyond Boundaries: Cartier and the Palace Museum Craftsmanship and Restoration Exhibition." June 1–July 31, 2019. https://en.dpm.org.cn/exhibitions/current/2019-04-17/2933.html.

Tsui, Christine. "From Symbols to Spirit: Changing Conceptions of National Identity in Chinese Fashion." *Fashion Theory* 17, no. 5 (2013): 579–604.

Tu, Thuy Linh Nguyen. *The Beautiful Generation: Asian Americans and the Cultural Economy of Fashion*. Durham, NC and London: Duke University Press, 2011.

Victoria and Albert Museum. "Christian Dior: Designer of Dreams." February 2–September 1, 2019. www.vam.ac.uk/exhibitions/dior-designer-of-dreams.

Weinstein, Jeff. "Is Clothing Art?" In *Fashion Statements*, edited by Ron Scapp and Brian Seitz, 69–72. New York: Palgrave Macmillan, 2010.

Welters, Linda, and Arthur C. Mead. "The Future of Chinese Fashion." *Fashion Practice* 4, no. 1 (2012): 13–40.

Wilson, Eric. "Asian-Americans Climb Fashion Industry Ladder." *The New York Times, Fashion & Style* section, September 4, 2010. www.nytimes.com/2010/09/05/fashion/05asians.html.

Wilson, Kimberley, and Cheryl Desha. "Engaging in Design Activism and Communicating Cultural Significance through Contemporary Heritage Storytelling: A Case Study in Brisbane, Australia." *Journal of Cultural Heritage Management and Sustainable Development* 6, no. 3 (2016): 271–286.

Wu, Juanjuan. *Chinese Fashion: From Mao to Now*. Oxford: Berg, 2009.

Zhuang, Zi. "Ren Shi Jian." *Zhuang Zi*, December 20, 2019. https://baike.baidu.com/item/%E4%BA%BA%E9%97%B4%E4%B8%96/2110596?fromtitle=%E5%BA%84%E5%AD%90%C2%B7%E5%86%85%E7%AF%87%C2%B7%E4%BA%BA%E9%97%B4%E4%B8%96&fromid=10162802#2_3.

10 New Old Stories

The Temporal Landscape in Fortnum & Mason's Digital Heritage Storytelling

Federica Carlotto and Andrea Tanner

> Being 310 years old, we have hundreds of stories to tell.
>
> (Fortnum and Mason, 2017)[1]

Introduction

As highlighted by the extant body of research on corporate heritage, companies and brands that leverage their past take a very specific approach to time.[2]

Instead of merely 'going back' with an archaeological focus to retrieve facts as they happened, heritage companies 'go back while looking ahead' and select past-related cues in light of their relevance, which they hope to retain in the future. Heritage companies, in other words, have "a concern with the future."[3]

In assessing relevance, however, such companies also need to have a deep sense of the time present. Arguably, relevance is not intrinsic to historical provenance; rather, it is contextual; that is, it lies in the 'eyes of the beholder.' In order to turn their history into heritage material, therefore, companies need to identify historic cues or traits that are meaningful to current stakeholders. As the business context is constantly changing, heritage creation becomes an ongoing search for a 'past content with a present salience.'[4]

Looking specifically at marketing, heritage creation both informs and merges into heritage storytelling, meant here as the organized and purposeful formulation of heritage narratives situated within a market-oriented communication landscape. Effective heritage storytelling requires marketers to relate closely to the consumer audience and to shape the heritage content in a way that resonates with their semantic and emotional view of the past.[5] Equally important is the management of the storytelling process, with the selection of meaningful channels, timing, and modes through which the heritage content is narrated.

This chapter explores the case of London luxury retailer Fortnum & Mason's (F&M) heritage storytelling as delivered on the company's website and main social media networks (SMNs). Specifically, the chapter aims to provide an analytical account of the temporalities underpinning F&M's digital discourse about heritage.

After outlining the case methodology, the chapter will move on to provide an overview of F&M as a "heritage brand"[6] with a high "heritage quotient,"[7] showing how F&M has been developing stewardship of its past, incorporating heritage in its value systems, positioning, marketing mix, and communication. The main body of the chapter will then illustrate the conceptual framework created to navigate the storytelling landscape of F&M and discuss the empirical results of the e-fieldwork conducted on the digital platforms. Here, F&M heritage storytelling will be assessed according to the temporal narratives and engagement dynamics it generates.

The conclusion will highlight this case's contribution to the academic literature on corporate heritage and digital storytelling, and signpost implications for strategic heritage management.

The Heritage Stewardship at Fortnum & Mason

F&M is a 300+-year-old store that has operated on the same site since its foundation. It first sold candles and developed a reputation as a 'magasin de comestibles,' offering customers food and drink from across the globe. In the 1920s and 1930s, the shop expanded into a department store, including some surprising new specialties, such as the Expeditions Department. While it has adapted to changing times over the past three centuries, its core business concentrates largely on the same sorts of products that its founders first offered. The flagship store in Piccadilly is self-consciously historical in both architecture and interior design, and the front-of-house staff dress in a traditional manner, as do the staff in the three Fortnum's outlets in St Pancras, Royal Exchange, and Heathrow Airport, Terminal Five.

The company heritage has been largely uncovered through exploitation of the in-house corporate archive, augmented by research in outside archive repositories, oral history interviews, and secondary published sources. The company archivist and deputy also purchase past products and packaging for use in storytelling and in visual merchandising in store and online. The posts are situated within the marketing department, where are also found the design manager and the social media team.

New members of staff are introduced to the history of the company on their first working day in the hope that the stories will capture their imaginations and prompt strong identification with the brand. This includes direction toward the historical content of F&M's social media activity. Activation is prompted by requests for information on specific products or past activities from both inside and outside the business. Stakeholders within the business include the board, retail, human resources, hospitality, customer services, and buyers, as well as the host marketing department. External queries come from journalists, museum curators, amateur genealogists, and academics, in addition to customers.

Storytelling has been at the heart of the brand since at least the mid-Victorian era, when the little advertising the company commissioned emphasized the age (and therefore reliability) of the business.[8] At the beginning of the twentieth century, when the founding families had died out and F&M came under new management, the longevity of the company became a central feature of advertising, perhaps to reassure customers that their favorite shop was not going to change.[9] The history of the business, and the stories behind the goods for sale (both real and imagined), dominated the direct mail advertising campaigns that Fortnum's pioneered in the 1920s and 1930s, masterminded by the public relations genius of Hugh Stuart Menzies and Marcus Brumwell.[10] When the company celebrated its 250th anniversary in 1957, a short illustrated history pamphlet, *The Delectable History of Fortnum & Mason*, was made freely available to all and any enquirers, and the catalogues and advertising for the whole year concentrated on the venerable history of the company.[11] The Tercentary in 2007 inspired a whole range of products and a short history book, filled with stories about products, staff, and customers, heavily illustrated from the archive.[12] The book was sold in store and through the company website and put into Christmas hampers, and its stories were the basis of interviews with the domestic and international press and customer Tercentenary events. Both significant anniversaries saw a two-way traffic of storytelling; the memories shared with customers prompted letters and telephone calls from customers, recounting their stories of encounters with F&M, many from childhood—and without exception fond and positive.

Since then, the company website and social media output have become insatiable users of historical stories. Nurturing of the company's past and the stories gleaned therefrom is undertaken within the archive department both physically and digitally. The most heavily used sources have been digitized, the concomitant tagging and metadata allowing every stakeholder to conduct efficient access to the information in the collection. Heritage is an important element of social media campaigns, reaching out to old and new audiences. To a large extent, the archivists are the guardians of the brand, ensuring integrity in the use of the company's heritage and compliance with brand values, and the social media team are the interpreters of those to a global audience. Catriona Maclean of the team describes it thus:

> We are trying to recreate the in-store magic online into comms and online. The silver lining is that in those platforms and with those audiences, the numbers are overwhelming in comparison to visitors to the store. Many of the people we are reaching online may never have been to the store. They might dream of coming here, but they are still so excited about the brand—they are in love with it.[13]

The Fieldwork

The case is based on the thematic analysis[14] of the digital content shared on F&M's website and main SMNs: Facebook, Instagram, and Twitter.

In order to profile the F&M corporate approach to heritage storytelling, we first organized a group interview with the company's marketing and social media team. The interview took place at F&M headquarters in Piccadilly on May 17, 2019, and it lasted approximately one hour. The questions followed a semistructured order to enhance the natural flow of the conversation and allow the spontaneous exchange of opinions between the three interviewees.

Subsequently, we moved to F&M's digital platforms. The e-data collection was carried out in July 2019 and concerned textual and visual content shared by the company and other online users: articles, posts, comments, replies, tweets, hashtags, emojis, pictures, and videos. The website was examined in its entirety, as was Instagram, for a total of 2743 posts covering a six-year timespan (from May 24, 2013, to July 22, 2019). The search on Facebook and Twitter covered a balanced number of posts, 829 (from the end of 2018 to July 24, 2019) and 821 (from May 31, 2019 to July 24, 2019), respectively.

In the first stage of the data collection, we included every item containing past-related cues—old visuals or words such as "vintage," "history," "tradition." The data corpus was further screened in order to isolate 'rich items,' that is, communicative units with semantic pertinence and/or generating meaningful resonance. As a result, 452 items were validated for thematic analysis.

Despite the numerical exiguity, the final data set has been of substantial quality for our research. The website has provided a coherent overview on heritage as integrated into the brand's official story. Twitter and Facebook serve primarily as digital catalogues for F&M products—mostly food and drink. In such commerce-driven platforms, past-related cues are implemented as products' descriptors, but they don't seem to generate any significant response from the audience. Among the SMNs, Instagram has proved to be the most valuable tool to map users' engagement with heritage storytelling.

To orient our data collection, we elaborated a framework based on constructs from digital sociology, corporate heritage studies, and consumption theories. The framework was also put into use in the subsequent stages of data coding and theme searching. Our analytical lens has been zooming from micro-units of meaning—for instance, a single emoji—to the composite semantics of a conversation thread, where the meanings of individual comments blended into a composite, polyphonic narrative. A certain degree of interpretive flexibility, however, was maintained to capture undetected themes or codes' clusters.

The interpretation of the data worked two ways: from the framework to the fieldwork and from the fieldwork to the framework. The thematic analysis presented here integrates the patterns of meaning deductively identified through the desk research as well as those that have been driven by empirical insights from the digital platforms.

Digital Heritage Storytelling: Conceptual Framework

The framework proposed for the analysis of F&M's storytelling (Figure 10.1) addresses the heritage as storytelling content and explores it in interaction with other infrastructural elements of the storytelling process—the communication context, the storyteller–audience dynamics, and the horizons of reference.

Content: Heritage

Our understanding of heritage builds on the taxonomy of past developed by Hudson and Balmer.[15] This model profiles brand heritage along four main facets, each one characterized by a specific corporate approach to time both past and present:

- Structural Heritage: focuses on the linear causation between past and present. This dimension covers the details surrounding the brand's origins, that is date, circumstances, key people in its foundation. As in the sentences "Fondè en . . ." or "Established in . . . ," it stresses the legacy dimension of heritage.
- Implied Heritage: outlines the continuity of past attributes to the present. The display of historical artifacts in corporate museums, the celebration of brands' anniversaries, the reference to a brand's age or timespan of activity ("Since . . .") validates the congruous development of a brand through time. Here, it emphasizes the longevity dimension of heritage.
- Reconstructed Heritage: works with the individual's tension toward an historical past that in comparison with the present times is remembered as or imagined to be better/more appealing. The revisiting of a brand's past products, packaging, and advertising campaigns evoke consumers' nostalgic feelings ('the good old days'). It is the longing dimension of heritage.
- Mythical Heritage: transcends the past in its historical occurrence, focusing on its archetypical forms as residing in our collective imagery (the Victorian era, the Versailles Époque). Mythical veneer products, consumption environments, or communication contents connect with a past that is not necessarily part of the brand's actual history. Heritage, here, crystallizes as legend.

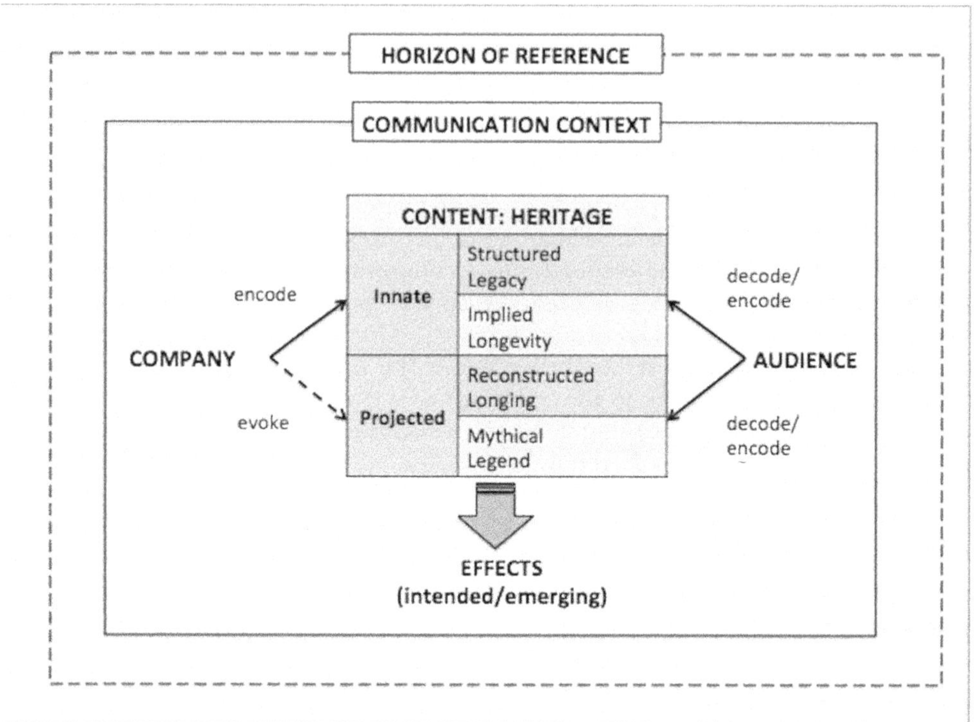

Figure 10.1 Framework of analysis.

In a storytelling context, structural and implied heritage can be considered "innate"[16] facets, because they are based on facts that are inherent to a company's actual history. Conversely, reconstructed and mythical heritage are "projected"[17] facets, as they are generated by the audience, based on their perceptual connection with the past that is evoked.

The Communication Context

Every communication act happens in a specific context. The analysis of any storytelling practice thus cannot overlook its spatio-temporal coordinates, as they impact both the production of the content and the way storytelling as a practice is carried out. Here, we are concerned with Internet communication technologies. Far from being mere transmission channels, Internet media have generated an entirely new communication environment, with its own "cultural forms,"[18] power dynamics, and expressive modes.

By compressing the space, the Internet media have exponentially increased the outreach and connectivity between online users, widening the audience with which every storyteller interacts. Additionally, the digital environment—and especially SMNs—has subverted the storytelling agency. In traditional marketing, storytelling is firmly in corporate hands, with the audience being at the receiving end of the communication process. Online, consumers are not only reading content about the brand but are also sharing their own content. As such, digital storytelling breaks the unidirectional, encoding-decoding order of meaning circulation in classic media,[19] as the audience is decoding others' contents while simultaneously encoding their own. Online users are, in fact, "co-creating brand stories."[20]

The spatial compression of the web sphere also accelerates the tempo and the speed of content creation. Online communicative acts—feeds, comments, stories—work on both immediacy and frequency, with their communicative currency existing and being exhausted in the "hyper-now":[21] the very present moment.

As a result, digital storytelling can be defined as a networked and interactive "produsage"[22] of units feeding—and fed by—likes, comments, and reposts by multiple sources.

These aspects, however, have a different relevance depending on the media considered. With reference to the platforms under analysis, there are certainly differences in terms of content variability, authorship, delivery mode, and context. The content provided on a corporate website is mainly the final output of a one-way storytelling process: it is usually self concluded, and it is relatively consistent in time. This also provides the users with a general context of reference for the individual stories presented on the website.

Very different is the environment of Facebook, Instagram, and Twitter: their content is generally self-concluded in a post, with no narrative continuity built in. This is particularly true of Instagram, with its focus on visuals and its Stories feature, and Twitter, whose communicative units are limited to 160 characters. The content is ephemeral and very quickly consumed. Both platforms, however, rely on the active participation of their users. As such, storytelling here gets close to a conversation, continued and amplified through the users' comments, reposts, and hashtag naming.

Heritage Storytelling at Work

In analyzing storytelling in action, there are still a couple of elements to keep in mind. First, as mentioned previously, heritage is a "tripartite"[23] temporal construct, where the time past is evaluated from a present perspective for future value. While the past provides the content for heritage storytelling, only the present dimension is able to make it resonate. It is the present, in other words, that makes the past "as we know it."[24] Time present, with its trends, practices, beliefs, and symbols, is therefore the temporal horizon of reference for both the company and the audience in encoding and decoding heritage.

Second, corporate storytelling is always purposeful, that is, directed to specific audiences to obtain certain effects. The actual effects generated by a company's storytelling, however, will depend on their communication strategy and style, the timing of storytelling, and the audience's actual decoding. Scholarship has profiled the general effects of corporate storytelling for both brands and audiences, according to short-term and long-term outcomes.[25] Here, we consider the effects based on the agency of content encoding/decoding. When creating storytelling content, a company might envision certain effects to be generated: we name those 'intended' effects. 'Emerging' effects are instead those actually generated only at the moment of the storytelling.

The chapter now moves to explore the temporal landscape, or "timescape,"[26] of F&M heritage content as emerging from the company's digital platforms.

Rich and Augmented: The Timescape of F&M Heritage Storytelling

In shaping history into heritage content, F&M pays specific attention to the innate dimensions of heritage, that is, legacy and longevity.

The company's founding date is already included in the mark: "Est. 1707," and it is further explored as an element of continuity on the Twitter bio: "Since 1707, Fortnum & Mason has been home to joy-giving things, exceptional food and unforgettable experiences" (@Fortnums, Twitter).[27]

Details related to provenance and continuity also feed into the description of F&M individual products: Empire Tea was "[f]irst sold at Fortnum's in 1934 and once presented to Queen Mary by Empire Tea Growers" (@Fortnums, Twitter, July 18, 2019);[28] Scotch Eggs were "[f]irst invented at Fortnum's in 1738"(@Fortnums, Twitter, June 20, 2019); the Breakfast Blend "has been a teatime favourite since the mid-1800s" (@Fortnums, Twitter, July 16; June 10 & 26, 2019); Potted Welsh Rarebit is "[m]ade to the same Fortnum's recipe for decades"(@Fortnums, Twitter, June 5, 2019). By clarifying both the historical origins of its products and their congruity in time, F&M ultimately validates the authenticity of the brand.

Discourses of longevity also play an important role in legitimizing F&M's status in the luxury industry. In a piece about the Diamond Jubilee Tea Room on the company website, afternoon tea is presented as "[a] Fortnum's tradition for centuries, and delicious proof of our endless obsession with extraordinary tea."[29] Here, F&M's expertise in tea purveying appears to stem from an "obsession with extraordinary tea" that has stratified in time. The term "extraordinary," in addition, positions F&M in the luxury tier of the business, conferring this quality to related offerings—such as afternoon tea. Past visits to F&M tea salons by Queen Elizabeth II and French couturier Yves Saint Laurent, as documented on SMNs, are for the audience particularly persuasive testimonials of F&M prestige: "Even the queen loves fortnums" (Instagram, March 1, 2017); "was good enough for Queenie" (Instagram, March 1, 2017); "Of course [YSL] had great taste so he drank the best tea in the world xxx" (Instagram, July 27, 2017). As the adjective "endless" suggests, however, this passion for excellence trans-passes any historical coordinate or temporal contingency, crystallizing the F&M brand as an absolute in the tea sector. This is fully acknowledged by SMNs users: "The only 'tea' in London" (Facebook, May 21, 2019); "Still the best tea in the world" (Facebook, May 21, 2019); "Always timeless, always a perfect gift!" (Instagram, February 4, 2017).

By anchoring the brand to its actual history, this kind of storytelling makes use of the past as a "[source] of truth and merit,"[30] growing simultaneously the audience's appreciation of the brand's stability across time.

While enhancing its pedigree, however, F&M keeps looking for change. In a dedicated article on the corporate website, we are told that innovation is the actual driving force behind F&M's longevity: "At Fortnum's we have been in the business of innovation for centuries, from crafting pioneering blends for monarchs to continuously sourcing the very best from around the globe."[31] Here, the seemingly oxymoron between change ("pioneering") and consistency ("for centuries") is reconciled. Because innovation is at the very core of F&M, it is only congruous for the company to refresh existing products and develop new ones—as with the Sparkling Tea, which is launched in the market both as "an earth-shaking revolution"[32] and "the latest evolution in our 312-year history in tea" (@Fortnums, Twitter, July 9, 2019). Furthermore, because F&M's expertise in innovation spans in centuries, new products are already infused with the flavor of a long-standing excellence: "Since 1707, our passion for innovation has been at the core of everything we do. . . . So whatever culinary creations Fortnum's future holds, you already know they're going to be DELICIOUS!" (@Fortnums, Instagram, April 13, 2019).

In launching new products, F&M is also mindful of their heritage potential, which the company curates in its SMN postings: "Time flies when you're eating chocolate. . . . Today marks one year since we introduced Ruby Chocolate to the United Kingdom—just as we did the Scotch Egg in 1738, and The Knickerbocker Glory in 1955"(@Fortnums, Instagram, April 13, 2019). By celebrating the first anniversary of the ruby chocolate release alongside other F&M classic 'inventions,' F&M starts consolidating new legacies for the future.

When exposed to innate facets of heritage, SMNs users generally react with a sense of wondering fulfillment. The comments about the Scotch Egg invention by F&M are quite topical: "interesting fact!" (Instagram, November 15, 2015); "never knew this..!" (Instagram, July 9, 2017); "how wonderful" (Instagram, October 12, 2018). At times, users participate in the storytelling. One user confirms the information about the Scotch Egg by referencing it back to Fortnum's 'The Cook Book': "page 259, invented by . . . F&M. . . . Congratulations!" (Instagram, October 12, 2018). Conversely, another user challenges F&M about the invention.

Oftentimes, this kind of storytelling engenders affective statements toward the brand, again in the case of the Scotch Egg: "who knew?! My favorite store in London!" (Instagram, November 15, 2015); "We did know that & we adore your Scotch eggs. They are eggcellent! #worldeggday" (Instagram, October 12, 2018).

Users may also fully immerse in the story and prompt for further details. When told that in the 1930s, F&M used to have a store in Madison Avenue (NYC), users are thrilled: "really?" (Instagram, January 22, 2019); "what happened to the NY store?" (Instagram, September 6, 2017). One user even contributes with a link to an archive picture of the NY store (Instagram, August 23, 2018).

While innate forms of heritage storytelling are based on historical detail and factual information that a company shares with the specific objective to educate the audience about the brand's authenticity and consistency, projected heritage storytelling is audience driven; that is, it relies on past-related cues that are meant to plug into the audience's personal or collective memories. Visuals retrieved from the F&M archive (Figure 10.2) are key prompts for this kind of storytelling: black-and-white pictures, illustrations from past catalogues, decades-old advertisements, and original finds are mainly shared on Instagram and tagged with #TBT (Throwback Thursday), #History, and #Archive. The asynchronicity between the contents and the medium of communication is what activates the users' perceptual and emotional response.

A picture of a F&M sewing kit ('the housewife') discovered by the company's archivist in San Francisco (Instagram, July 21, 2016) evokes detailed accounts of how 'the housewife' was once used by grandfathers and fathers and eventually passed on to children attending boarding schools. When showed a 60s picture of the F&M delivery van (Instagram, January 11, 2018), a few recall their parents or acquaintances driving the same model.

Sometimes the audience verbalizes the sense of longing that emerges from remembering their past. To a post introducing the Flying Saucers with the hashtag "BackToTheFuture" (@Fortnums, Instagram, October 21, 2015) one user reacts: "Nostalgic!!; Ah these take me back #yum #retro #treat" (Instagram, October 21, 2015). This feeling of loss is not necessarily anchored to any specific fact or event directly experienced, as shown by the following comments about pictures from the 50s–60s: "Those were the days" (Instagram, January 18, 2018); "Love the old world" (Instagram, January 18, 2018); "#thosewerethedays#60s Great times! #memories" (Instagram,

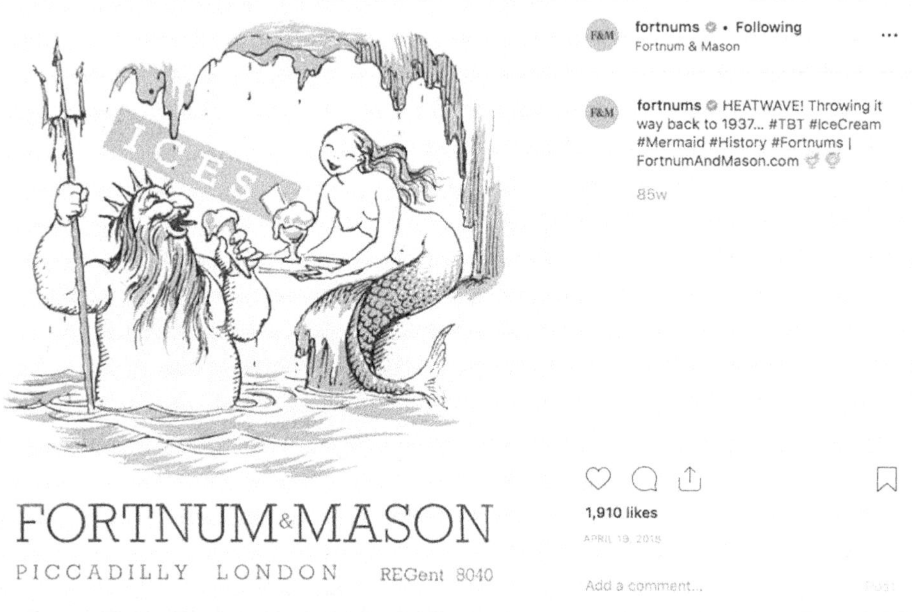

Figure 10.2 HEATWAVE! Throwing it way back to 1937 . . . #TBT #IceCream #Mermaid #History #Fortnums. Fortnum and Mason (@Fortnums), Instagram, April 19, 2018.

Source: Image Courtesy of Fortnum and Mason.

February 15, 2018); "Such style in those days" (Instagram, January 4, 2018). The vagueness of the expressions "those were the days" or "in those days" suggests that nostalgia can have very blurry temporal contours.

There are also cases where users take a more playful stance and place themselves in the temporal space evoked by the pictures. For instance, in a post asking: "What provisions would you love to try from this 1931 catalogue? #TBT #Mermaid #Archive#Illustration #Fortnums" (@Fortnums, Instagram, September 6, 2018), one replies: "May I order some celery & cheese wafers please?" (Instagram, September 6, 2018).

Similarly, about a post showing a 1925 dessert menu with the pun: "Prunes in Gin, anyone?" users joke: "If you insist" (Instagram, January 7, 2016); "I really must" (Instagram, January 7, 2016).

Rather than longing to go back to the past, users often want to 'bring back' the past. The term "cool" is a semantic indicator of this re-evaluation of the past's appeal in the present, and it is used extensively on F&M digital platforms. Interestingly, SMN users even get to the point of commodifying the past's coolness by themselves suggesting ideas for the development of 'retro-merchandising:' "Adore this illustration. Another one that would make the perfect tea towel. Come on F&M feed my passion for tea towels and produce some new designs. Xx" (Instagram, February 25, 2016); "Have you thought about a limited edition Christmas decoration, just a thought??"(Instagram, December 31, 2015); "LOVE! Please tell me these could be available as prints . . . #keepmeinformed"(Instagram, December 17, 2015).

As highlighted by F&M, a three-century-old company "[has] hundreds of stories to tell" (@Fortnums, Instagram, July 27, 2017). As such, by sourcing mainly genuine archive-based content for its digital stories, F&M makes very limited use of the mythical heritage facet.

One instance of mythical heritage is the case of the County Biscuits, celebrating the heritage diversity of the British counties. The narrative developed on the official website frames County Biscuits as the output of F&M traveling "from the bottom to the top of the map" and gathering "stories [from the local folklore] along the way."[33] The audience is invited "to discover legends old and mysterious hidden in a little booklet inside your tin."[34] Compared to other product descriptions analyzed so far, the use of terms such as "mystery," "legend," "hidden," and "folklore" immerses the audience in a British epic past, whose allure stems from being remote without being historical.

There is also a mythological aura surrounding the F&M flagship store in Piccadilly. While being a very tangible exhibit of F&M historical existence, the store is often described as "iconic" by the company and SMNs users alike: "one of Britain's most loved icons" (@Fortnums, Instagram, February 24, 2018); "a legendary piece of history" (Instagram, February 24, 2018); "A London Landmark" (Instagram, April 26, 2019); "Magical inside and out" (Instagram, February 24, 2018). "Magic," "legendary," and "iconic" almost transfigure the sturdiness of the building, turning it into a symbolic gateway to abstractions such as London or "history."

This is most evident when F&M brings into its storytelling another heritage brand: the British monarchy. The monarchy, an example itself of staged heritage storytelling,[35] nonetheless provides Great Britain with historical and visual identity by embodying quintessential Britishness at home and abroad. There are instances where F&M counts its longevity not in years but in reigns: "This is our 12th reign in which we are proud to serve" (@Fortnums, Instagram, April 21, 2016). In other cases, F&M syncs with the royal calendar by sharing celebrative postings on the royal jubilees, which are very well received by the users: "Amazing! [crown emoji]" (Instagram, June 9, 2018); "Love This! [British Flag]" (Instagram, June 9, 2018); "[England, cake, crown emojis]#ilovefortnums" (Instagram, April 21, 2016). In order to further associate itself with future royal jubilees, F&M releases new tea blends for special occasions—as happened with the christening of Prince George in 2013 and the wedding of HRH William and Kate Middleton in 2011.

Here, we depart from the faux character of mythical heritage as modeled by Balmer and Hudson to identify another facet of projected heritage: the 'synergic' heritage, which leverages the historical links and cultural commonalities between two heritage brands. In the case of F&M, this narrative stream leverages the brand's historical relationship with royalty to secure access to collective constructs, such as the idea of Britishness. For different reasons, this appeals to both F&M's domestic and international customers.

As mentioned previously, heritage storytelling is the narration of a past with 'present relevance.' This requires F&M to connect with the current *zeitgeist*, fine-tuning its stories with the myths, values, and beliefs resonating in contemporary society at large.

Female empowerment and gender inclusivity are among the contemporary topics F&M heritage storytelling ties into. Among the women-related stories shared on SMNs, particularly effective is the episode of suffragette Helen Craggs, daughter of the F&M chairman at the time, who was imprisoned for smashing F&M windows in the Edwardian era. With regard to gender inclusivity, in summer 2019, F&M featured on SMNs the story of Bunny Roger, drag queen, war hero, and F&M couturier during the 50s.

Here, F&M is not only retrieving episodes from the past. Those stories show the brand's allegiance to causes that historically might have been perceived as disturbing or disruptive but that are now intrinsic social values. The fact of having been there since the very beginning provides gravitas to F&M statements and sanctions its role as time precursor: in the same way F&M used to send hampers to the suffragettes to support their cause, the company now consistently "stand[s] with each and every woman and continues to support the fight for a more equal world" (@Fortnums, Instagram, March 8, 2019). Similarly, by considering Bunny Roger's quirkiness "a perfect fit at Fortnum's," the company validates diversity as part of its brand identity.[36]

The comments to these stories—often visualized through clapping hands and red heart emojis—convey a deep sense of admiration toward F&M: "This is amazing and makes me love F&M even more" (Instagram, March 8, 2019); "Thank you Fortnum's . . . this history is why you have endured and prospered for over 300 years! #FueltheFight" (Instagram, March 8, 2019); "I'm very impressed about the hampers and the suffragettes! Bravo! My deepest respect"(Instagram, February 6, 2018); "That is why Fortnums is my favorite store on earth" (Instagram, November 10, 2017).

To enhance audience emotional engagement, storytelling timing is also crucial. Women-related stories tend to be shared on Women's Day, while Bunny Roger's story was featured on July 6, 2019, in celebration of the Pride Jubilee and the fiftieth anniversary of the Stonewall riots in New York City. During the Pride period, F&M usually propose on SMNs a playful pun about having welcomed "several queens" through their doors in the years, an irreverent association between the establishment and the queer.

As a digital user itself, F&M must also sync with the trends circulating in the SMN environment. At the beginning of 2019, the digital community virally engaged in the '10-year challenge,' whereby users had to post a throwback photo of themselves from 10 years ago along with a recent pic. F&M participated as well, with an old print of the Piccadilly flagship store (Figure 10.3): "300 year challenge. Keeping it [hundred points emoji] since 1707 . . . #TBT#10YearChallenge #Heritage #GOAT#Fortnums" (@Fortnums, Instagram, January 17, 2019). In the posting, F&M playfully brags about its longevity: while 10 years is already quite a timespan in human life, F&M sets the bar way beyond, with the hashtag #GOAT (Greatest Of All Time).

It is worth reporting a few comments from the audience, as this shows the multilayered semantic fabric interwoven in only one post: some users point out F&M's legacy ("Fortnums ancestors would b very proud of you [ok hand emoji]") and longevity ("Historic preservation at its finest; Yet another reason why fortnums is the epitome of perfection"); some others become nostalgic ("Thank goodness you haven't bowed to the pressure of 'change' and kept the store wonderful like it always has been. It's so lovely to visit F&M it's like stepping back into a time when shopping was a pleasure and sales assistants cared. Well done F&M keep it going [two hearts emoji]"; "In uncertain times we need to take reassurance from things that stay constant and familiar. You're always there for us @fortnums"); some others associate F&M and the British royalty ("[5 British flag and 5 crown emojis]";"My youngest daughters favourite store she's 11 and loves the traditional style #queenvictoriafan").

By looking at the timescape of F&M digital communication outlined previously, we contend that F&M heritage storytelling is rich both in its temporal stretch and its semantic reach. As a storytelling content, heritage deals with a past that is presented

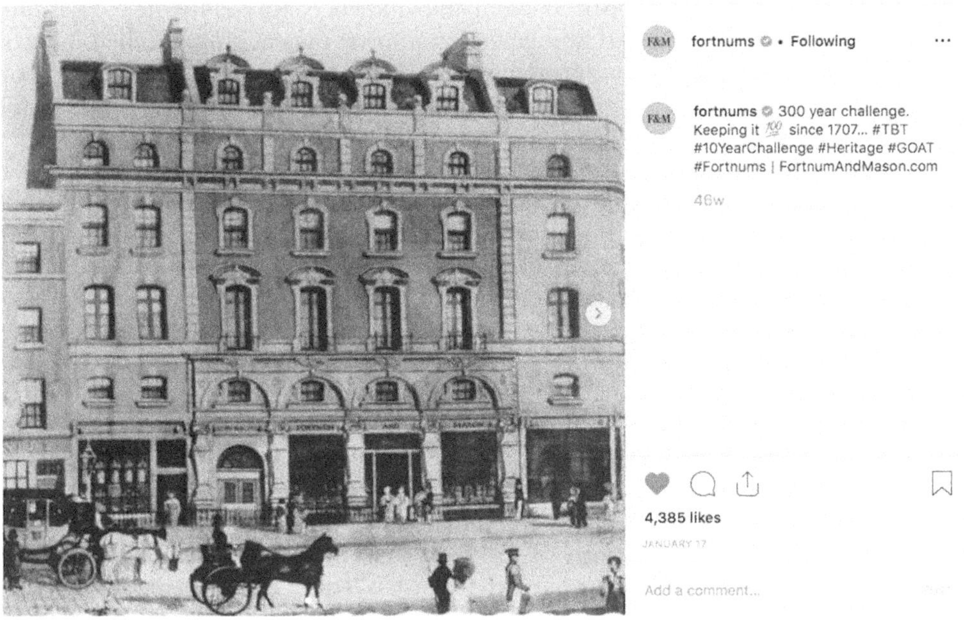

Figure 10.3 300 year challenge. Fortnum & Mason (@Fortnums), Instagram, January 17, 2019.
Source: Image courtesy of Fortnum & Mason.

at times in its historical occurrence; at times in continuity with the present and extension toward the future; and at times as an emotional vessel for individual projections of longing and belonging, memories and reveries. Heritage content weaves complex discourses about brand authenticity and integrity, innovation and change, timelessness and perfection, nostalgia and fantasy. As effective communicative acts, heritage stories harness the cultural spirit of the present: appealing episodes, engaging formats, and suitable timing infuse old stories with a contemporary flair, thus making the past meaningful to the audience.

In addition, F&M heritage storytelling takes full advantage of the communication potentialities of the digital environment. Because of the audience's constant and active participation in content production, F&M storytelling can also be defined as 'augmented,' with streams and strands of heritage stories by multiple sources blending in, while at the same time amplifying, individual temporalities, societal temporalities, corporate temporalities, universal—therefore timeless—temporalities. Thus, red-heart or British-flag emojis posted to comments about F&M sending hampers to the British army during the World Wars open simultaneous semantic windows on global historical events, Armed Forces Day in the United Kingdom, Britishness, family memories, approval for the brand's commitment to social causes, or reflections on patriotism and self-sacrifice.

Conclusions

Storytelling is a situated practice of content creation and communication directed to a specific audience. This chapter has delved into the 'situated' aspect of storytelling and has explored heritage content in interaction with a corporate digital communication context. By including aspects such as company–audience storytelling agency, timing of communication, and intended and emerging effects, the chapter has shed light on the dynamism of heritage content production. As such, rather than a construct, heritage needs to be seen as a construction, emerging from a plurality of perceptual and conceptual stances toward past, present, and future.

The analysis of the heritage timescape in the case of F&M digital storytelling has provided practical instances of how the temporal discourses by both the company and SMN users interweave constantly and spontaneously, eventually profiling different dimensions of heritage. This has allowed us to identify a specific 'heritage mix' for F&M storytelling, partially different from the Hudson and Balmer's taxonomy: a limited use of the mythical facet of heritage, as opposed to an extensive reliance on the 'cool effect,' a positive variation on reconstructed heritage. Also, we detected an additional heritage facet: the synergic one.

This methodological approach has implications in the field of digital heritage communication. As mentioned previously, digital technology has empowered users as co-creators of digital storytelling, leading to an increased relevance of peer-to-peer content in the corporate marketing communication.[37] In this scenario, corporations need to undertake the vicarious role of 'enablers' by developing the ability to "solicit consumer narratives and create a contextualized landscape of experiences shared by the community."[38]

As the F&M case shows, delivering 'rich' heritage content is the first step to generating customer engagement. With innate aspects of heritage, it enlivens information transfer into an informative learning experience. Projected forms of heritage arouse the users' escapist imagination toward alternative pasts—pasts they feel actually or fictionally connected with.[39]

The timescape analysis devised here can be a helpful tool for marketers to map their heritage content and to implement strategic decision-making in their storytelling practice: whether to plan a consistent narrative across the platforms or to differentiate it, whether to diversify the heritage facets considered or prioritize one facet of heritage over another and on which platform. In the case of F&M, the company might want to explore the opportunity to differentiate the facets of heritage storytelling on Twitter and Facebook or to harmonize the frequency of its heritage content on SMNs.

With regard to the actual engagement of the audience on SMNs, F&M might appear a lucky outlier: not only are SMN users' responses positive—with little to no criticism registered—but the F&M community is fully committed to storytelling co-creation, as shown by the intimacy of the stories people volunteer on SMNs and by the spontaneous and affectionate tone of voice of their messages. The F&M marketing team, however, is well aware that "we have them to lose,"[40] so the challenge for the company is to find new channels of communication—such as animations or videos—to keep the dialogue alive.

As such, heritage storytelling is not just a marketing deliverable, but it stems from a specific value-based approach to the passing of time in storytelling. If the past is a source to exploit, the passing of time is content-value in the making. Heritage storytelling becomes a strategic arena for the company to capitalize on the past in the present by creating meaningful narratives while harnessing elements with heritage narrative potentials. It is about the creation of "New Old Stories."

Acknowledgments

The authors thank Bimal Tailor, Catriona Maclean, and John Ovans for their assistance and support during the research project.

Notes

1. Fortnum & Mason (@Fortnums), *Instagram*, July 27, 2017.
2. Anna Blombäck and Olof Brunninge, "Corporate Identity Manifested through Historical References," *Corporate Communications: An International Journal* 14, n°4 (2009): 404–419, https://doi:10.1108/13563280910998754.
3. John M.T. Balmer, "Corporate Heritage Identities, Corporate Heritage Brands and the Multiple Heritage Identities of The British Monarchy," *European Journal of Marketing* 45, n°9/10 (2011): 1380–1398, p. 1396, https://doi:10.1108/03090561111151817.
4. John M.T Balmer and Mario Burghausen, "Explicating Corporate Heritage, Corporate Heritage Brands and Organisational Heritage," *Journal of Brand Management* 22, n°5 (2015): 364–384, https://doi:10.1057/bm.2015.26.
5. Fabien Pecot and Virginie De Barnier, "Brands Using Historical References: A Consumers' Perspective," *Journal of Brand Management* 25, n°2 (2018): 171–184, https://doi:10.1057/s41262-017-0076-y.
6. Mats Urde, Stephen A. Greyser, and John M.T. Balmer, "Corporate Brands with a Heritage," *Journal of Brand Management* 15, n°1 (2007): 4–19, p. 5. https://doi:10.1057/palgrave.bm.2550106.
7. Ibid, 5.
8. *The Morning Post* (London, England), Friday, December 15, 1848.
9. *Graphic*, Saturday, December 13, 1902.
10. "Books and Booklets," *Art and Industry*, June 1, 1924, 48.
11. The pamphlet was written by John Paddy Carstairs and illustrated by Edward Bawden.
12. Tim Lawler, *Fortnum & Mason: The First Three Hundred Years* (Fortnum & Mason, 2007).
13. Interview with social media team, May 17, 2019.
14. Virginia Braun, and Victoria Clarke, "Using Thematic Analysis in Psychology," *Qualitative Research in Psychology* 3 (2006): 77–11, https://doi:10.1191/1478088706qp063oa.
15. Bradford T. Hudson and John M.T. Balmer, "Corporate Heritage Brands: Mead's Theory of The Past," *Corporate Communications: An International Journal* 18, n°3 (2013): 347–361, https://doi:10.1108/ccij-apr-2012-0027.
16. Ibid, 354.
17. Ibid.
18. Vincent Miller, *Understanding Digital Culture* (Los Angeles: Sage, 2011), 21.
19. John Storey, *Theories of Consumption* (London: Routledge, 2017).
20. Stephen Brown, Robert V. Kozinets, and John F. Sherry Jr., "Teaching Old Brands New Tricks: Retro Branding and the Revival of Brand Meaning," *Journal of Marketing* 67, n°3 (2003): 19–33, p. 30, https://doi:10.1509/jmkg.67.3.19.18657.
21. Robert Hassan, *Empires of Speed* (Leiden: Brill, 2009), 103.
22. Miller, *Understanding Digital Culture*, 30.
23. Balmer, "Corporate Heritage Identities," 1386.
24. David Lowenthal, *The Past Is a Foreign Country* (Cambridge: Cambridge University Press, 1985), 26.
25. Aistė Urboniene, "Storytelling in Country Branding: A Semiotic Approach," *International Journal on Global Business Management and Research* 5, n°2 (2016): 17–30.
26. Barbara Adam, *Time* (Cambridge: Polity, 2004), p. 143.
27. Fortnum and Mason, *Twitter Account*, last accessed August 21, 2019, https://twitter.com/Fortnums?ref_src=twsrc%5Egoogle%7Ctwcamp%5Eserp%7Ctwgr%5Eauthor.
28. In quoting posts from SMNs users directly, we will omit their account names to protect their privacy. We have maintained to original typos and the original English spelling. The descriptors for the emojis are those of Emojipedia.

29. Fortnum and Mason, "Take Afternoon Tea. Diamond Jubilee Tea Salon," Website Landing Page, last accessed August 21, 2019, www.fortnumandmason.com.
30. Lowenthal, *The Past Is a Foreign Country*, 369.
31. Fortnum and Mason, "New! Fortnum's Sparkling Tea: A Marvellous Tea Total Tipple," *The Journal|#Fortnums*, last accessed August 16, 2019, www.fortnumandmason.com/fortnums/fortnums-sparkling-tea.
32. Ibid.
33. Fortnum and Mason, "Fortnums' County Biscuits: Take a Delicious Tour of Four British Counties with Our Ever So British Biscuits," *The Journal|#Fortnums*, last accessed August 16, 2019, www.fortnumandmason.com/fortnums/our-new-county-biscuit-tin.
34. Ibid.
35. Balmer, "Corporate Heritage Identities."
36. Fortnum and Mason, "Proud to be Queens' Grocer: Neil Munro 'Bunny' Roger," *The Journal|#Fortnums*, last accessed August 21, 2019, www.fortnumandmason.com/fortnums/bunny-roger.
37. Renée Richardson Gosline, Lee Jeffrey, and Urban Glenn, "The Power of Consumer Stories in Digital Marketing," *MIT Sloan Management Review* 58 n°4 (2017): 10–13, sloanreview.mit.edu/article/the-power-of-consumer-stories-in-digital-marketing/.
38. Mine Üçok Hughes, Wendy K. Bendoni, and Ekin Pehlivan, "Storygiving As a Co-Creation Tool for Luxury Brands in the Age of the Internet: A Love Story by Tiffany And Thousands of Lovers," *Journal of Product & Brand Management* 25, n°4 (2016): 357–364, p. 359. doi:10.1108/jpbm-09-2015-0970.
39. Anne Rindell, Fernando Pinto Santos, and Ana Pinto de Lima, "Two Sides of a Coin: Connecting Corporate Brand Heritage to Consumers' Corporate Image Heritage," *Journal of Brand Management* 22, n°5 (2015): 467–484. doi:10.1057/bm.2015.20.
40. Interview with social media team, May 17, 2019.

Bibliography

Adam, Barbara. *Time*. Cambridge: Polity, 2004.

Art and Industry

Balmer, John M.T. "Corporate Heritage Identities, Corporate Heritage Brands and the Multiple Heritage Identities of the British Monarchy." *European Journal of Marketing* 45, n°9/10 (2011): 1380–1398. doi:10.1108/03090561111151817.

Balmer, John M.T., and Mario Burghausen. "Explicating Corporate Heritage, Corporate Heritage Brands and Organisational Heritage." *Journal of Brand Management* 22, n°5 (2015): 364–384. doi:10.1057/bm.2015.26.

Blombäck, Anna, and Olof Brunninge. "Corporate Identity Manifested through Historical References." *Corporate Communications: An International Journal* 14, n°4 (2009): 404–419. doi:10.1108/13563280910998754.

Braun, Virginia, and Victoria Clarke. "Using Thematic Analysis in Psychology." *Qualitative Research in Psychology* 3 (2006): 77–11. doi:10.1191/1478088706qp063oa.

Brown, Stephen, Robert V. Kozinets, and John F. Sherry Jr. "Teaching Old Brands New Tricks: Retro Branding and the Revival of Brand Meaning." *Journal of Marketing* 67, n°3 (2003): 19–33. doi:10.1509/jmkg.67.3.19.18657.

Emojipedia. Last Accessed August 21, 2019. https://emojipedia.org.

Fortnum and Mason. *Facebook Account*. Last Accessed August 21, 2019. https://en-gb.facebook.com/fortnums/.

Fortnum and Mason. "Fortnums' County Biscuits: Take a Delicious Tour of Four British Counties with Our Ever So British Biscuits." *The Journal|#Fortnums*. Last Accessed August 16, 2019. www.fortnumandmason.com/fortnums/our-new-county-biscuit-tin.

Fortnum and Mason. *Instagram Account*. Last Accessed August 21, 2019. www.instagram.com/fortnums/?hl=en.

Fortnum and Mason. "New! Fortnum's Sparkling Tea: A Marvellous Tea Total Tipple." *The Journal|#Fortnums*. Last Accessed August 16, 2019. www.fortnumandmason.com/fortnums/fortnums-sparkling-tea.

Fortnum and Mason. "Proud To Be Queens' Grocer: Neil Munro 'Bunny' Roger." *The Journal|#Fortnums*. Last Accessed August 21, 2019. www.fortnumandmason.com/fortnums/bunny-roger.

Fortnum and Mason. *Twitter Account*. Last Accessed August 21, 2019. https://twitter.com/Fortnums?ref_src=twsrc%5Egoogle%7Ctwcamp%5Eserp%7Ctwgr%5Eauthor.

Fortnum and Mason. "Take Afternoon Tea. Diamond Jubilee Tea Salon." Website Landing Page. Last Accessed August 21, 2019. www.fortnumandmason.com.

Fortnum and Mason. "Website." Last Accessed August 21, 2019. www.fortnumandmason.com.

Graphic (newspaper), 1869–1932.

Gosline, Renée Richardson, Jeffrey Lee, and Urban Glenn. "The Power of Consumer Stories in Digital Marketing." *MIT Sloan Management Review* 58, n°4 (2017): 10–13. http://mitsmr.com/2qAM9mU.

Hassan, Robert. *Empires of Speed*. Leiden: Brill, 2009.

Hudson, Bradford T., and John M.T. Balmer. "Corporate Heritage Brands: Mead's Theory of the Past." *Corporate Communications: An International Journal* 18, n°3 (2013): 347–361. doi:10.1108/ccij-apr-2012-0027.

Lawler, Tim. *Fortnum & Mason: The First Three Hundred Years*. London: Fortnum & Mason, 2007.

Lowenthal, David. *The Past Is a Foreign Country*. Cambridge: Cambridge University Press, 1985.

Miller, Vincent. *Understanding Digital Culture*. Los Angeles: Sage Publications, 2011.

The Morning Post, 1772–1837.

Pecot, Fabien, and Virginie De Barnier. "Brands Using Historical References: A Consumers' Perspective." *Journal of Brand Management* 25, n°2 (2018): 171–184. doi:10.1057/s41262-017-0076-y.

Rindell, Anne, Fernando Pinto Santos, and Ana Pinto de Lima. "Two Sides of a Coin: Connecting Corporate Brand Heritage to Consumers' Corporate Image Heritage." *Journal of Brand Management* 22, n°5 (2015): 467–484. doi:10.1057/bm.2015.20.

Storey, John. *Theories of Consumption*. London: Routledge, 2017.

Üçok Hughes, Mine, Wendy K. Bendoni, and Ekin Pehlivan. "Storygiving As a Co-Creation Tool for Luxury Brands in the Age of the Internet: A Love Story by Tiffany and Thousands of Lovers." *Journal of Product & Brand Management* 25, n°4 (2016): 357–364. doi:10.1108/jpbm-09-2015-0970.

Urboniene, Aistė. "Storytelling in Country Branding: A Semiotic Approach." *International Journal on Global Business Management and Research* 5, n°2 (2016): 17–30.

Urde, Mats, Stephen A. Greyser, and John M. T. Balmer. "Corporate Brands with a Heritage." *Journal of Brand Management* 15, n°1 (2007): 4–19. doi:10.1057/palgrave.bm.2550106.

Index

For Product Safety Concerns and Information please contact our EU representative GPSR@taylorandfrancis.com
Taylor & Francis Verlag GmbH, Kaufingerstraße 24, 80331 München, Germany

www.ingramcontent.com/pod-product-compliance
Ingram Content Group UK Ltd.
Pitfield, Milton Keynes, MK11 3LW, UK
UKHW050753180926
475701UK00007B/1023
9780367638054